OCCUPATIONAL INCLINATIONS OF TRIBAL WOMEN IN MEGHALAYA

About the Author

Ms. Y. Satya, Ph.D. in Consumer Behaviour, Marketing Management is recognized scholar, teacher and speaker on market applications and execution. Currently she is working as an Associate Professor in the Department of Commerce, St. Anthony's College, Shillong, which is one of the most renowned colleges in North-East. She is associated with North Eastern Hill University, Centre for Distance Education, NEHU and IGNOU, Shillong for their Post Graduate Degree and Diploma Programmes at different capacities viz., Curriculum Preparation, Counselor, Visiting Faculty and Project Guidance. Her areas of specialization are Market Research, Strategic Marketing Management, Market Intelligence and Markets-in-Pursuit etc. As an aspirant researcher she is consistently engaged with research programmes associated to North-East for more than a decade and worked in the areas of Decision-making, Market Communications, Women's Issues, Resource Utilities, Transit Markets and currently working on the Skills Development. Her research articles were published in Journals like IASSI Quarterly, New Delhi, Journal of Marketing Trends, Institute of Public Enterprise, Hyderabad and with Concept Publishing Company Pvt. Ltd., New Delhi etc. With reference to the research presentations she articulated her research deliberations at various forums ranging from regional, north-east and national level seminars, workshops and conferences held by NIRD, Hyderabad; SMVDU, Jammu; Institute of Chartered Accountants of India, New Delhi; Planning Commission, New Delhi, North Eastern Council etc.

Occupational Inclinations of Tribal Women in Meghalaya

Dr. (Ms.) Y. Satya

CONCEPT PUBLISHING COMPANY PVT. LTD.
NEW DELHI-110 059

ISBN-13 : 978-81-8069-770-8

First Published 2012

Published and Printed by

Concept Since 1974

Concept Publishing Company Pvt. Ltd.
A/15-16, Commercial Block, Mohan Garden
New Delhi-110059 (India)
T: 25351460, 25351794, *F*: 091-11-25357109
E: publishing@conceptpub.com, W: www.conceptpub.com
Editorial Office: H-13, Bali Nagar, New Delhi-110 015, India.

Cataloging in Publication Data--*Courtesy:* D.K. Agencies (P) Ltd. <docinfo@dkagencies.com>

Satya, Y., ***Dr.***
Occupational inclinations of tribal women in Meghalaya / Y. Satya.
p. cm.
Includes bibliographical references (p.) and index.
ISBN 9788180697708

1. Khasi (Indic people)—Economic conditions. 2. Jaintia (Indic people)—Economic conditions. 3. Women, Garo—Economic conditions. 4. Women—India—Meghalaya—Economic conditions. 5. Women—India—Meghalaya—Social conditions. 6. Occupations—India—Meghalaya. 7. Women in economic development—India—Meghalaya. I. Title.

DDC 338.900820954164 23

Foreword

It gives me great pleasure to write this brief foreword to Dr. (Ms.) Y. Satya's book entitled *Occupational Inclinations of Tribal Women in Meghalaya*. The book is a comprehensive attempt at understanding the complex interplay of socio-economic, cultural and psychological specificities of the major tribal communities viz., Khasis, Jaintias and the Garos of Meghalaya in view of their occupational inclinations, sought after choice and decision-criteria. The study is mainly empirical where it frequently brings insightful theoretical considerations to bear upon the understanding of the data which was so meticulously collected. The most interesting aspect of the communities that she has studied is the matrilineal system that they all share, practice and applaud in common. Matriliny in Meghalaya is an extremely complex phenomenon which gives these communities an ethically established community cult, customary and time-honoured living styles form a proven dimension which is entirely their own, even though it allows subtle differences among them. Of the many publications over the themes of employment, services, labour etc., in recent years which pose similar to Dr. Satya's, this book stands out for its penetrating analysis, fresh insights and excellent articulation of the profound reflexes substantiating occupational preferences of these ethnic groups.

To the reader the book unravel the contemporary issues influencing the status of progressive modernities in relevance to the conditional feminine conscientiousness revealed women folk in terms of their participation, contribution, and deeper sense of employable adaptabilities. The research outlook ensures to be very useful resource for further studies in to the associated areas promptly raised by Dr. Satya.

Mrinal Miri
Member, National Advisory Council
Former Vice Chancellor, NEHU,
Shillong

Preface

A conceptualized ethnic ordering in modern convergences shaping magnitudes of understanding arraying different dimensions of socio-economic progressiveness and its implications over ethnic-bound structures. The value extensions of these systems pleatued are both situational and variable in their applicabilities. These with due concerns associate segmental effects over the issues-of-importance remain proximate to influence over the changeable modes of impact-sourcing. The configurations of dominant themes and the reactive tendencies based on the externalities pertinent to regional factors of priority in the framework of shaping as well as structuring the so-called inevitabilities reflect the practices adopted-approaches preferred, the challenges trailed are the determinants leading to a decision-routing. The synergistic consequences of the penetrating change have no definite direction but the pervasiveness of its impact remains as a means of its growth and rapidity with which the growth competencies occur or adapted and accept for its own merit.

Ethnicity of Meghalaya, the remote north-eastern domain, as such by itself contribute towards the values systems and beliefs remain the core due to the reason/s based on the social experiences enable to imply pre-dominances, complexities which form vitalities in participatory trends of tribal bound life trajectories are most revered and sought of. Reaching the ethnic definitions amid diversities need to be understood as an exasperating recitation of the ethical impact over the developmental issues.

"Women" as a focal issue and as a prerogative characterized to the ethnic symbol and their lifestyle options remain vital to tribal living-culture adaptation systems. The strong feelings of encircled culture are represented in their familial and community environment can possibly be understood by the gamut of situations prevailing, the cultural experience is the insistence on incidence-based living patterns. Do the women in their turn try to bring cultural change and will such adaptations contribute to the individual lifestyles? Does it deem to be the singular decision or at-large try to assign a shape-in to a transformation or new generation of ideologies? If women as such represent a vitality, the fair sex in Meghalaya has a distinguishable identity of being the adaptors of matrilineal / matriarchal system symbolized by their title, deemed as a privilege to be continued and each girl-child is the most preferred as being a clan promoter that enables her the embedded responsibility inculcated in her as a part of their aspirational culture. A born Meghalayan is perceived to be having the familial and clan-based responsibility implied in un-skewed form making them i.e., women as decision makers, powerful and responsible towards all of their surroundedness in "relevant" environment. Their individual decisions persevere to be the natural impact of their families and of clans as life, they need to recognize as significantly contributing component of the clans and communities rather than just being their self. Lately, the decisional effects of the women in terms of their knowledge-based condition, the opportunities and growth clauses having been triggering the already prevailing micro-managerial and micro-organizational competencies into a definite shape facilitating them to think towards the ambitious and achievable life-patterns based on occupational preferences. Can they be understood as signifying contributors towards developmental progressions of the state?

The research enabled to provide an intrigue into the preferential options of occupational living style references seemed to be variant to what actually persists and what is been perceived. The context-building, reception discrimination and the pervasive approach are few complexities came into the focus which were not realized until the understanding of the talks, meetings with women in individual and groups by means of a survey undertaken for this purpose. The vitalities of the research is to understand the women's preferences towards career decisions in their in-depth patterns and each woman represent the personalized versions, experiences and forms without confining themselves wholly to the questionnaires or their limitations.

The state basically has a rural dominant character with minimal urban influence but its locational advantage enables it to share inter-state and international boundaries and channels pass through it towards interiors of north east. All the areas which have been exposed to the externalities have a behaviour different from its counterparts which are deep inside and have minimal rapport. The context-based differences are natural enough to enable the ethnic women to be adaptive within their set cultural frame. The women chosen for the sample being 3600 and odd comprised both rural and urban and the sample cover all the seven districts barring the variations of size, demographics, inter and intra cultural rigidities in the districts. The geo-demographic and infrastructural difficulties have been partly natural and partly self-prescribed have their extensive impact visibly define the women's self-advancements towards the situations. The idea is not to review the prevailing conditions critically but to attend towards the bare realities emerging in the process of persevering the women's role significance in different contexts viz., deprived and opportunistic. The criticalities have become a part of tribal system and living with perfect imbalances have taught them to live with life realities emerging in day-to-day consequences within which they need to search for life values. The primary and foremost factor being understood is non-deviation or separation from the community as majority believes that the association and mutual-dependency remain as prerogative within the state. The unexpressed, suppressed reluctances and aversion to mingle freely with other communities associated with extreme self-centredness and mutual dependencies within the clan/community seemed to be the prominent factors reflecting isolation, lack of communication and interaction etc., available among majority of women. We visited the habitats of the respondents and their work place, some we have accompanied them to their business understanding and to gleam from their experiences which are important for their occupational decisions and the merging of life decisions with regard to occupations. The experiences have taught us that the women is a phenomena rather than an individual and the talents which they have exhibited in the producible and non-producible spectrums can be channeled towards effective development in several social layering.

The journeys are tedious and some areas where the hilly tracks, paths and non-motorable lanes, lesser developed areas have been intrigued leading to the women's world. Barring few in several places we received good treatment with kindness and courtesy. The interpreters have done their best job and the tribal involvement was much felt in few areas which the historical traces of non-conversion, tribal dominances, areas which are beyond the trace of modernity. A complete cut-off from the rest of the world, the lack of understanding surfaced the attribute of "closed system" was much felt in the central areas where the women are less mobile and not keen for exposure. The women's concept what we find in other parts of the country is different and these filled with ethnic differences are much loaded and burdened with community based impositions and self-constraints raised out of ignorance, lack of knowledge and understanding. The in-depth understanding also revealed its positive dimension as women are been positioned as big business magnets from Jaintia, Khasi and Garo Hills, as agriculturists, as international brokers, as members of NGOs and even as micro-participants but are still incomparable as the ethnic domain in its stances demand an occupational understanding which is totally unique and distinct. These are networked on the criteria of different emotions, values and difference of opinions towards the ethnicity and perseverance of clan culture. The isolation, seclusion and fear for new environmental challenges seem to be a vibrant force which has been subserved with in the ethnic framework and need to be awaited to be prepared to lead successful lives.

Methodology and Limitations of the Research Study

Keeping in view the coverage of both urban and rural segments of Meghalaya, the tribal state in the Northeast India, parameters was drawn to adopt empirical patterns suitable for the conduction of research study. The data prescriptions include the tools, design, sample size and methodology. Questionnaires were chosen as primary tools to be supported by interview, judgment and observation methods to gain information from respondents. In this reference the usage of questionnaires was as follows: questionnaire-I to gain the elementary detail/s of the chosen respondents, questionnaire-II to identify the temperament of women with positive and negative statements that include the general opinions over relevant issues chosen for the study, questionnaire-III for general awareness with reference to women and her environment, questionnaire-IV concentrates over the rural women; questionnaire-V attends to business women, questionnaire-VI for urban women in service, questionnaire-VII for general and questionnaire-VIII for specific occupational understanding of women. The questionnaire-I provides the information about the status of women and about women's status by being engaged in formal/ informal occupations with consideration (i.e., employment/ job/ service/profession) which forms the foremost criteria to select the respondents. Meghalaya has been divided into seven districts with nine urban areas identified as class-I, II, III, IV and V cities by its Urban Administration and its prominently significant rural comprise the rest. New blocks added recently making the total blocks mounting to thirty-nine (inclusive of both urban and rural segments). The total urban and rural population data was sourced from the published information by Economics and Statistics Evaluation Centre, a State Government Department of Meghalaya and the Census details from State Secretariat.

All thirty-nine blocks from seven districts were covered in which the blocks are treated as strata. The sampling design used in the study is stratified two-stage sampling with proportional allocation. At the first stage, three villages were selected for SRS (Simple Random Sampling) within each stratum (block). At the second stage 2 per cent households in urban areas and 1 per cent households in rural areas were selected by SRS without replacement using random numbers table. Only one woman preferably working was selected from each household using convenience sampling within the household. It did not pose much problem barring few occasions as majority of the women are work-oriented in some form or the other irrespective of their status. A total rural population of 1898 and urban population of 1715 were chosen for study making the total as 3613 respondents i.e., sample size. Besides these, two case studies were also undertaken as supportive studies i.e., the spinsters and adolescents' studies. 224 spinsters for Case – I and 210 teenagers (young women) for Case – II were chosen as sample size. Convenience sampling was adopted to undertake representations of all three tribes i.e., Khasi, Garo, and Jaintia. The interpreters' training was a repetitive affair and there was a common complain about the length of the questionnaires. The data was analyzed by means of statistical tools and keeping in view the vastness of information it was felt feasible to provide it in the form of percentages. Inferences from data were sought by using statistical techniques viz., Multiple Regression, Anova (Analysis of Variance) , tests of significance (t-test) and tests of homogeneity (γ^2 - test) and variability (F-test). The data representations were also made by using the judgment and observation methods, informal interviews, situational analysis and by means of references. Besides the statistical information and analysis, the data was also presented by using "mapping" for socio-psychographic expressions of occupational context in both rural and urban.

However, it was found that the option -5 of any other and no opinions were used as most convenient alternatives while attempting the questionnaires without suitable justifications and this witnessed a massive 40-60 per cent response rate. The typical ethnic rigidity of strong disagreement was another tool was put to use without mentioning much of their discontent as it also provided as an easy form of expression resorted by majority of respondents. The judgment and observation methods to some extent overcame this deficiency and remained informally supportive along with elaborate personal narratives, complaints, aspirations relevant and irrelevant which became a part of the data collection.

The new introduction being the occupational opinions expressed with reference to the background and context of the respondent to grasp the living styles expressed by women. Besides giving the statistical supportives the investigator is also enthusiastic to provide the information by means of mapping the data which helped to express the variability. For majority of the women the entire exercise is a first of its kind and did not really respond as they were too new to the context, reluctant to reveal, shy away from parting information, asking return questions and passing off etc., were found. The ground preparations needed were elaborate and vast majority indeed tried to respond but the replies were too brief, different and out of context. The interviews were held at farm, in the shop, while travel as a group and at times by means of interactivities with the help of gram sevaks, co-traders, head men, shop-keepers etc., inclusive of interpreters. It was found that they preferred to reply as a part of group, felt-need for support and it need to be agreeable that there is marked difference when they replied as individual or as a part of group.

The limitations of the study are the rigidities expressed by means of scaling techniques and questionnaire methods adopted were felt to be limiting factors restricting the dimension/s of the research study but the same enable as a facility to the investigator to draw parameters of coverage to be done as per the information detail. The questions regarding to the parents, family, clan promotion, migration and more sensitive issues viz., of partnering and living together, health, nurturing , finance, investment, credit, religion and competition etc., posed too personnel and displayed personalized and contextual bias in their reactions. The domain chosen was too vast which can be angled from too many dimensions. The current study narrowfied its jurisdiction to the vital aspects of the women's occupational preferences and selectivities in the context of ethnicity, culture, social and familial reasons as well as the respondents' persona. The context adopted was more shallow rather than in-depth as it posed the character of multi-perceivables touching too many dimensions of rural, urban, service, business but ignored the other economic, social involvement, family disturbances, degree of exposure, peer group influence, knowledge, education which have their very own relevant or irrelevant influences over their past, present and future behaviour and anticipations.

The study touched only few relevant dimensions out of the total focus and outcome consequences of the sources. Neither the ethnic occupational domain nor its prescriptives can be used as comparatives with the occupational set-up elsewhere and the patterns adopted as the living styles, approaches and behaviour in Meghalaya is totally different and the pattern/s naturally adopted a prototypical means and vitalities referred to new definition/s of understanding. The influencing factors are aligned in structured or unstructured cannot be understood as the subconscious decisions which are difficult to mark out even by respondent.

Justifications of the Limitations: The prime difficulty arises due to its overall impact of privatization at every level be it natural assets, resource ownership, property, markets, infrastructural facilities and massive business transactions etc., leaving no authority to the formal government. This deprives any access of information, involvement, regulation, promotion and it is simply the people's paradise, individualism and informality as most prevalent condition.

The overdose of cryptic condition in the society bars any information, communication, interactivities and interconnectivities in inter and intra-system levels.

The policy of co-existence with other non-ethnic groups is an imposed experience reluctantly tolerated as they fear insecurity and lack of competency, exposure and knowledge parity create a serious rift instead of anticipated harmony and co-ordination.

The extent of entrepreneurial activity cannot be considered as a natural consequence as its extensions are reserved and applicable in the familiarized context but the true spirit of entrepreneurism is not vigilant as the level beyond micro approaches such enthusiasm seemed to be fading away. The spirit however stands alive and brilliant to the extent of survival needs of women which is the point of contentment beyond which the tribal segments are reluctant to yield in.

The changes sought by the youth are merely aspirational but temporal condition without much base as the change may have insignificant effect, as much of the society is still complacent with the traditional systems popular now. There is no SWOT analysis, no opposition nor criticism in adopting them and the system goes without much reaction. This is due to the limited knowledge, non-availability of alternatives and where no total transformations are expected.

The tribal adamancy is prominently visible while replying the questionnaires where the strong agree and strong disagree was depicted as they posed very minute difference for range expression. The occupational preferences were not rigid as the women seemed to be shifting the occupations as per convenience, adapted as per the situation and are dependent on several occupations at a point of time. The micro-portfolio is been speculated as per the convenience and system permissiveness was not adopted without much sentiment nor attachment permit them to shift to another system. The fundamental motivator being the survival instinct and majority of the rural segments prefer money only to meet the domestic purchase of day-to-day needs such as oil, salt, tobacco, soap etc., and occasionally clothes, shoes and health check ups. Otherwise they prefer to estimate the total consumption of the time and settle up the life bargain to work only to meet their minimal necessities and refuse to budge beyond that. This character of extreme adamancy was reflected in their response towards attempting the questionnaires viz., reluctance in interaction, in parting with self-information, participation and early withdrawal from situation etc., resulted in partially filled, unfilled and attempted questions etc. The women were enquired with the experiences, narrations and initiations towards occupations and for very many it is a barter experience, a charity and seasonal preference. It is considered that the employable experience they gathered is not very different with the time, size or even parities as they maintain and choose the generational change has not much really made any impact on their occupational abilities. For majority of women it is observed that their occupational saturations have been fixed at very low profiles. There arises too many trivial parameters which prove to be too vital to them as place of birth, Church, leased land, even pets, annual rituals, graveyard, monoliths, forced habits including "teer" (local gambling), music, arrack and beetle nut (Quai), passion fruit, visits to weekly market/s etc., deemed to be the influencers of occupational decision. The variations with respect to age, gender, education, financial background, access to power, resources, distances, location (including rural and urban), prototyped technologies, practices and local knowledge-based systems out of trial and error were more preferred due to their familiarities, reliability of sources (heredity) and access of ready reference of seniors who supervise or guide the trends. Acceptability to the familiarity of the well set practices which have even though seemed too old they prefer to adopt them. Keeping in view the in-built system mechanisms which have a wider invisible hand preventing them to adopt the new innovative changes barring few who are exposed to the knowledge pace and can make comparatives with both living circumstances are still few to draw the wiser attention to bring the occupational transformations so as to keep pace with the modern changes.

Acknowledgements

I am highly grateful to Rev. Fr. I Warpakma, Principal, St. Anthony's College, Shillong, for his constant support and encouragement to initiate and continue the research project. I am deeply indebted to him not only for his generous approach but also for his advise in critical moments.

I wish to express my deep gratitude to the Indian Council for Social Science Research for giving me this opportunity to successfully undertake the current major research work and their co-operation by liberally financing to pursue the research work and constant encouragement. In this reference it is well in context to extend my deep acknowledgements to Dr. K.L. Khera, for his commendable motivation towards research promotion in the North-east has become the source of my inspiration enabled to bring this occasion. I also extend my sincere thanks to Prof. H.C. Gautam, Gauhati University, Guwahati for being a constructive critic and evaluator of this report in most proficient form.

Special mention of thanks are due to Prof. Surinder Singh Dean, Deptt. of Geologoly, and NEHU to all the respondents, interpreters, government and non-governmental officials, and special mention to the NGOs and associates from different agencies and organizations who spared their valuable time in answering the formal questionnaires and informal discussions and those who extended unstinting cooperation in collecting the essential data for the successful completion of this study.

I reveal my feeling of appreciation would like to the students, host of my friends and colleagues who proved to be very cooperative and helpful but whom I am not able to acknowledge by name. I am indebted to many personnel who have been responsible for the inspiration, direction and execution of the present study. Many others, especially the names of my colleagues in the college need special mention but I hope and trust they will understand and appreciate their omission is nothing more than an investigator's quest for brevity.

Finally, I express my appreciation to the dedicated project team and especially to Baruah, the research assistant, and Ms. Susmita, for her diligence in typing and others who extended their wholehearted cooperation with which the project gained ease and admittance in several ways.

Shillong **Y. Satya**

Contents

List of Tables and Chapter Annexures

Annexures

List of Figures, Maps, Charts and Photographs

Figures

Maps

Charts

Photographs

1

Introduction

Constantness is neither deemed nor implied as a perpetual condition in activated situations and social structure often representing considerable dynamism adept to the prevailing rapidity of convergences either in proactive or reactive behavioural character or otherwise most pertinent to the situations. The social transformations therefore are a natural phenomenon being a part of supra-systems enable the change-impact assent to influence to the extent responsive, receptive and accommodative. The extent of accessibility over the situations spread over the concerningly dominant-level/s reciprocate the impending change viz., social acceptability, willingness and social inclinations favouring the innovative situations help determining the parameters of acceptable levels over the given segments. Societal reactions represent direct or phased relaxations in reservations towards the change-promulgating mechanisms depend on their own self-potentialities viz., historical reasons, resource competencies and locational variables including the radically foreseeable contribution/s by human intervention. The highly interactive societies accept novelty as a positive condition due to their positivities and adaptative flexibilities but it is different in closed segments characterized by their definiteness and conditioned preferences. Self-initiated change is purely contextual leads to transformational changes as it result in societal decisions based on reciprocal and multi-transformational effects.

Reasoning unique with self-centric attributes, compositions—opting secluded approaches, views and acceptances provide an ideal understanding over the focus on ethical identity preservations, inhibitions and anticipated complicacies in adaptabilities of prevailing, anticipatory or innovative situations. The ethnic structures subserve some distinctive patterns viz., socio-behavioural dynamics (Davies, H. and H. Joshi, 2002), ethnic reflexes, generic feasibilities and occupational deviations perceive the change and accommodate it as per its own understanding. These ethnic rigidities imbibed in conditional environments proximate to the societies from intrinsic reasons of understanding seems to promote only limited outlook towards developmental issues as against progressions of growth measures comparable to the extent of intensifications evidenced in developmental or advanced state of affairs. The pace at which the convergences in global context massively being marked in diversified portfolios forcing their way to penetrate their role-significance in those least-responsive segments which are more prone, sensitive and are beyond the jurisdiction of the localized conditions. The contexts which support innovative societal-orientations tend to get reacted with situations viz., transformations initiated in these areas. The progressiveness of such entirety depends on approach-initiations consummate to be the lead. One can observe the vast majority enabling to be reactive to innovative situations tend to be presenting minimal influence lacks appropriate understanding leading to criticalities in interactive conditions i.e.,

- Understanding the adaptation styles of most desired and undesired state of affairs in change context.
- Embarking on compromises over stringency and severity in terms of which facing time testing and restricted alternatives.
- Elaborated time spaces and challenging external pressures which made the ethnic segments especially the vulnerable groups non-reactive towards their cultural dilutions and situations prone for change.
- Majority of the impending changes seemed to be a felt-need or a necessity due to remoteness or isolation created due to the non-changing situations of social-self and its components.

- The prevailing factual gaps creating non-aligned situations with minimal or lack of parity in social divisions on the criteria of convertible conditions.

Competencies of Localized Character and Occupational Proneness

The socio-cultural changes and constructives need to consider processes and domains of influence should perceive these interactions rather than the more vital phenomenon of character or behavioural adamancies and volatilities (of the system concerned).

Dualities in System Determinants : The Constantness Vs. Adaptative Variations

Resource-based dependencies are one of the prime conditions support the generic and explicit anticipations of ethnic-systems. It is perceived that the resource ownership is a variable condition and majority of these resources are under private management viz., the syiemship or lyngdohship (kings), community and private lands leaving minimal authority to local governments for decision making. These utility conditions in their extent are much dependent on the resource access ranging from meeting basic livelihood and survival needs to structural and functional contribution to its economy. Much of the decision-manoeuvre contrived by resources-owners from the final authority result in prescriptions of opportunistic conditions of minimal effort at individual levels. The occupational implications seemed to be vibrant at the source where the value-extensions are seriously understaken due to lack of progressional modernities.

Impact of Value Determinants and Occupational Competencies

The widespread diversities in the State's geo-demographics can be implied over its topographical and climatic impact on its flora and fauna. Its contribution can be evidenced not only on its rainfall, water resources and soil but also on its plantations and crop patterns, horticulture, forest and livestock growth etc., depict the economic and socio-cultural dependencies which have been accommodated not perceiving these as "occupational variation" but as a part of their culture. The repercussions of such impact are also felt on its provisioning of the basic infrastructural and progressive adaptations by the government, uniformity in the access of assets, services, opportunities etc.

Essentialities of Informalities

The socio-cultural and familial systems are influenced by the (Yapi-Diahou, A., 1995) accultural, multicultural combinations especially in the Capital City Shillong, the inter-district, state and international domains enabling to promote trade, industry and commerce. These areas have not been restricted to the cross-cultural institutional effect but also promoted multi-stimulus reciprocal business dependencies viz., collaborations and partnering, promotional tie-ups, live-in arrangements to boost the market activities enabled a hyper-cosmo environment encouraging vast scope for micro and meso business strata

Gender-role Contributions and Extended Status

The ethnic effect and its impact on the women is immense due to the customary laws, traditions and ethnic framework in its likelihood character of forward growth by means of enforcements insisting on the multi-mode living styles, asset-distributions, shouldering family liabilities resulting in horizontal extensions, proneness to neo-traditionalism, attending to behavioural dynamics (Vlasblom Jan and Schippers, 2006) and transaction-effects on its occupational understanding and self-approach. The cultural dominance over promoting the occupational cult insisted on the major role-play of "clan promotion" as an ethnic liability deemed to be the most influencing contributor in this dimension.

Urban and Rural Divisional Arena

The spatial means defined on the jurisdictions (Yahama, D. and Shekamang, P., 1986) based on domain cannot be an ideal estimator for natural growth consequence and its rapidity over the zonal implications enable the comparatives practically non-feasible. The present case reveals the urban-based restraints and limitedness is least effective with minimal incidental forms where much of which are overcome by external supportives. The rural positions depict self-sufficiency in their character with massive possessions and meagre means whereas their urban counterparts represent the ownership over "all pertinent dependencies" of ruralities due to its multi-dimensional growth and interactive effects. These dependencies seemed to be varying in direct and indirect access conditions based on contextual dependency-character prevalent in the state.

Role-definiteness in Resource and Market Based Dependencies

The core market activities influenced by the externalities penetrating into the closed systems have been witnessing disproportionate contributions viz., market systems, religious and social-supportive systems advocating new perceptions in occupational choice-options and preferences. The value-determinants have been dependent on the intervening segments diluting the spatial rigidities of both focused and non-focused systems chosen in the current study.

Occupational Supportive Radius (OSR)

The feminine OSR seemed to be a determinable condition over the perception of ethno-societal—character, attributic contributions of domain, the systems provisioning towards creating an occupation-prone applicability, self-approaches and new definitions in the synergestic combinations create "tier" systems of occupational scope and condition. The occupational determinants are those which happen over the definitions of new value chains prescribed with variant orientations and suitabilities in terms of application.

Hierarchy of Occupational Designs (HOD)

HOD enable the occupational differences based on multitude of mechanisms prescribe the gender-based generic conditions which create pre-determinants of occupation-based core views (historical) and evaluate the contribution by means of core-competencies. The occupational entry therefore can be understood as to be of gender, race, religion, ethnic and social-based statuses contribute to the "scenario-building" of the current and future occupational portfolios.

The synergistic forum in which the occupational interest, creativity keeping in view its visible role of requirements replacing materialism to the shallowed values of ethnicism form into a central issue which behave towards sensitivities enable to perk into the societal felt need towards meeting its requirements. Shaping contribution of the occupational components enable to identify and highlight the **objective-range** based on issues-of-priority which rule the sub-sub-condition may querry over the following :

Objective Wrap-up

- What are the prone forces which actually determine the priority of occupational highlights?
- What are the parameters of the operational capacities of extensive (selective) situations in terms of societal contribution to the occupation?
- What environmental forces enable to define the work-preference in different environments?
- What are the suitable determinants of occupational entry and exit measures?
- What are the new measures that are help changing the occupational divisionalisation open only to specific segments?
- What are the determinants of occupational market? What links actually make the markets meet, evaluate and materialize the value chain analysis?
- What occupation markets permit direct participation? What occupational growth/occupational deepening and access frontier is the rates of occupation expansion?

The Multi-effective Provisioning Model : The Situational Why's and Why not's

At macro level the occupational proneness is a general reflective situation when the opportunities enable to

- Identify the requirements of given locations in terms of occupational needs.
- The local demand which comes forth to prefer the occupations.

The constant and volatile ethno-social stature presenting reflections effective to its socio-compositions enable to define the ethnic stature as to its vitalities in terms of :

- **Societal character :** The component of occupational casualty leading to the minimal expectation and self-involvement in the aggressive forms. The social character is conditioned by its provisional and confirmed influencers. These factors are understood in different dimensions enabling to perceive the socio-rationalities in heterogeneous forms.
- **Level of perception :** The brand of ethnicity is partially successful in creating a consistent image but the internal transformations have been quite prominent. The horizontal inequalities are competent to generate a shallow but wider occupational environment.
- **Looking beyond one's own capacities :** The accelerated growth is restricted in selective occupational options enabling the majority to opt for "dependent measures and alternatives" for selective groups and selective options.
- **The feminine organizational and administrative contribution :** The micro approaches which are complacent irrespective of urban-rural divide enable the social segments show a reverse influence of urban dependencies (for specificities) on rural rather than *vice versa*. The ethnic socio-compositions and

transformations enabling promotives are suggested in Figure 1.1.

Figure 1.1 : Ethnic Stature Vs. Ramification Model

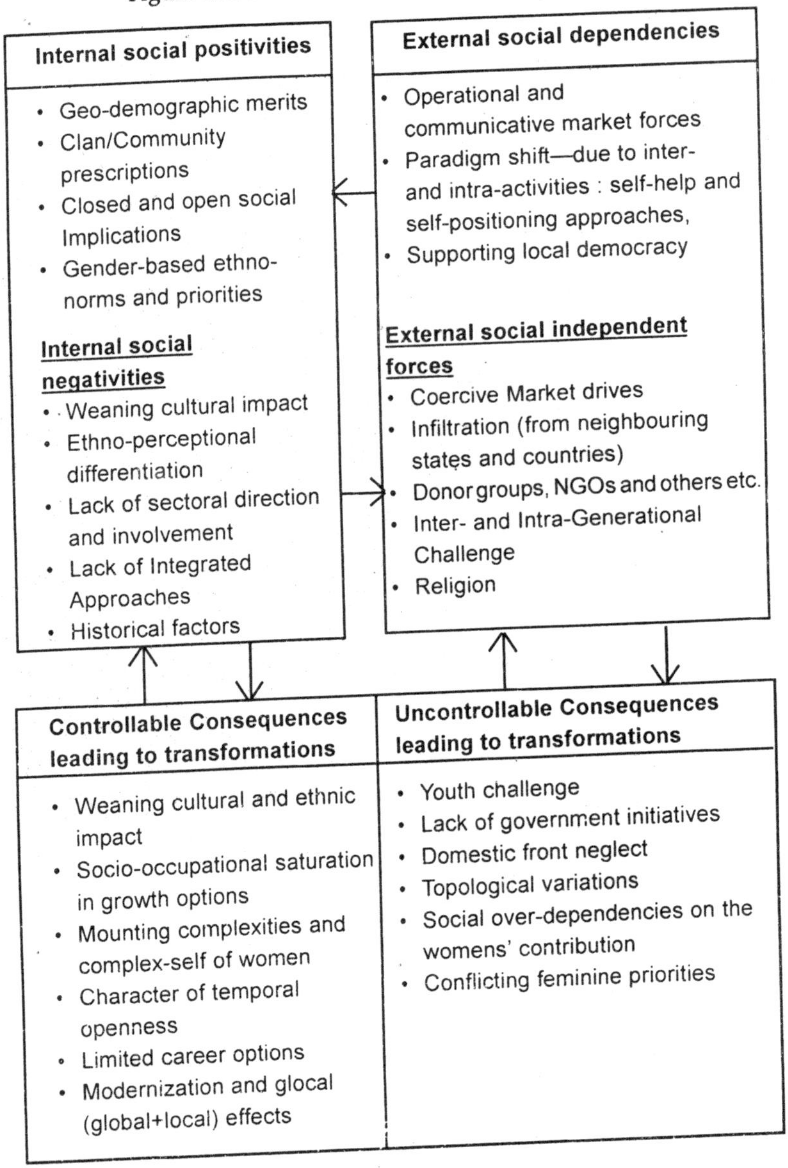

Orientations and Profiling : Concept of Stabilization

The perceptions, temperaments, personalities, value systems, socio-cultural factors and role ambiguities etc., enables to create the activity level towards the general lifestyle patterns of the social segments. The occupational beliefs and decision formulations sue to be the reflections of such lifestyles which remain at parity or opt for elevated or depleted levels. The social behaviour is the interactive reflection of the social equations layered and prescribes the determinable behaviour helps creating the "socio-occupational spaces".

Occupational Ethics and Ethical Issues

The employable competencies are based on the regional locational factors, its affordability and coping abilities of generating a resource frame, its exposure and interactivities define the typical ethnical values and occupational ability form a dual appeal of both restrictive and encouraging forms. The occupational determinants, the functional framework, role-orientations preferred determine the level of occupational ethics. The occupation as such can be viewed as a measure of survival, power, prestige, skill, money or any other economic, social, cultural or environmental need disposition can be explained in terms of the value codes, generosity, universality, conversion, cross-cultural satisfier enable to perceive the ethnic-temperament.

Socio-value Dimensions and Occupational Promotions

The former parameters valued as social dimensions be it traditional or modern based on the family, gender, age, race or position in social segment became less significant rather than the family concepts and mutualities, cross-culturalism, communal solidarity, convergence, occupational aesthetics, reciprocity and behavioural dispositions etc., on attitudes, values, situational compassion, implicit culture or isolates etc., have been the latest to influence the occupational framework.

Urbanalities vs. Ruralities : A Social Assessment

The urban advancements, opportunities and access to the occupational dependencies other than the land based assets discriminate these on technological or convergent issues. The areas where rural resource forms a base the urban is dependent on rural for mega issues and rural's self-potentiality enable to be of minimal dependence on urban but this remain a singular context applicable in appropriate conditional status.

The rural and urban association also depends on the multiple urban opportunities available to the rural and these alternative patterns aiming minimal need gratification of rural display—one can be understand that the rural in its simplistic form is more independent rather than being dependent. The alternative emphasis over the non-agricultural forms, leveraging equalities, vulnerabilities and minimal pursuit represent the requisite conditions enable contextual understanding based on the access and adequacy conditions.

Social Cohesion (Consistency)

Contextual Cohesive Levels (CCLs)

The consistency levels are deemed :

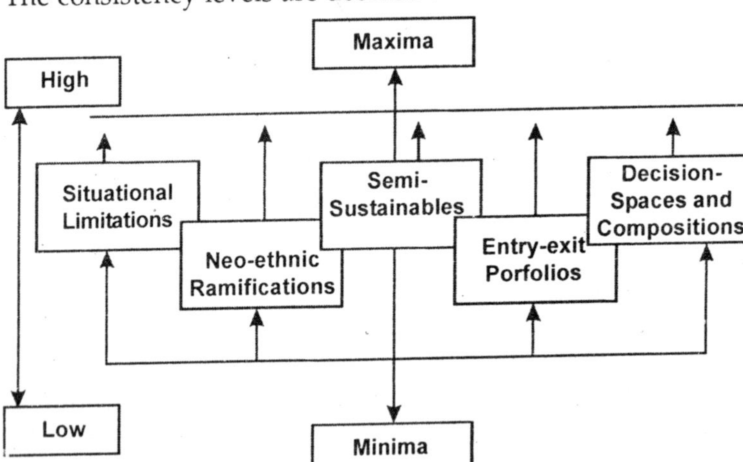

Figure 1.2 : Context-based Social Consistency Model

Conditions that concentrate on the (a) situational limitations which are predictable or contingent depict multi-effective implications synchronizing both traditional and modern situations; (b) neo-ethnic ramifications are the most sensible and reactive trends favouring or rejecting the nuances of benefit minutes/spaces.

Socio-ethical Affiliations : A Mutuality of Services

An inter-relationship with the occupational preferences enable to classify the occupations as :

- **Service Segment :** The gamut of service profiles in the state can largely be classified into the institutionalized (state, centre, local bodies and institutions of variant nature), networking (by means of branching out and creation of spaces either by enforcement or due to specific motives and informal categories form the itinerary of variant order spreading from large to small/ pigmy categories.
- **Business Segment :** The exclusive local talent of business has insignificant representation in the spectrum of business spread. The business as a massive external motivator and regulator is a force beyond the jurisdiction of any regulation as the market forces are penetrating and reflective provisioning a precise but reciprocal advantage towards the incoming and outgoing market activities. Much of the business activity is managed by private factors without much enforcement, supervision and promotional appeal.
- **Ethnic Professionalism :** Represented by skills and offer of professional services the local talent is still in infant stage and are restricted to urban areas. The formal allocations of professional facilities made available at rural make a surrogate effort of survival. Several professional service offers are collaborative or contractual in nature are meagre and inadequate with limited condition.

- **Seasonal** or periodical employment, temporal in nature and partial need gratifier in which the much popular, locally highly demanding and resource dependent occupations viz., agriculture with its allied occupations of horticulture, floriculture, pisciculture, mining, forestry, livestock etc., are pre-dominantly internal and occupations based on external supportives promoting local talents and skills.

Meriting the Realistic Performance : Magnitude of Competitive Advantage

Creation of Occupational Spaces : Variant and Vulnerable

The occupational vitalities in the ethnic domain characterize the functional framework suggest the "segmental dependency ratio" depicting multi-occupational dependencies i.e., occupational portfolios for different purposes. It is observed that the occupation is much a prerogative for survival—be it in rural or urban and the situations pose lack of alternatives, or alternatives beyond the reach, alternatives demand extensive compromise and is beyond the capacity of acceptance. The occupational comparatives enable to decide on specific occupation till a new lucrative offer arrives or make a temporal compromise or settle with the occupation available at hand which satisfies majority of either occupational or non-occupational specificities.

Developing a Value-based Decision Point (as rated by Social Segment/s)

In the process of survival, the occupational-proneness can be witnessed in direct/indirect, advantage, creative or even aggressive forms the occupational temperament can depict the nuances by means of differentiation. The occupational strategies are the combined effect of accepting those which match the needs and situations aiming maximum benefit with minimal effort. The occupational perceptional differences tend to opt a situation of "unique occupational image" created by judgmental means. The occupational context however poses wide variation between occupations which are tangible (structure and benefits), abstract (alternative and cryptic (hidden) merits) and situational (contingent or context-based).

Perceived Differences in Micro and Macro Occupational Markets

The pre-requisites associated to geo-demographic, socio-economic and ethno-cultural etc., shape the favourable and unfavourable perseverances towards the ethnic mindset and perceptional variations based on the segmental context of aiming towards "preparedness" and "suitability" from the angle of employable competency of the domain determine the synergistic outcome of an occupational positioning. Both external and internal factors matter to a large extent as motivators for the initiation, continuity, modify or even liquidate the situation.

Setting Occupational Brand Position

Image created by brand remains foremost. The attributic range (choicest occupational option), spirit of participation, administering (the generic initiations desirable) and manageable ability (competencies/skills—to gain employability) are the framework which create a congruent image. A position then is a location where the occupational brand is positioned relative to its alternate image-builders. Leveraging the occupational image building and decision-making process keeping into concern the influential and involved contributions create a particular occupational base in terms of arriving the continuum of satisfaction (based on character, brand, image or a combination of all) determine the "occupational decision intensity".

Occupational Focus

The approximations prescribed by the social angle of ethnicity enable to purview the occupation as a construct to appeal the norms of tradition. The supremacy of the ethnic identities enables to determine the corresponding reflections of each proven decision-context. The implicit conditionalities to a large extent have been promoting transformations at micro levels in a massive way but the overall implications of the social dimension enable to position the ethno-influential occupational stances as the generic articulations in prominent forms.

Mapping Occupational Sustainable Trends

The segmental framework by means of 5-A Preference matrix is as follows :

Table 1.1: 5-A Preference Matrix

Attribute	*Appeal*	*Atmosphere*	*Accommo-dation*	*Ambience*
Occu-pation	Level of Involvement	Personal status	Self-Image	Associated Risk
Ethnicity	Implicit culture	Inclined to clan	Community-Preference	Conventional/ Dependent
Resource Access	Existence of Base	Multiple Deci-sion Option	Self-regulated	Wider Prefe-rential status
Compati-bility	Exposure	Differentiation	Hetero-geneous	Exclusive/ Selective
Perform-ing Skills	In-depth character	Premium	Involvement-continuum	Situational predominance

The social mapping enable to understand the segmental framework towards features accessible or inaccessible determining point-of-occupational positioning based on the occupational brand and merits of the system concerned depict the :

- Composite vulnerabilities are the identifiable characters of the geo-demographic and infrastructural deficiencies mired the "occupational capabilities (coping + abilities)" of the domain.
- Character of Informalities which can be perceived at variant social layering enable them to accommodate an occupational compromise of varying degrees.

- Penetrating diversities from different dimensions *viz.*, accultural, neutralizing and casualisation deemed to be "culturally acceptable" and at-convenience behavioural patterns have much concern even on occupational trends.

A massive social contracting which highlight the deprivations, growing individualism, imbalanced gender concepts, ethnic shock due to hi-cosmo character etc.

Fig. 1.3: Preferred Lifestyle Model

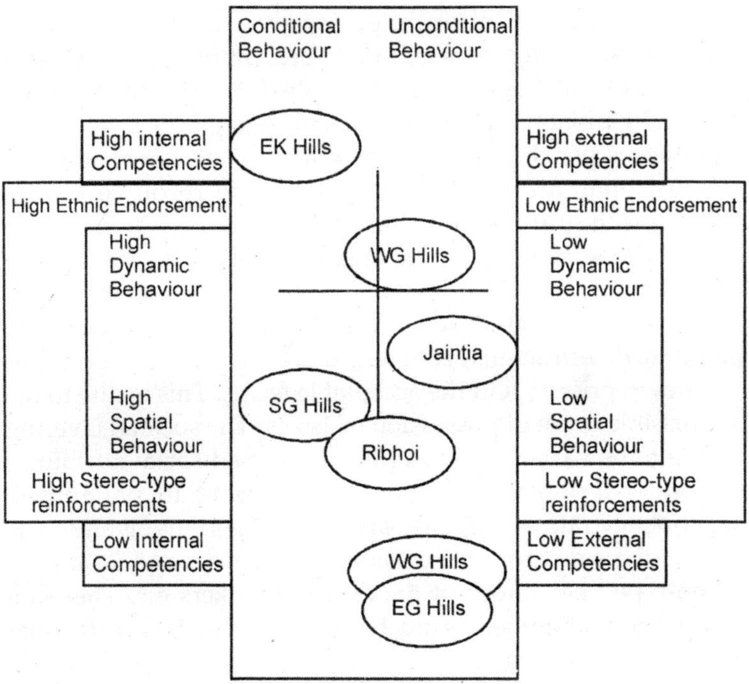

The representations of societal character in general depict the preferable lifestyles and the occupational compositions have their implications over the prevailing framework in the temporal and sustainable forms. The state experiences a coordinated multi-income trend which boosts imbalances at individual developmental levels at the cost of integrated growth. It is found that the fundamental "resource base proneness" ignore the rural and urban discriminations in the context of mutualities. Even in the conditions of value-determinants reaching minimum—yet the most is sought from agriculture, forest and mineral resources continue to bear hi-value conversion capacities attracting not only internal i.e., as survival option for large majority of urban-rural dependencies but the external penetrating forces viz., dominant and compelling market forces even under rigid conditional terms.

Alignment of Contributory Reflexes

Understanding the historical perspectives (Arce. A., 1998) of occupational preferences and in its present operant reflexes—the state depict fragmented but context-based opinionalities. The occupational orientation enabled to align the trivials and vitalities as per the social layering arrived on the condition/s of most open and hidden situations. The resource fixities determine the purpose for which the occupational dependency can be prone to limit "value chains" evolved as the level of involvement i.e., the internal, inter-district, inter-state, border trade (international). The conversion factor which matter as the value determinants are assessed at individual level—as per one's own priority and the acceptable terms. This is due to the permissible norm of possession of assets. The societal layering enable to be variant on the criteria of closed social attributes, perceptional differences based on inter-generational appeal, dependency ratios of micro-participation and involvement as well as the synchronized decision-making dependent on the stereo-typed behaviour of the decision-makers etc. The state occupational alignment is much observed as to its occupational options based on the :

- quantum of the preferred and consequentially preferred occupational means
- revocable/irrevocable conditionalities applicable as per situations
- distinctive localized appeal of integrated external and substantiated internalities

- status-based decision framework negotiate voluntary acceptances
- underlying consciousness reflect in the realistic applications

Critically the situations reveal lack of nurture, supervision and regulatory means where the systems have been directed by the movement of forces which are autonomous and attend to the self-centred behaviour rather than systematic progression. The societal appeal of matriliny is nothing but hype of the segmental attribute applicable in at-convenient shape in terms of its occupational fulfilment. The internal forces claim to be robust *viz.*, the community (Kenny, S., 2002) or clan have to some extent imply prescriptions as to the allocation of the most precious resource *i.e.*, the land and the autonomy to use it as the competency of the segmental components. Practically the segments are leading a simple and saturated lifestyle which is not supported by ambition or aggressiveness. The requirements are minimal as well as the opportunities. There is a perfect match with the people status code as well as the developmental progressions which create a minimal demanding condition. But within the desirable means each segment is competent enough to be engaged in multiple occupations that fetch a direct value or a near value-status based on conversion competencies of resource-base.

Entry and Exit : A Portfolio of Potentialities

Barring the service segmental offers of the security the rest of the occupational contingencies in applicable framework have been bearing the risks and uncertainties as typical as to any predictable condition. The occupational character posing a temporal factor due to the individual's self-centric decision-approach enable the negativities as a part of the game and the conflicting role-ambiguities form a vital system. The preference structure is stretched from a massive to micro representing a pareto effect in its growth and developmental forms.

The occupational forms preferred on the criteria of survival, prestige, power, recognition, appreciation, an expression of freedom and as an integrated perceivable need as per one's own understanding. The role-responsibilities assigned to the occupational-preference segment enable to determine the core parameters which are often more than one to influence the occupational spectrum in totality. Very many situations were found to be the limited choice and maximizing the compromise levels when it comes to survival. The next preference being the familial, clan-based associations and the most preferred comfort zones of familiarity and identity. The constructive parity in mind set and thought process enable a collective strength rather than individual strength.

Integrated Structural and Unstructured Social Movements

The occupationalities have not been a singular situation in which the decision-dimension can be perceived. It is an evolved condition based on multiple measurements subconsciously weighing each reference in its own strengths and weaknesses. The conflict-prone evaluative means enable to imply the base-conditions over which the assessments are made. The judgmental effects reflect the formal and informal tenacities adopted as life values in the process of criteria definitions. Each segment within the variables of understanding of its priorities and preferences determine the extent to which the acceptance or rejection is permitted. The convergences are those synchronized posit of events manipulating to pursue a favourable condition as preferred by the segments.

Within the span limits of occupational decisions, the ethnic segments of Meghalaya are competent to arrive their life lessons most applicable to the living conditions. The micro participation is being structured systematically which has been enabling the state to progress with the teeming population as majority of the ethnic groups have limited access of the natural resources. The overburdened responsibilities of the young, old and other family members which have been enforced by the customs are strictly followed. The occupation in the extended family structure is more a necessity which is to be undertaken as a part of family contribution. The macro-level of understanding therefore enable to define the occupation as a social necessity for the ethnic segments as they draw their parameters for providing a meaning of living in association. The sharedness, community survival and progressions have been the prerogatives which have been well understood by the segments to draw wider meaning of clan survival and clan promotion as the major and most significant factors to be met by the women. The occupational forces which form a secondary issue enable to define the living needs, growing needs, positional needs and survival needs of the clan members rather than being thinking in an individualistic view. The clan priorities, and behavioural compositions aim at much more higher order of ethnic struggle for the survival needs of the community at large rather than being identified as an individual decision.

Sum Up

The introductory reference unravel the vitalities of structural compositions of these ethnic segments, the survival norms in its wider framework being demarcated into several sub-segments having been differentiated on the criteria of the asset access, resource producibility and decision approaches feasible for adoption. The variations are based on the positional differences of the segments which at large have been standing on the uniform framework of the supreme need gratification of clan and community survival. The presence of the traditional regulatory means still hold good to partial extent to support equilibrium when it comes to the question of survival of the much fragmented ethnic brand identities. The orientations towards sustenance endorse appropriate yet stereo-typed alignment/s in the contributory factors resulting in multitudinal decision approaches based on the applicable context and appropriateness as per the developmental understanding towards the communities' survival and growth needs.

2

Occupational Consequences : Understanding Focal Group Interpretations

Introduction

Understanding the ideologies of femininity in gender-based contributions preferably in matrilineal segments persevere the unique and distinctive conceptual framework, associated developmental context in which the feminine intellectual, operational and psychographic abilities to be perceived in most feasible and understandably vivid classification in gender analytical systems. The pronouncements of these multi-layered singular contributions facilitate exploration of feminine entrepreneurial, organizational and managerial talents articulated into micro and macro developmental channels. The ethnic enforcements into the matriarchy enabled, molded, feminine life-perceivable styles as being most honourable, predominant and custodial forms idealize traditional values and customs. The parametric view enables to exhibit vitality but there are transformations in the system as the feminine **role-description** enables to define the role-complexities as follows :

- The concept of matriliny is much advocated only to the youngest daughter of the family. The daughters other than the youngest have not been bounded by the family-based responsibilities.

- Since three generations we have a single girl child. The girl child is responsible to look after all the surviving members of the family.
- We give what all we have to the youngest daughter. After all if something happens—it is she who has to take care of us.
- The youngest daughter has to look after the senior members of the family. She is the custodian of the property of the household or even clan.

The ethnic view defines the role-responsibilities of (Willis, K., 1996) women especially the most prominent women in the family being **(i)** the **mei-ieit** (the seniormost surviving women in the household); **(ii)** the **daughter** of the family other than the youngest daughter {initiator of the new iing (house)} and **(iii)** the **Ka Kadduh**, the youngest daughter of the family, by being the virtue of her position hold the clan imposed responsibility of looking after the family. The **families are** mostly of extended form comprising the grandparents, parents, maternal aunts, cousins, unmarried brothers and sisters, separated or divorced brothers, husband and children (in case of married ka kadduh) etc. A typical household includes maternal uncles and clan members as frequent visitors.

The role-predominances enable to reveal the supremacy of the *mei-ieits* to undertake the overall monitoring and supervision of the family. The daughters of the family are being assigned with the "responsibilities" ever since childhood is nurtured to be prepared for the load of relationships accepted gracefully. The daughters other than the youngest daughter move out of the parental **iing** (household) after their marriage. They are independent and prefer self-decision while making the selection of the husband and also the post-marriage lifestyle to be adopted. However, a separated or divorced daughter may well opt to return back for shelter becomes the responsibility of the youngest sister. It is critical for the "youngest" daughter who is married or unmarried (including separated or divorced) to be relieved from this privileged responsibility assigned by tradition.

Familial Decision-making

The familial situations enable to reveal the stability of marital status for the first and subsequent is the highlighting character. The clan/community and religion remain silent when it comes to the interference into the private lives of its members. This freedom is interpreted in different forms resulted in "decelerating" family values and concepts.

- My brother has a broken family. His wife married again and his children are now my responsibility. His drinking habit is uncontrollable. In order to keep my children away from this mess I moved out of my parental iing and formed a nuclear family. But everyday I still visit my house to look after my family members.
- I had to stay in a rented house because of my school going children. My parental house is too far away and is becoming inconvenient for them. Either me or my husband visit my parental house almost everyday to look after the necessities.
- I am married to the youngest daughter. She got agricultural land which is taken care by her maternal uncle and me. However, my role as husband remains limited when it comes to her family affairs. I withdraw myself from their exclusive family meetings.
- I have two unmarried sisters and two unmarried step-brothers from my step father. One brother returned back from his wife's house. My sister-in law—is a government employee and holding a good post. My brother is younger to her and is in private job. She insisted on him to look after the household which he didn't like.
- I remained as a spinster throughout my life. All my sisters and brothers got married except me. Being the youngest daughter my responsibility is to look after the grandmother and my aunts. We have an electronics shop in the market.

Irrespective of the role-responsibility the system enabled to promote mutually merited conjugal acceptances of both legitimate and illegitimate forms and these are formally accepted and honoured. The practices are much prevalent in the urban areas due to its cosmo environment in inter-district, inter-state (with Assam) and international (Bangladesh) border areas where the interactivities are visible in momentum. The resultant feature being single ladies with children (as preferred by the women) depict casuality in relation, short-lived and relationships without responsibility. Majority of men withdraw from household responsibility from either side (of wife's or parental) and prefer a carefree lifestyle or maintain nominal involvement.

The women's role in this context becomes crucial as the care of self and children (including spouse, if any) enable her to accept the dual role responsibility towards nurturing the family and opt to be selective in occupational choice which does not clash with her interests in the family. The personal reasons in no way abrupt the status of youngest daughter in accepting her responsibility towards her iing. However, the family members share the burden by engaging in different tasks to earn their livelihood.

The **role** of tribal women :

- as Clan Promoter
- as Custodian
- as Iing (Home) maker

define the occupational interest (to look after self, her immediate family, and extended family) keeping in view the supportives as to what actually forms her inherited property—be it a house, land (urban or rural) utility of land (used for agriculture or non-agricultural activities i.e., mining, forestry, plantations etc.). The "asset backing" by self-means or ancestral (loaded with responsibilities) provide materialistic relief as to make an occupational decision. The male involvement in this reference remain by being a father, maternal uncle, husband or any other living relation by enabling support to the process of maintaining cultural advocacies by means of rituals, ceremonies, traditions etc.

Character Analysis of Tribal Women

It is observed that the limited maturities and adopted lifestyles with the much granted autonomy has lost its sanctity of family stability and security otherwise serves as cushion/protectives for the women. The personal freedom towards leading one's lifestyle by women relieved the men from bearing all responsibility except few cases of genuineness. The character of possessing property and maintenance is being supplemented by men, where the higher order of activities are taken care by women i.e., money matters and vital decisions. The women, therefore,

- Look after the self, familial needs and responsibility and also to create a provisioning for it,
  - o To hold the responsibility of the assets (if any) inherited which form a core or source of supplementaries to the regular source of income.
  - o To enable the administration of household functional with other earning members of family.
- But the situational extremities influence occupational decision when :
  - o Custodian is not inherited and without any property or nominal property to share similar burden.
  - o Relieved due to non-residential status and foregone the claim over clan property for ever.
- Occupation remain inevitable in which the lead role played by youngest daughter and all other family members.
- The other than youngest has to initiate a new home need occupation for establishing a new iing.
- The matriliny insist on clan promotion as "cultural responsibility" rather than sparking ethnic professionalism of the women—who also innately has the desire to promote her title by producing offsprings.

The Occupational Layering

The clustering of women's occupational initiatives is as follows :

- **Service Spectrum** : This comprises the state and Central Government, government undertakings including local bodies and few private organizations etc.;
- **Professional/s** : This form into a nominal group comprising both urban and rural professionals;
- **Business** : It includes (i) **Producibles** (including extractive) and manufacturing : Lumber, coal, limestone, Broom, Livestock, Tejpatta etc.;

(ii) **Moderate** : Cement, horticulture, potato, smoked meat, bakery items, dry fish, beetle nut, beetle leaves, tobacco, ginger, turmeric and other spices;

(iii) **Micro** : (inclusive of itinerary) orchids, herbal and medicinal plants, fresh and dry mushrooms, bamboo items, ready-made garments, décor, wooden and bamboo utilities, jam-jelly making, pickles, poultry, spices, dry fish, rice liquor, dry garlic, hides and skins, bristles, wooden utilities, tailoring, computer skills etc.;

(iv) **Business Serve** : Large and small scale retailing, foreign goods, second hand goods, smuggled goods etc.;

(v) **Modern Professions :** Rural real estate, brokering (including international broking), trafficking, rural tourism, developing theme and techno-parks, money lending and financial services, security, domestic help and private rural transport, gambling and wager, arrack making, border trade (inclusive of illegal trade i.e., smuggling gold, arms and banned material) floriculture etc.

The decision effect is the result of convergent factors based on the personal and family possessions, the reasonability of exploration/exploitation as per one's own segmental exuberance. But the closed societal effect of the state with its limited levels of performance scope enabled to provide conditioned lives. For majority of the women the foremost condition is being reluctant towards mobility (Pisati, M. and A. Schizzerotto., 2003).

Fig. 2.1: Mapping Ethno-decision Options

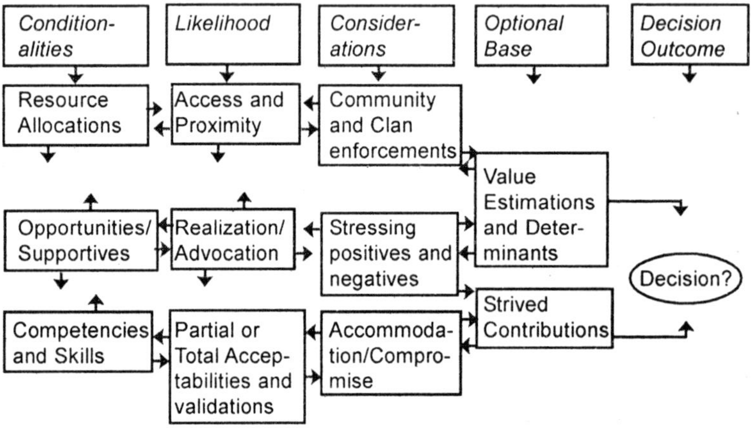

The extremities in reactivities, behavioural patterns, the associated trends (Jacobs, S., 1999) and adaptation towards the positional advantage lack consideration and an appropriate base leading to formulations over the occupational valuations, identities and transformational challenges. Determining structural trend towards the prone cause-and-effect reasons which have cultural issues enabling to reduce the sanctity of value systems and cultural positions get dampened up by transformations. The cultural rigidities and external transitions have the following :

Incidence of Situational Definiteness

The enabling environment favouring the progressive growth seemed to be under severity. The activities prone for occupational promotives pose definiteness giving way to the opportunities to external forces is one of the major factors of situational limitedness. The ethnic trends, value determinants, internal conflicts, lack of aggressive growth-orientations and strategic outlook have been the contributors for ethnic rigidities.

System Polarization

The accultural behaviour to a large extent brought revolutionary changes much supported to the ethnic prescriptions. The occupational preferences to a large extent have been influenced by these polarized behavioural cult otherwise became an integral part of ethnic system. The prevalences, however, are reserved to the urban segment but its repercussions have no high reactivities even in rural sector.

Table 2.1 : Model of System—Schism

Prerequisites and Contradictions	*Neutralizing effect*
• Urban-rural variation	• Resource access and possession
• Preference and perseverance	• Ethnic enforcements
• Signifying optional effects	• Context-based value definitions
• Initiatives and compromises	• Level/s of ethnic shock
• Social and circumstantial limitations	• Stereotype adaptations
• Homogeneity and heterogeneity	• Equality in opportunity

Social-layering and Effects of Informality

The societal layering is based on the criteria of exposure to external systems, understanding the consequences of interactivities with diversified segments enabling horizontal/ vertical integrations, pervasiveness of effective knowledge and communication systems. Lack of appropriate infrastructural combinations, low system versatilities created social-tiers and promoted occupational decision variation. The ignorance of occupational tactics, selectivities and minimal negotiation towards life values provoked massive micro stimulations as current day occupational consequence.

Leveraging Ethical and Occupational Consequences

A combined set of "social reconciliations" which may be observed :

- I did my MBA from a reputed management institute. I got a job in a multinational company. My pay was quite handsome. But I still prefer being here as I belong to this place.
- Being in State Capital is my privilege. I originally hail from a remote village and always dreamt of having a job here. I accepted my first job in Calcutta and served there for 2 years. They posted me here and I am the branch manager now.
- I left my home town to continue my studies. There are no specialized institutions in the subject I opted for. After my studies I got a job in Bangalore which was accepted by me. Staying outside the state in the initial periods is no problem but in long term I didn't prefer it.
- My retail business is going pretty well. I wanted to expand but I need to travel quite a lot all over Meghalaya. But I prefer being in Shillong and became contented with my business level.
- I am dealing in decorative pieces useful in interior décor. I get good deals within Shillong. The dealers bring the material to Gauhati and we go to pick it from Gauhati. I know my choice is limited by being in Shillong but I am reluctant to leave the place.
- I am a vegetable vendor. I import onions from Nasik and potatoes from Assam. My business flunks when there is flood in Assam. I am used to be dependent on the brokers who supply the "mal" since several years. I cannot ditch them.
- I am a doctor by profession. I am posted in a rural area and my old parents stay in the city. I attend my duties and prefer to remain in the city as they need me. (Doctor who visits the rural area only on the village market days i.e., 2 days in a week).
- I am an auto dealer. The pony carts look shabby in the city and became successful to enforce the law that no pony cart is permitted in the city limits. The

> consequence being that all pony carts have been shifted to far away district and that could boost my business.

reveal the social inflexibilities and the relative concern towards social sensitivities and administering the "contextual" compositions which have an ideal bearing on the decision-values and trends.

Decision Spaces : Events and Uncertainties

The prevalence of organizational and managerial talents as imbibed qualities the ethnic women (segments) have cultural interpretations which formed much to their life decisions. The occupational preferability to make the functional area different to the familiar situation, the acceptance or tolerance limits to the extent to be borne with the segments other than their own communities are a task difficult to several women. The concept of short-vision is much in momentum rather than futuristic view which prefers them to think for immediate need gratification rather than follow up a more contributing developmental view.

Dearth of effective communication and personality development skills enable them to withdraw from the lucrative offers and learning practices from other communities. Meriting the occupational analysis, coping with critical consequences, augmenting tact and exploring the opportunities as well as the total commitment to the realistic views enable to glorify the womens' entrepreneurial talents but proved to be adopted in negligible forms.

The ethnic segments demonstrating the character of closed economies procreate the ideologies of isolation.

Arena of Ethnic Positivities

Prescribed behaviour- straight forward-sincere-cooperative-at-ease lifestyles-prefer elaborations-least concerned about unrelated issues-expect reciprocal behavioural ethics-associate events with ethnic purview-definiteness and quick decision-making.

Arena of Ethnic Negativities

Perceptional reservations—difficulties in coping up-slow pace of understanding-limited outlook-resist change-strong in-built beliefs and value systems—preferential difference in communication, inter-personal relationships, motivational approaches and outlook.

An "occupational situation" needs to be understood in the context of comprehensive ethnic understanding and knowledge towards the ethnic clans and cultural values, customs, priorities and experiences which create a wholesome familiarity of the ethical context. Creating an **occupational condition** as per the ethnic choices and assessments of its worth not in the typical context but signifies the ethnic prospects. This enables to perceive the :

- non-occupational perceivables and priorities vigilant in the work conditions.
- occupation demand ethics to be matched with available ethnic possibilities and the likelihood of ethical context with milieu.
- with respect to the people, their occupational opinion in terms of the needs, desires, satisfactions and dissatisfactions, assessment, expectation from occupational environment in which the work—the employable terms—expectations and associated means need comprehensive insights.
- lack of in-depth understanding of the "practicing ethnicity"—ethnic demands, requirements and negotiations are prone to the limited grasp/ understanding of given occupational context.
- the "performing skills", of occupation/s—their initiations, sequences, operational purview need to be assessed and differentiation to verify the occupational fulfilment by undertaking an ethical and non-ethical forums. This should accord the significance in the variation.

Nurturing and Accommodating of Response Channels

In the ethnic standpoint it is quite difficult to be non-ethnic. The ethnicity factor in the ethnic domain angle the perceptions in ethnic viewpoint and to the originals who have imbibed only ethical culture it remains too difficult to understand the non-ethical viewpoint. The segments which are least exposed tend to be sensitive to cultural facets and develop a deep sense of complexes with co-existing cultures *viz.*, the variation in Khasi cult in East and West Khasi Hills, the accultural symptoms of Assam and Garo in the Garo region and influence of Bangladesh in the border areas of Khasi and Jaintia Hills etc.

Why interactivities are rigid?

- The ethnic segments are ethically rigid
- Prefer to remain in community comfort zones
- Unwilling to compromise or adamancy
- Lack of parity in understanding
- Developing complexes and self-centredness
- Preference ratios as per their limited understanding
- Mismatch of reciprocal priorities and work preferences
- Communication gaps

Besides these Figure 2.2 perk into the effective situational-response as under :

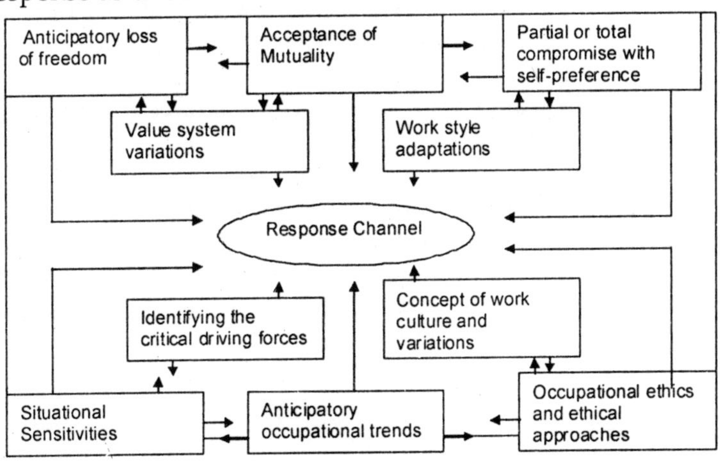

Fig. 2.2: Response Model

Generic Transformations : Feasibilities and Advocations

What is the extent of the possibility to make the comparatives (Heath, A. and Cheung, 1998) of a subconscious internal system and the volatile external system remains parallel? Should we consider occupation as a women's dependent or interdependent condition? What are the motives of being their dependent and independent status? The competency of employability influences the situation as follows :

(i) At macro level the occupation as a dependent factor is restricted to the extent of the independent (ethnic, social, cultural, economic, legal or environmental) motivating factors.
(ii) Its dependent status is wholly influenced by the partial or total influence of independent variable/s.
(iii) Each independent variable is effected by multiple dependent variables which is not an uncommon feature.
(iv) The dependencies relate over independent factors in proportionate or disproportionate forms.
(v) Series of factors of dependency tend to vary as its influence ratio advances towards being deemed independent.
(vi) There exists a possibility of intermediary stage/s remain as passing stage prevail both in long and short span of influence.
(vii) An integrated dependent effect will have to be partial or total solution.

It can be observed that both dependent and independent variables are not a permanent condition and are purely context based. There exists no single barometer which enables to accurately validate the effect of these variables especially in women's behavioural patterns.

Table 2.2 : The Component of Heterogeneity

Character	*Ethnicity*	*Occupation*
1. Incidence	Insist as an imbibed permanent attribute	To be earned or acquired by means of determinable parameters
2. Evidence	Character of rigidity and in-depth condition prevailing	Choice decision can give up flexibility and enforce permanency—as its drives
3. Illustration	Accepted as a part of living style, honoured, provide an identity	Adopted, temporal and preferred-occupation is a barometer of performance image
4. Organize	Has nothing to do by being arrived in hierarchy it is an accepted norm, cult adopted from the source of generic dependency	An array of occupational diversities persist and continue to prevail as per one's own accommodations
5. Intimacy	Honoured as it reflect the inter-relations, bonds based on values within the limits of one's own understanding.	Indicate the employable relationships, positioning role and contribution.
6. Skill/s	**Impressions Substantiated :** Affinity, identity, permanent, pride, originality, representation, symbolic, realistic etc.	**Impressions Substantiated :** Pressing requirement, zeal, need, necessity, compulsion, initiative, enthusiastic, thrilled, reluctant, disappointed, compromised manipulated etc.

The transformational needs enable to quarry out the quantum and criteria of preferred occupations. How many could really begin with the preferred occupation. If the occupational condition is revocable then the validity is dependent on the exposure, evaluation of decision option really need an external motivating force? There is innumerable numbers of possibilities as to the presence of hidden character and their variable influence or the prevalence of open factors which enables to establish an open relation with the determinants result in employable condition/s.

Table 2.3 : Internalities *vs.* Externalities

Internalities	*Externalities*
• Massive resource base dependencies	• Major and minor market forces
• Community strategy for occupational development	• Government affairs
• Temporal or permanent partnering favouring occupation-based relations	• Donor groups, NGOs
• Competency to look beyond the capacities	• A miniature form of international arena and the dependent neighbourhood
• Occupational ethics *vs.* the ethical issues	• External regulatory to promote the internal practices
• Stereo-type reinforcements	• Penetrated diversities and glocal impact
• Ethnic endorsements and demonstrations	• Part-fulfilment and limited focus over deliberations and schedules

The Gender Role

The gender-based orientations in the socio-ethnicity in relation to personal and professional norms and standards based on the :

- **Socio-ethical considerations** framed in tight-knit clan and community-based assumptions define the social behaviour. The social division based on the resources/ asset-ownership and strategic utilization patterns form a natural necessity. The absence of other socio-dependencies *viz.*, the technological or economic drives haven't created much of a positive image. The experience towards unilateral or multi-lateral socio-positive and negative experiences reflect the retention or rejections.
- **Community-based standards** encourage division of ethnic professional outlook which set the code of standards and identify the constructive forces behind the occupational intent. An interactive social forum need to maintain rapport with the dependent and

independent forces present an overall social impact on the women's occupational base. The ethnic standards, self-image, materialism and cultural pollution aiming towards the vulnerable target groups influencing their need-based systems. At individual/familial level/s, they comprise ethnic motivators seemed to be experiencing the self-concept, the occupational endorsements, comparatives, ethnic shocks and inappropriate stereotyping.

Role-participation of Men in Matriarchal Systems

Privileged as uncles, husbands and sons the men claim a distinctive and adaptive relationship in different positions. Their role-demarcation is witnessed in money, political power and status consciousness, information and knowledge systems. A micro study with a sample of 60 men revealed by temperament that they are ambitious, pleasure-loving, amicable and accommodative. Data collection was done by means of convenience sampling where the representation included respondents from three tribes *viz.*, Khasi, Jaintia and Garo. The respondents' representations are that 36 per cent are below 30 years and 14 per cent are > 30 - < 40 years and 23 per cent are > 40 and < 50 years, 17 per cent had rural background and 22 per cent are graduates. The occupational preferabilities suggested that their inclinations over mobility (27%), equality in tasks (42%) with women, preferred matriliny (27%), skills acquisition (68%), preference in service (14%) preference in business (38%) and preference towards resource access (56%). The rural-urban demarcations were admitted by 24 per cent, supremacy of rural over urban (37%) and *vice versa* (41%). 49 per cent preferred to be occupationally independent, 23 per cent preferred to work in association with women. 89 per cent of respondents agreed that the working styles of men makes a difference with women and all men displayed natural interest in work preferences. They revealed that economic independence (46%), family responsibility (21%) and status (8%) remained as most influencing determinants while selecting occupations. An overall impact reveals that the admission of the women supremacy was accepted but limited to the household and other activities beyond this jurisdiction are undertaken as men's privilege or in association with women. An overall status of equality, uniformity and gender-based allocations seemed to be the prevalent criteria of work preference and any deviation is deemed to be the effect of personalized decision/s.

Sum Up

The "women's occupational intent", therefore, can be understood as an ethical context (Varley, A., 1996) posed complexities as the occupational plateau drawn and accepted is purely based partially on the psychographic backgrounds and partially on the prevailing situations of individual/familial-self in group-interactivities need to satisfy multi-effectual forms. In short, each occupational decision need to satisfy a portfolio of determinants perceived as per their vitalities in the context of women's perceptional priority and necessity within their knowledge and competencies consequence an outcome in terms of immediate need gratification rather than any other criteria.

3

Positioning of Micro-Perceptions and Neo-Social Supportives

It is more appropriate to define the status of women in a comprehensive definition which enables to create a multi-dimensional image of women and pervasiveness at different social layering. They offer different connotations for the term occupation as for majority of them it is as natural as any other life function. Inculcating the cultural prerogatives the ethno woman accepts it as a passion towards her own relevant environment and responsibility as a natural way to attend the needs and responsibilities of the core domain of priority or influence sensing and routing as a dimension of domestic and familial assignments. Imbibed with natural entrepreneurial and leadership qualities sourced from the ethical and cultural enforcements over these women segments enabled them to become adept towards accommodating themselves into the "context-based preferences" in which they placidly being accommodated in the array of occupational self-assignment with the character of cultural and community-based responsibilities.

These contextual variations under multiple situations are adaptative and accommodating—as they need to be explicit for ethnic women in their most versatile, volunteering, honourable, powerful and responsible characters but at the same time remain unfulfilled, gullible, depressed, religious and compromised. The tribal women's position of reverence is limited to the extent of empowerment implied in terms of materialistic, knowledge-based resource access and competent to make independent decisions in variant situations. The typical character of prominence in the positional role-significance in its fundamental form and character enable the tribal women contribute differently in their role-justifications towards their own-self, family and clan etc.

Spread of Occupational Intent

The opinions expressed by the women refer occupation as a **congruent event** rather than a single task.

(a) In **urban** area it suggests a means to earn on the decisive factors of formal education, skills, service provisions, facilitation, intermediation and alternative dependencies. However, the investment orientation towards rural natural resources, infrastructural, services and long term financial investments *viz.*, transport, housing, hospital, tourism, professional education etc., and are instrumental which claim transformations.

(b) in **rural** area it is a means to earn different forms of supportives needed in the familial context *viz.*, agriculture along with allied activities such as bamboo, broom, beetle nut, beetle leaf, spices etc., rearing livestock, kitchen garden/ orchard, leasing or subleasing the community land for domestic or commercial use, alternative micro-opportunities to work as labourer in agricultural, coal and lime mining, stone chirping, small time retailing etc., form a combination to meet core life perspectives rather than a change means.

Combined opinions over the proportionate/ disproportionate parameters of education, age, resource access, distance and mobility or any other criteria seemed to be thoroughly violated as it posed difficulty to associate the segmental character with the occupational decision option.

Ethnic Predominances over the Occupational Environment

Defining the distinctive identities of tribal women as being a part of day-to-day life being engaged in the process of shared-assignments. A strong base of ethnic networking can be observant in the situations of family/clan calamities *viz.*, sickness, condolence, burial or death are strictly observed and brings the work concept totally to zero. Women by themselves form as an institution and embodiment of cultural and ethical representations believe it firmly by means of self-valuations or due to prevailing environment. The perceptions are moulded to hold them ethically, mingled with femininity and correlate them to be belonging more towards satisfying the community norms rather than self. In the process of submission towards avoiding social exclusion the decision-making process and its effect corresponding does not antagonize with clan enforcements. Degree of relaxation in decision-making can be limited to the extent that the decision alternatives or options have an impact. Extremities by means of violation of self-norms which are submissive to community norms are considered to be ethical but not *vice versa.*

Occupational Specificities

Prototyping the typical feminine ethnic beliefs suggest

- The **Concept of Centricity** at macro approach is strongly believed even at the internal differentiation-levels arrived due to language, religion, cultural compromise, exposure to accultural sequences etc. The in-built secluded temperament enable them to retain the community-based image as being a brand image of ethnical identity is well honoured and priority to ethnic networking rather than work.
- The **Concept of Immobility** is the foremost and vital belief among the tribal communities in general and women in particular. Uniformity in belief can be perceived among all segments in different proportions irrespective of their stature, education, occupation, resources, economic status and interactivities etc.
- The **Concept of Informality** is being attended due to the limitedness in the access towards opportunities, modified conditions due to multitude of enforcements which have their impact to accept the adaptable

condition, income diversification and livelihood measures etc.

- The **Concept of Externalities** : These restrictions imposed over external entry dependent factors like business dependencies/independencies conditioned could be to a large extent have a positive impact for independent and negative effort for dependent conditions.
- The **Concept of Micro-participation** : Lack of considerable exposure, reluctance and lack of knowledge of the occupational intricacies and an overall understanding of the tasks involved, utility and value analysis etc., reduce the occupational involvement. The vitalities which are the day-to-day priorities seemed to be more pressing determine the short-sighted vision over the long term consequences of even relevant issues.

Short-term Vs. Long-term Effort

The external intrigue arise due to "mutualities" and reciprocal dependencies enabled to be the determinants of singular formula of benefits to participatory segments. Estimating the extent of benefit is rather difficult to be expressed in measurable terms but the bargain seemed to be more skewed towards the externalities whose involvemental initiatives needed larger compensations for their concern in terms of satisfying the possessive groups' *viz.*, the business and market effects. The floating occupational environment seemed to be dependent on the concept of "temporariness" due to the absence of any rigid norms which run the entire segment aiming towards specific (low profile) targets. The system of informality prevailing as each benefit segment has been drawing its own norms and prescriptions keeping in view what is the arrivable benefit and attending to the activities which help them in gaining approaches towards their targets. This to a large extent contributing towards diversified short-term gains rather than a structured long-term benefit to the participant-groups.

Contribution of Women

The degree of contribution towards both occupational and non-occupational factors depend on the competency of contribution, the reciprocal consideration/s, the situational co-operation and co-ordination to the extent to which these contributions are needed etc., are the most pertinent considerations.

Based on these the women's **contributory levels** can be understood as follows :

Dimensions of Contribution

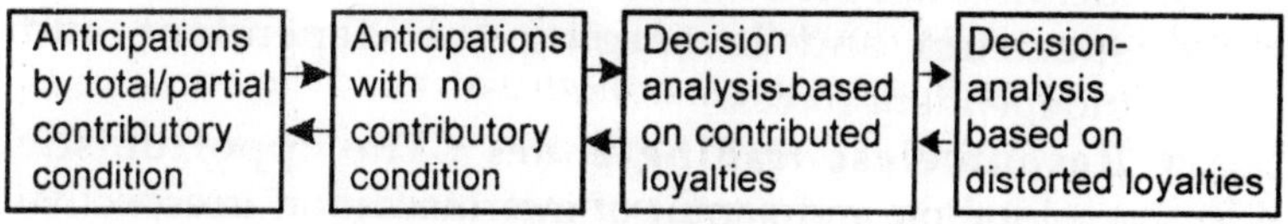

Degree of Decision Option

The evaluative criteria ultimately result in the decision options as to the occupational reference is based on the domain of psychographic and socio-cultural reflections define the decision alternatives. The compromise and valuation of the decision-continuum enable to finalize the most optimum situation. However, this criteria is overloaded by the occupational or even non-occupational impact which rule the decision-criteria.

Prototypical Conditionalities

At domestic level the occupational platform permit the entry of different players with different backgrounds and anticipations make an entry. This help determining the off-screen motives initiated by typical behaviour.

Local Preference towards Occupational Channels

- **Border Areas :** Prefer good rapport with the neighbourhood district, state and country.

- **Areas near State Capital** : Heavily influenced and dependent on the State Capital.
- **Areas proximate to national highways** : Areas of booming markets and most adaptable and customer-centric orientation and mostly succumb to constraints.
- **Areas in between two state capitals** : Highly accultured and are gained with the pros and cons of both systems.
- **Resource-prone areas** : Mostly interiors but are highly developed due to constant economic activity. The most lucrative hot-zone for internal and external contractual spectrum and leveraging the dependent and independent forces.
- **Resourceless trading zones** : The opportunistic exploration and gamut of intermediation irrespective of the presence of any positivities is prone for survival skills due to the versatility arised due to their constant exposure with external situations.
- **Closed zones/economies** : Self-impositions, rigidities and lack of adaptativeness with extreme self-centricism remain congruent and adamant with any new situation and ignorant about the wider views and visions of survival and growth.

Externalities and Domain of Preference

The external forces inclusive of governmental, private segments and those with business mind set especially market-prone forces, religious groups, NGOs, other service layering inclined towards the resource-base and its reflexes, dependent market and exchange activities, collaborative ventures, projects and all intermediary (facilitative) activities including contracting, leasing, franchising etc., are equally vital in creating a "wider" range of occupational domain with total or partial involvement. A mixed group of internal (local) and external (non-local) partnerships are quite rampant is one of the striking features supporting the occupational character.

Occupational Proneness : Inclinations and Reflections

The regional cult is predominant even though all clans uniformly maintain the norms as they concern the women and their position in the clan promotional and nurturing priorities. The associated freedom in decision-making, the economic stability with responsibilities and the deep personal occupational inclinations arose with the motivational factors of non-descriptive and sub-conscious determinants act vital in deciding their occupational choice. The women's typical condition in which the social segments determine their general status—

(i) Occupational choice in the prescribed limitedness partially self-imposed and partially by the cultural/ social systems.

(ii) The autonomy and independent thinking process remain submissive to the wider framework of ethnicity and cultural norms.

(iii) The expectations of growth and development remain difficult to be achieved at individual levels outline a system of external dependency is the prominent character visible in every angle.

(iv) Understanding the self-positioning helps developing suitable strategies and need appropriate inputs other than the economic incentives seem to be insignificant.

The reflections of the secluded preferences and attitudinal limits reveal proneness towards entertainment, religion, clan-based enforcements; familial responsibilities enable women to restrict their ambitious work expectations. Language and communication barriers with other communities, barrier on settlement, acquisition of property by non-locals, social insecurities discourage any external intervention. However, the business relations charter market demands, bilateral exchanges especially barter systems and settlements etc. are still rampant in day-to-day practices.

- Strengthening the group and ethnic concept seemed to be the foremost priority.
- To remain complacent in community/group and family concept rather than the individual approach.
- To promote and nurture the families and participate in every social/cultural occasion.
- To minimize and condition the interactivities with non-local members.
- To remain secluded due to lack of knowledge, understanding, skills resulted in rigid mindset and attitudinal framework.
- Lack of confidence towards new skills, new situations, less adventurous and restricted but identifiable preferences.

Fig. 3.1 : Framework of Women's Macro Occupational Decision

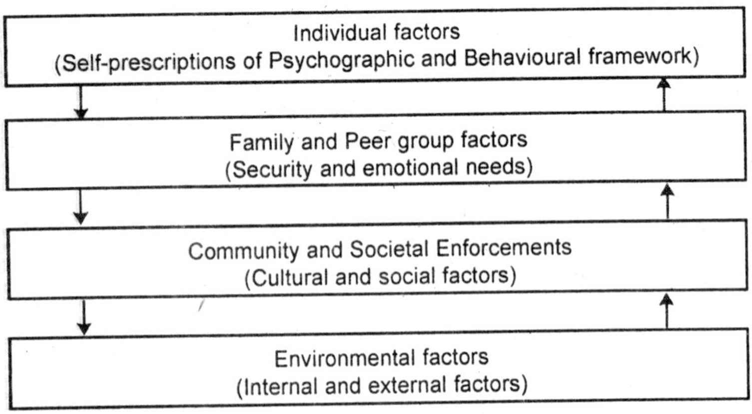

This system preference criteria shaped the "occupational comfort zones" creating an occupational divide into the exclusive occupations which promote means-ends channels totally controlling and regulating an occupational environmental layering based on **(i)** priority; **(ii)** dimension; **(iii)** opportunities; **(iv)** self-initiatives and innovation; **(v)** accommodated environment and **(vi)** short *vs.* long-term relevant environment. However, the domestic value system believe that the occupational-intent in its frame of reference remain unique even in the ethnic dominant areas enable to show tolerance, refineness, comradeship and even the occupational preference as the priority with considerable wholesomeness (clubbing function), as having minimal rapport of considerable stake or as part interest (partially deviated function), as no interest (totally deviated function) or as one among multiple-dimensions prescribing that living function is independent to the occupational function. The framework reveals that the women's occupational decision is dependent on the comprehensive set of activities initiated with the self-competencies and progressive make-up reflected with the association of dependent domains such as family, society and environment etc. This is a dualistic relation *viz.*, a pre- and post-determinant reflections constantly present their impact define the decision-option.

Temperamental Status of Women (Tm)

Table 3.1 : Temperamental Patterns of Respondents

Code	*Attribute Category*	*Stake prone perception*	*Response*
Tm-1	Pragmatic	• Demographic differences tend to show variation on occupational preference	(23.6%) (14.9%)
		• Competitive skills should be a part of learning to seek gainful occupations	(23.0%) (14.9%)
Tm-2	Analytical	• Feminity in the education does not allow the girls to develop in an open environment	(23.8%) (13.8%)
		• Our cultural implication need to be changed to transform ourselves	(21.9%) (14.1%)
Tm-3	Creative	• In a closed social structure women's creativity remain insignificant	(21.6%) (14.5%*)
		• New generation aspire on innovative occupations	(20.6%) (15.7%*)
Tm-4	Social	• The ethnic impositions act as gate-keeper for any development	(21.6%) (14.6%*)

Code	*Attribute Category*	*Stake prone perception*	*Response*
Tm-5	Dynamic	• Exploring the possibility of micro-participation of women lead to social transformation	(22.1%) (15.8%*)
		• The traditional community concept is potential for integrating development	(21.8%) (13.3%*)
Tm-6	Conven-tional	• The new technology movements of on-line jobs need to be welcomed	(23.7%) (13.9%*)
		• Each individual should invest in developing the social capital	(22.3%) (13.4%*)
Tm-7	Ambitious	• Females are considered as clan promoters as it is culturally accepted	(22.0%) (16.0%*)
		• The ethnic culture is weaning out slowly from tradition	(22.6%) (16.1%*)
Tm-8	Dependent	• Tribal women are more competent than men in managing complex activities	(22.9%) (15.8%*)
		• In matrilineal society females are honoured due to tradition	(21.0%) (16.8%*)
Tm-9	Frustrated	• The growth options are saturated but we prefer to remain where we are	(20.0%) (17.1%*)
		• Infiltration from other places is the root cause of inflation	(19.7%) (16.2%*)
Tm-10	Pessimistic	• The government has not been doing anything for our development	(17.5%) (16.9%*)
		• The tribal women fall under minority and our interests are not taken by centre	(22.2%) (16.9%*)
Tm-11	Hesitant	• Without external support our people cannot cope up with radical changes	(21.9%) (15.8%*)
		• Today's youth faces the challenge of learning new skills to gain new occupational opportunities	(22.7%) (17.2%*)
		• The self-help groups are an innovative self-directive mechanism	(18.3%) (18.5%*)

Code	Attribute Category	Stake prone perception	Response
Tm-12	Self-direction	• Career Guidance is one of the popular means promoting self-direction	(18.2%) (21.7%*)
		• The under skilled performers remain as socio-cultural isolates	(20.9%) (21.2%*)
Tm-13	Postponer	• A paradigm shift to be recommended to cope up with non-performing youth	(20.7%) (22.2%*)
		• Promotion of local democracy helps preserving traditional systems and also the community interests	(22.2%) (21.9%*)
Tm-14	Rigid	• Only an integrated approach among youth promises an over-all support to new generation	(20.5%) (19.8%*)
		• Adult and continuing education for women leads to reorientation	(22.8%) (19.7%*)
Tm-15	Planner	• In a tribal society women face conflicting/dominating/ submissive or aggressive roles	(23.7%) (22.6%)
		• Appropriate decision-making in the family is possible when decisions are made by concensus/women/clan members or older members	(21.7%) (20.6%*)

Note : The figures in (*) represent urban response.

It is observed that on average the category A represented by10 per cent response, B by 15-18 per cent. The no opinion is too prominent around 19 per cent in urban and 35 per cent in rural areas. The strongest "total disagreement" came with robust figures of 20 per cent in both urban and rural segments. The non-agreement stood on average ranging between 55-60 per cent in rural and urban areas and agreement ranged between 20-25 per cent were positive and agreeable.

The data has been redefined taking into concern its positive and negative statements which are provided in Fig. 3.2 reveals the response pattern of respondents in the entire state. The data represent a sample of 1898 respondents in rural and 1715 in urban area (see Annexure 3.1).

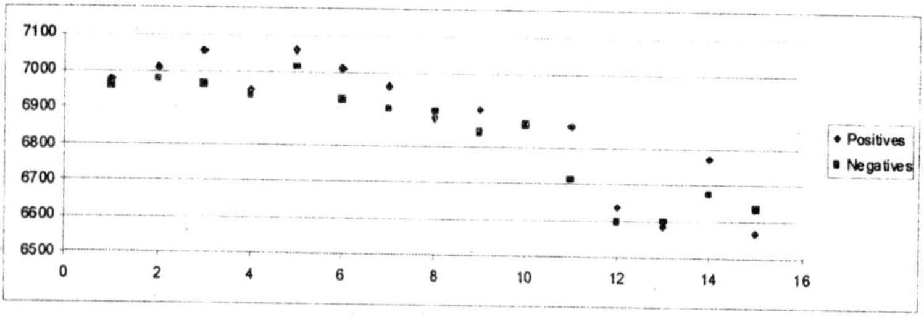

Fig. 3.2 : Rural-Urban Temperamental Response Patterns

The coverage of domain-prominence include the (i) women's preferences towards making investments, (ii) foresightedness restricted to decision-making, (iii) occupational decision-limits wrap into the future role of marriage, (iv) marriage and motherhood is no significant end for women's career, (v) return-to-work after the temporary break from occupation arises due to personal liability, (vi) situation witnessed only provoke thought perceival, (vii) feminity as constituted within the constructive age negate achievement in occupational decision, (viii) prominence of sub-cultural differences among young women, and (ix) typical determinants of women conventional interest in occupational branding.

The statistical tools used are tests of significance by t, test of variance by F are provided in appendix and ANOVA (Analysis of variance) to support the justifications. The multiple regression equation of the dependent variable RTM (Rural Temperamental variables) - 1.1 on : RTM-1.1 = [2.008 + (.186 RTM-1.2) + (.089RTM-2.1) + (.043RTM-2.2) + (.06RTM-3.1) + (.074RTM-3.2)].

Using the wider perception of representation of dependent and independent factors is as follows :

(i) **Dependent Variable** : Demographic differences to influence the variation on occupational preferences (RTM-1.1).

(ii) **Independent Variables** : (a) Need of competitive skills for gainful occupations (RTM-1.2), (b) Pursuing growth in open environment (RTM-2.1), (c) Role of culture in self-transformations (RTM-2.2), (d) Negating the closed environment (RTM-3.1), and (e) The aspirations of new generations in innovative occupations (RTM-3.2).

It is observed that all the regression coefficients are significant at 5 per cent level of significance. Moreover the regression coefficients of RTM-1.2, RTM-2.1, RTM-3.1, RTM-3.2 are significant at 1 per cent level of significance with the F ratio 29.485.

Table 3.2 : ANOVA-1 (Rural)

Model		*Sum of Squares*	*df*	*Mean Square*	*F*	*Sig.*
1	Regression	155.787	5	31.157	29.485	.000(a)
	Residual	1999.337	1892	1.057		
	Total	2155.124	1897			

a Predictors : (Constant), RTM 3.2, RTM 1.2, RTM 2.2, RTM 2.1, RTM 3.1
b Dependent Variable : RTM 1.1

Coefficients

Model		*Unstandardized Coefficients*		*Standardized Coefficients*	*t*	*Sig.*
		B	*Std. Error*	*Beta*		
1	(Constant)	2.008	.152		13.216	.000
	RTM-1.2	.186	.022	.190	8.356	.000
	RTM-2.1	.089	.023	.089	3.871	.000
	RTM-2.2	.043	.023	.043	1.887	.059
	RTM-3.1	.060	.023	.060	2.614	.009
	RTM-3.2	.074	.022	.076	3.359	.001

Dependent Variable: RTM-1.1

Using the same variables for urban segments the Urban temperamental variable UTM-1.1 as dependent and UTM-1.2, UTM-2.1, UTM-2.2, UTM-3.1 and UTM-3.2 as independent variables the F test observes that all regression coefficients are significant at 5 per cent level of significance and the regression coefficients of all independent variables are significant at 1 per cent level of significance with the F ratio 24.34. The multiple regression equation of the dependent variable UTM (Urban Temperamental variable) 1.1 on : UTM-1.1 = 2.298 + (.229UTM-1.2) + (.065 UTM-2.1) + (.046UTM-2.2) + (-.006UTM-3.1) + (-.006UTM-3.2)

Table 3.3 : ANOVA-1.1 (Urban)

Model		*Sum of Squares*	*Df*	*Mean Square*	*F*	*Sig.*
1	Regression	167.546	5	33.509	24.342	.000(a)
	Residual	2352.590	1709	1.377		
	Total	2520.136	1714			

a Predictors: (Constant), UTM-3.2, UTM-1.2, UTM-2.2, UTM-2.1, UTM-3.1
b Dependent Variable: UTM-1.1

Coefficients

Model		*Unstandardized Coefficients*		*Standardized Coefficients*	*t*	*Sig.*
		B	*Std. Error*	*Beta*		
1	(Constant)	2.298	.151		15.268	.000
	UTM-1.2	.229	.024	.227	9.532	.000
	UTM-2.1	.065	.024	.066	2.692	.007
	UTM-2.2	.046	.025	.046	1.854	.064
	UTM-3.1	-.006	.025	-.006	-.247	.805
	UTM-3.2	-.003	.025	-.003	-.117	.907

a Dependent Variable: UTM-1.1

Similarly taking TM-6.2 as dependent variable and TM-7.2, TM-10.1,TM-9.2, TM-9.1,TM-8.2,TM-8.1 and TM-7.1 as independent variables for urban and rural the regression coefficients witnessed high significance in the following tables:

Table 3.4 : ANOVA-2 (Urban)

Model		*Sum of Squares*	*df*	*Mean Square*	*F*	*Sig.*
1	Regression	157.623	7	22.518	15.943	.000(a)
	Residual	2410.948	1707	1.412		
	Total	2568.571	1714			

a Predictors: (Constant), UTM-7.2, UTM-10.1, UTM-9.1, UTM-9.2, UTM-8.2, UTM-8.1, UTM-7.1
b Dependent Variable: UTM-6.2

Coefficients

Model		Unstandardized Coefficients		Standardized Coefficients	t	Sig.
		B	Std. Error	Beta		
1	(Constant)	2.162	.190		11.356	.000
	UTM-7.1	.203	.024	.206	8.468	.000
	UTM-8.1	-.003	.024	-.003	-.144	.886
	UTM-8.2	.072	.025	.070	2.885	.004
	UTM-9.1	.022	.025	.021	.877	.381
	UTM-9.2	.054	.026	.050	2.100	.036
	UTM-10.1	-.006	.025	-.006	-.243	.808
	UTM-7.2	.043	.024	.044	1.760	.079

a Dependent Variable: UTM-6.2

Model Summary

Model	R	R Square	Adjusted R Square	Std. Error of the Estimate
1	.250(a)	.063	.059	1.071

a Predictors: (Constant), RTM-10.1, RTM-8.1, RTM-7.1, RTM-9.1, RTM-9.2, RTM-8.2, RTM-7.2

Table 3.5 : ANOVA-2.1 (Rural)

Model		Sum of Squares	Df	Mean Square	F	Sig.
1	Regression	144.999	7	20.714	18.059	.000(a)
	Residual	2167.899	1890	1.147		
	Total	2312.898	1897			

a Predictors: (Constant), RTM-10.1, RTM-8.1, RTM-7.1, RTM-9.1, RTM-9.2, RTM-8.2, RTM-7.2

b Dependent Variable: RTM-6.2

Coefficients

Model		Unstandardized Coefficients		Standardized Coefficients	t	Sig.
		B	Std. Error	Beta		
1	(Constant)	1.907	.172		11.084	.000
	RTM-7.1	.166	.023	.162	7.065	.000
	RTM-7.2	.055	.024	.054	2.310	.021
	RTM-8.1	.069	.024	.068	2.909	.004
	RTM-8.2	.019	.023	.019	.822	.411
	RTM-9.1	.036	.023	.036	1.550	.121
	RTM-9.2	.081	.023	.081	3.551	.000
	RTM-10.1	.053	.023	.052	2.296	.022

a Dependent Variable: RTM-6.2

The occupations preferred to be independent self, partnerships, casual and seasonal, part or full time, contractual and assignment, composite or multiple categories. The orientations being self, family, career, profession, opportunities, children, parents, grandparents, peer group, skills etc., which provide wider view of either one or more than one having influences over structured or unstructured forms. Very many really do not have long-term preferences but attend to the immediate need gratification. The gender-based issues get neutralized as the women hold more responsibility than man and prefer to remain self-dependent. This leads to self-decision-making which represent the entire family rather than self and most of the decisions are wrapped by "reasons of priority" which cannot be overlooked as limitedness in opportunity or choice. The temperamental status adopting the Likert's 5-point scaling is used to represent the category of women over the statements classified on the criteria of A for total agree; B for partially agree ; C for partially disagree; D for totally disagree and E for no opinion. The representative groups have been attributed with fifteen categories with different temperaments of women assigned to the statements (as in Table 3.1). The statements have an in-depth understanding towards the environmental effects, feminine status, emphasis on occupational-prone effect of tradition and traditional values, felt need of modernities. It covers the issues of progression of social (Schmidt, J.D., 1997) capital, parity between the tradition and modern role-differentiation in women and comparatives. The weaknesses can be witnessed as being admissions which provoke the current deficiencies by means of dissatisfaction, blame, and compromise insist the inclusion of new effects or preferences towards by means of government participation and support of seniors to look into the matters of decision-making. The statements have a grasp towards the role of culture and its effect of influencing the contexts as to their preference or reluctance which also suggest as to their keenness of attributing or shedding their current identities.

At **individual** level the women's temperamental status identifies few influencing reflections on the criteria of prominency of issues which are as follows :

- It is persevered that the occupational initiatives are disproportionate and tend to get diluted as per the situational dominance and permissiveness of individual self.
- Presence of conceptual and realistic discrimination of clan/community over the personal decisions *viz.*, mobility, accultural behaviour etc., of clan members.
- The level and extent of dependency over consequences within and beyond the geo-demographic variations.
- Understanding the concept of femininity in different references highlighting the occupational specificities.
- Multiple perspectives form a natural phenomenon in a composite situation where majority of people segments branched out from different environments.
- The minimal level of exposure determine the extent of closed status in societal expressions and character of isolation encourage rigidities and discourage external involvement.
- In matrilineal society the inter-generational perceptional differences deemed to be mild and less significant.

At **societal** level :

- Weaning tradition is perceived as religious conversions, accultural cult and dynamic market forces etc., making their way promoting the area as a happening domain.
- Infiltration consequencing due to illegal and unstructured inflow of people especially in itinerant, general, business and resource-based services.
- Lack of balanced local developmental activities resulting in extended expectations and anticipations from external supportive measures.
- Promoting a parallel local democracy with the formal administrative systems added only new layer of authority without responsibility.
- A prototypical understanding of the developmental issues only enable minimal extensions of the prevailing situations but have not been responding to the conflicting status of tribal women.

- Reflections of decision-criteria towards a comprehensive understanding over the outcome influencing different dimensions of immediate need are still in infant stage.

The highlighting temperamental aspects of women revealed that :

- The accommodations of traditional view as a part of life but not whole life.
- The geo-demographic variations did not really show much impact on occupational decision.
- Women's role deemed to be more crucial and complex—as decision-making between tradition, self-survival and modernity is still a waiver.
- One can perceive the prominent character of temporal openness in the closed system.
- The ethnic youth-priorities claim modernization/s and transformation/s with least cultural concern.

Fig. 3.3 : Model : Alignment of Situational Dissonance

Preference towards Supportive Situations	**Prevalence of Meek Conditions**	**Anticipated Transformations in Search of Opportunities**
↓	↓	↓
• New technologies • Social capital • Self-help • Career guidance • Paradigm shift • Integrated approach	• Micro participation • Tradition • Culture • Closed society • Demographic Differences • Clan Promotion • Female Business • Selective life options	• Pervasiveness of limitedness • Weaning culture • Saturation in growth options • Infiltration • Lack of government initiatives • Isolates and Minority segments Developmental Barriers *viz.*, meagre Infrastuctural, communication etc. • Insignificant and self-prescribed external support • Youth challenge • Lack of skills or Underskills • Rigidity in performance • Promoting local democracy • Conflicting tribal women's Decision-making process

The responses of women towards the temperamental issues revealed the areas which need attention and the anticipated transformations suggest the awareness levels of women segment with the underlining incompetence to change the prevailing system. However, the aura in situational characterizations is marked with initializations witnessing change-agents to perform as follows :

System of Occupational Preference Criteria (OPC)

Shaping the Occupational Comfort Zones (OCZs) enable to concentrate the occupational character in terms of level of self-requirements, extensions of marketability to the extent of fringe (Sullivan III, W.C., 1994) spared by means of producible scope and opportunities. The gearing of needed worth of occupational spaces through weighted priorities other than occupational decision of spend time, return, ease, extent, occupational stretch and possibilities in terms of contribution of each other to the total desirable limit. The differences in the ethnic approaches identified are :

The three dominant tribal segments chosen for the study *viz.*, the Khasi, Jaintia and Garo seemed to have adopted different lifestyles based on their cultural framework. Such division highlighted the language, temperament and living style preferences keeping the fundamental base of matriliny intact and is uniformly applicable in their family structure, the clan and familial responsibilities, economic independence, urban exposure and accultural interactivities enable the growth of specific segments which is as follows :

Khasis : The vitalities being presence of State Capital, prominent tourist spots *viz.*, Cherrapunjee and Mawsynram, the wider availability of resource base and locational advantage created a positive and developmental environment [Taylor,W.D (eds), 1981] perceive Khasi women segment imbibing most dynamic, hardworking and entrepreneurial qualities. Depicting vibrant occupational proneness the *khasi* women present themselves as self-motivated and ambitious segment engaged in multi-occupational framework.

Jaintias : Highly resource-based economy the women are blessed with born entrepreneurism supported by partial business and investment skills highly supported due to the ownership and access of large volumes of natural resources. The developmental activities wrap around the resource base which is the only but potential supporting factor enabling them to promote different forms of extractive businesses from mega to micro levels. The women involvement is significantly less as compared to *Khasis* but the feminine stances, beliefs and living philosophies are largely similar to that of *Khasis*.

Garos : Mostly dependent on education and regular occupations the Garo women form an excellent service segment. Absence of resource base is prominent except in South Garo, the women with skills and personal talents tend to remain comparatively mobile in search of occupations. The influence of acculture and cultural tolerance is high but the community has insignificant business and survival skills needed for their livelihood.

Bhoi : The recent addition with formal identity and deviated khasi segment has high locational advantage prone for numerous occupations yet the minimal exposure, language, communication barriers, lack of professional and business skills contributing to their low profile lifestyles and micro-living systems.

The occupational reflections enable to determine that

(i) The prominence of women is uniformly applicable factor in all communities resulted in submissive trend/s of masculine force enabling to fortify the feminine active role participation (Vance, I., 1987).

(ii) The concept of family and associated instabilities and feminine involvements has drastic repercussions over the youth preparedness, women's positioning, familial support and security in nurturing the occupational framework.

(iii) The geo-demographic and socio-cultural factors have their implications on women segments that mostly prefer to accommodate themselves for their survival needs. The secluded environments restrict their active participation from both external and internal forms create barriers which are prone for lack of development.

The differences in the occupational context can be perceived as follows :

Among **urban** segments, the external players like markets, accultural behaviour, interactivities, migration, (Shukla, V., 1988) relocation, transformations and comparatives, knowledge/awareness, non-resource-based dependencies, occupational alternatives and extensions etc., form the most influencing factors whereas, in **rural** segments the return migration, possession of resource-base, proximity to urban locations, education and personal/commercial/professional interactivities etc.

It can be perceived that in Meghalaya the urban areas are too limited leaving vast stretches of rural segments but the prominence of urban is mostly historical and create administrative convenience. Occupationally the urban zones have been facilitated with suitable infrastructure and amenities but the same are totally negligible in rural areas. Barring the growth component at and around national highways the market stimulus aroused the NGO's initiations induced to step into notable changes in some selective segments. The aspirant public and their enthusiasm remain in the closed economies which permit conditional entry of all external forces and withdraw from any active participation when it concerns the non-locals. This creates a vacuum prone secluded environment.

Table 3.6 : General Status of Women (GW)

Code	*Understanding the Background of Women*	
Gw1	• The inter-generational perceptional differences are very strong	(14.8%) 25.3%*)
Gw2	• Maturity by age only visualizes transformations as welcome change	(14.9%) (21.7%*)
Gw3	• The employment possibilities can be enhanced by means of occupational skills	(13.8%) (24.0%*)
Gw4	• The tribal women are in general lack of skill competencies	(14.2%) (25.0%*)

Code	Understanding the Background of Women	
Gw5	• External motivations boost proper direction and involvement	(14.3%) (24.0%*)
Gw6	• Self-motivation remains submissive unless glorified with suitable supportive	(16.0%) (24.2%*)
Gw7	• Personal development of women enable her to compete with non-feminine occupations	(14.8%) (25.7%*)
Gw8	• Neglect of domestic front is the result of women's occupational preference	(16.0%) (23.7%)
Gw9	• Gender is immaterial while evaluating quality considerations in work	(13.2%) (25.5%*)
Gw10	• Active work markets prefer only high skilled participants	(14.0%) (24.6%*)
Gw11	• In current changing scenario market forces deviate from stakeholder's interests	(13.5%) (25.5%*)
Gw12	• Rural systems need to be dependent on urban systems	(15.7%) (24.9%*)
Gw13	• Culturally women's career progression has not been fully appreciated	(16.4%) (28.4%*)
Gw14	• Women at any level enjoy lateral connections of informality	(15.8%) (25.4%*)
Gw15	• Women's senses in larger respects are more finely tuned than those of men	(16.3%) (28.8%*)
Gw16	• Women are biased towards gender inequalities	(16.9%) (28.7%*)
Gw17	• Women's ethics on lifestyle patterns depends on her confidence levels	(16.5%) (28.8%*)
Gw18	• It is believed that the social antenna of women always being on	(16.7%) (29.5%*)
Gw19	• Mentoring can be the source of employment for women	(17.3%) (26.9%*)
Gw20	• Women in male dominated environment reported worse mental health	(16.1%) (29.7%*)
Gw21	• Women associate power as a network of human connections	(17.1%) (29.7%*)
Gw22	• Dual and multiple career women are not able to do justice in domestic front	(18.4%) (28.2%*)
Gw23	• Empowered women are becoming a political fore	(22.1%) (30.6%*)
Gw24	• Women's optimal range of choice and flexibility to entry into professional fields is restricts	(20.5%) (28.9%*)
Gw25	• Women have a generic advantage for interpreting the nuances of social interaction	(22.2%) (29.5%*)
Gw26	• Underdeveloped economies fail to fully use the skills potential of women	(21.5%) (27.3%*)

Code	*Understanding the Background of Women*	
Gw27	• Modern women are competent to introduce radical changes	(20.0%) (25.5%*)
Gw28	• Women interpersonal orientations always misunderstood	(20.3%) (24.2%*)
Gw29	• Success of women in small business is now recognized as a phenomenon	(23.1%) (26.4%*)
Gw30	• Percentage of women seeking highest positions remains insignificant	(20.8%) (25.4%*)
Gw31	• Modern women are more versatile and talented than their predecessors	(23.6%) (24.8%*)
Gw32	• Presently the opportunities for under privileged are still few	(23.0%) (25.4%*)
Gw33	• Pro-women environment need to be adjusted as per the potentiality of women force available in the region	(23.8%) (27.0%*)
Gw34	• One should believe that female oriented reassessment of labour market	(21.9%) (27.8%*)
Gw35	• Increased participation by women in different fields tends to create new position of women	(21.6%) (27.0%*)
Gw36	• Cultural impositions matter much in women's life	(20.6%) (26.7%*)
Gw37	• Female orientations need re-assessment in the work markets	(21.6%) (27.8%*)
Gw38	• Skilled women show high levels of sensitivity and flexibility in problem-solving	(22.1%) (30.4%*)
Gw39	• Changing occupational scene provide greater opportunity for skills	(21.8%) (33.6%*)
Gw40	• Continuing under representation makes no impact on women.	(23.7%) (36.9%*)

Figures in (*) represent Urban

Occupational Stretch Points

The environmental insecurities which have been restricting the external entry or permitting a conditional entry on the fulfilment of local norms reduced the local validities in growth and developmental terms. The influence of prototypical systems could not justify their stances as the implementation remained partial and insignificant. But the external dependent sources which enable to reconciliate are successful to some extent in creating a positive environment. The combination of internal determinants of occupational worthiness with the external forces to a large extent became successful in creating an "occupational platform". Each of these situations are influenced by different controllable and uncontrollable factors leading to occupational extensions, volatile participatory trends encouraging occupational consequences based on non-occupational contexts etc.

It is therefore need to be understood that the relevant environmental forces which create a suitable background of understanding to the women—who by themselves get involved in their early life stages. The diversified backgrounds, the variant self and the influencing environment to a large extent determine the micro effect/s of the lifestyle adaptations, exploring the opportunities, developing interrelations and associated compromises defining the occupational choices and preferences. Differentiations based on the accessibility of resources, ethnic preferences and cultural thought emphasized in the formal working styles, definite/extensive acceptance towards change and the adaptive or conditional priorities to a large extent suggest the width of the occupational choices claim to be promoting appropriate leverage between the work life and lifestyle aspirations.

Sum Up

It is important to note that the women's micro environment is not an ultimate nor perpetually rigid as occupational brand conditionalities vary from limited individual character to constraint free frontiers of occupational possibilities inspire differences on the comprehensive situations over which the decisions are made and the consequences felt from different socially permissive layers. In Meghalaya, the women force is definitely positioned in a strong capacity but the natural prerogatives are exploited at the same time allow them to be downsized to the level of ordinary women. The typical women faces multiple life situations and the vivacity is both challenging and stimulating to shape into most sought patterns. The familial role responsibilities and self-positioning in the family and society accommodate the occupational spaces in relation to the family and cultural base determine the occupational intent and occupational sustenance as life determinants or life choice-options.

Annexure 3.1 : Temperamental Status of Women in Meghalaya

Rural	*Urban*	*M1*	*M2*	*t-value*	*P*	*N1*	*N2*	*SD1*	*SD2*	*F-ratio*
RTM 1 Vs.	UTM 1	8.845	6.893	6.733	HS	1898	1715	11.867	1.906	38.757
RTM 2 Vs.	UTM 2	7.468	6.892	6.172	HS	1898	1715	3.413	1.912	3.188
RTM 3 Vs.	UTM 3	7.484	7.015	5.010	HS	1898	1715	3.443	1.865	3.407
RTM 4 Vs.	UTM 4	7.415	6.978	4.636	HS	1898	1715	3.484	1.849	3.549
RTM 5 Vs.	UTM 5	7.513	6.906	6.476	HS	1898	1715	3.437	1.907	3.248
RTM 6 Vs.	UTM 6	7.390	7.011	4.825	HS	1898	1715	2.718	1.886	2.077
RTM 7 Vs.	UTM 7	7.354	6.935	5.249	HS	1898	1715	2.714	1.975	1.887
RTM 8 Vs.	UTM 8	7.255	7.099	2.643	1%	1898	1715	1.692	1.866	1.216
RTM 9 Vs.	UTM 9	7.238	7.153	1.539	Insig	1898	1715	1.640	1.648	1.010
RTM 10 Vs.	UTM 10	7.231	6.925	5.429	HS	1898	1715	1.674	1.717	1.053
RTM 11 Vs.	UTM 11	7.150	7.039	1.953	Insig	1898	1715	1.708	1.689	1.022
RTM 12 Vs.	UTM 12	8.897	7.080	4.872	HS	1898	1715	11.939	1.639	53.054
RTM 13 Vs.	UTM 13	8.472	6.905	5.384	HS	1898	1715	11.949	1.631	53.695
RTM 14 Vs.	UTM 14	8.212	6.924	5.106	HS	1898	1715	10.323	1.722	35.950
RTM 15 Vs.	UTM 15	7.445	6.943	2.888	1%	1898	1715	6.993	1.786	15.332

(Note : "t"-test of significance with df 3611).
RTM : Rural Temperamental Status; UTM : Urban Temperamental Status; Insig : Insignificant; HS : Highly Significant; 1% : 1 % level of significance (2.58) and 5% level of Significance (1.96), N1 and N2 : Sample Size of Rural and Urban; (SD 1 and SD2 : Standard Deviation of N1 and N2; F-test : Test of variability.

4

Articulating Feminine Role-Orientations and Occupational Selectivities

The feminine ideologies towards the occupations have been felt variable as per the prototypical understanding between the segments facing an urban exposure since historical times have international interactions, interrelations with the neighbouring districts and states enable to provide reasonable exposure to dilute the behavioural patterns (Van Dijk, M.P., 1983). The behaviour is not limited to the environment, but to the family and the women concerned—is able to accommodate in the context of cultural, religious, and psycho-graphical dilutions. Language, food, dress code, living styles, appearances and adaptations etc., enable to define the broader environmental and narrower form of occupations that develop the concept of occupations in numerous forms.

The Occupational Initiatives

Do the behavioural patterns remain same towards the occupational forms even through the variable backgrounds or *vice versa*? This suggests the occupational understanding has been diversified irrespective of the personal reasons, competencies and circumstances. The generic foundations seemed to be stronger in the familial and clan-based environment especially for women as they are imbibed to develop the sense of responsibility ever since a nipper. There are hardly any predictions as to the category of occupation preferred but it is most accurate that the women naturally tilt towards secluded positions of security of family, clan/ community or ethnic or cultural assurances ensuring ease. Hardly their decisions are backed by uprooting the prevailing culture, nor against family and cultural norms etc. The initiation of the occupational preference towards in their own experience to a large extent commenced in their early life cycle stages—presupposed to be contributing to their decisions towards occupations. The narrations which have been made an in-depth analysis as to the criteria of vitalities enabled the women segment to charter the advocations of working definitions and talents.

Familial Environmental Realizations

With reference to the beginnings of the women, too positive for the behaviour prediction which enables them to decide as to the (a) form, (b) nature, (c) scope, and (d) occupational context which played vital but majority of the women could not even identify as to what exactly defined or influenced their decision-making. Significant majority of the women could not ensure the justifiable reasons of occupational influence during their early life stages but the context of homogeneity in reactivities is visibly prominent to be the assumed condition. For several, it is identified that the occupation is a natural state as for very many it just occurred as a casual thought or feeling supplemented with appropriateness. In the tribal bound segments being in occupation is an imbibed condition of their culture to be engaged in the work since childhood and the earmarking is not too specific but for majority, their beginnings were too modest suggesting the preferred nature of unstructured work which is the very part of lifestyle. The family background and the work context which are being defined by them form as motivator to proceed with the work. Being a component in the larger environment of extended families, each of the members feel implicit assignments of some task/s or the other motivate or force them to be engaged in any deviated economic activities irrespective of size or status. The work and school go together as early as their early years and the work which earns in kind by pigmy engagements *viz.*, piggery, gotary, poultry, horticulture, spices etc., are being bartered in exchange to the goods needed to the family. It is understandable that the ethnicity, religion, clan based enforcements and aptitudes which matter much in gaining a priority towards contributions based on the personal initiatives and also of immediate influencing family being a composition of all segregated familial factors :

- We own hotel business both in the urban and peri urban areas. My parents and several members in the family are engaged at different positions in this business. I am exposed to multicultural environment as several tourists used to visit our hotels. I like travelling and also interested in learning about new cultures.
- My mother and father are engaged in wholesale and retail business. Several of my cousins are also engaged in our business. Since childhood I am seeing people engaged in business activities and I never felt of leaving anywhere out from here.
- My mother is a Doctor and my father looks after the shop in the market. I have a contrast environment in the house. I preferred to do business like my father.
- We have a small land where we own limestone mine. My family is engaged in limestone export to neighbouring country Bangladesh. We all speak 4-5 languages. This adds to our business.
- I was in the hostel for my schooling in Shillong. I did my further studies outside the state and returned to look after the family business of coal export. My parents want me to remain here and I too preferred it.
- We have a small patch of beetle nut orchard. My mother and father lease more orchards and these beetle nuts are processed in our own processing unit. I am extremely motivated by the activities since childhood and decided to take it as my profession too.
- We don't have any assets but our clan is engaged in the broom stick business. We get a single crop per

annum which we own by auction and later my parents need to search for some alternative occupation for our livelihood. We have also been engaged in processing the broom but it is still in a small way. I prefer to expand the broom processing but the moisture here is not good for business.

- We rear pigs but do not process them here. My mother and aunts are busy both in trading and piggery which is our main source of living. We have a small orchard where we grow some vegetables and fruits. I too help them however; I do not prefer to be engaged in the same trade when I grow big.
- My both parents are not highly educated. We stay far from any urban influence but our living style is not inferior to them. We have been engaged in agriculture and horticulture. We grow spices and export them to Bangladesh and Shillong.
- My mother owns some forest land and we leased some more land used for agriculture. We are also engaged in charcoal business which is much fetching than agriculture. I prefer to continue in this trade.
- My parents are separated. My mother is not educated and is engaged in supplying smoked garlic, smoked meat and spices to the weekly markets. My grand-mother is very active business women but now too old and cannot move to get engaged in business activities.

For majority of the women the childhood influences based on parental background with respect to their education, employment, age, the parental perception of occupation, income levels, perceivable levels of the family status maintained, growth status of the family and family members, the occupational likes and dislikes and occupational dependency to maintain the life-style patterns preferred formed into life-turning decisions.

- We hail from a land-locked village which has neither external link nor influence. Our headman is very particular in permitting any outsider into the village. Except the Catholic Church there is nothing which can really associate us with outside world. I pursued my studies only due to our interaction with the Priest.

- We were originally from rural area. Living in the State capital is something very great for all our villagers. After my graduation I could not get any suitable job. I started distributing the newspaper and within 2/3 years we started our own local newspaper. The competition is too much in this line but still we are able to survive.
- We have one taxi and one auto which are run by my family members. The auto has limited area but the taxi is used even to go to border areas and also to Guwahati (Assam). It is also been hired by local officials of banks and tourists. Business is not regular but we are able to manage.
- My father is in Government service and my mother runs a shop. We are eight children. I had to give up study to cope up with family expenditure. I am engaged in supplying stationary to government departments. There are few practical problems I did not find more suitable occupation than this.
- I work as a commission agent for different products especially seasonal products to be channelled from interiors to the urban areas. I also own two small and one big truck for this purpose. I am very ambitious about expanding this business.
- After my graduation in arts stream my parents want me to settle in the village. I am settled to look after my family members and the property. I wanted to study further but I am engaged in doing retailing in readymade garments. I can't say I am contented with my occupation but I am able to look after my family.
- My mother is a Garo and my father is an Assamese. I can speak both languages. We could expand our business to Assam due to my father and my mother is a housewife. I prefer to be a Christian like my mother even if I marry a non-tribal.

- My mother is a staff nurse. We are five children and our step father is not very keen in keeping us. He is a temporary labourer and I know that I cannot continue in this family for long and prefer to be engaged in any private job.

It can be observed that the language proficiency, nature of the family, parental decisions about their own living styles, life experiences, non-member influences, relationships and value systems, the localized opportunities, the tolerance and struggle towards maintaining the expected living patterns matter to a large extent in occupational preferences.

- There is only one primary school in the neighbouring village. Most of the villages are acutely short of infrastructural support. We cannot improve our life standards by being in the village. I won't mind struggling but I prefer to live in better place than this village.
- I am not confident by quitting the village as I am attached to this place. Our resource base is so strong that we can comfortably survive by being dependent on it. Our major source of living is agriculture but we also supply rice liquor to the weekly markets.
- I used to live in Shillong doing a private job. The living conditions were not comfortable there and after developing much rapport I observed that the urbanites are keen in rural investments especially the land. I initiated the process and today am a successful real estate agent in this rural area.
- Our village is awarded as the neat and clean village in the Meghalaya and people from different corners of the country come here to visit it. We have plans to develop it as a tourist spot. But we don't have elementary facilities like medical or market etc. Life is very tough here.
- The village comprises only two clans. Our main occupation is horticulture. We grow bananas and sell

in the weekly markets. This became our profession and we don't prefer any change in it.

- Our whole family is engaged as agricultural labourers. In the off season we go for stone chipping or even as coal mine labourers. Distance is not a problem and we migrate for one season and come back to our villages. We prefer change but do not know how. The government has to do something.
- We are associated with an NGO. They pay money to us to collect the herbs and orchids in the forests. We are also engaged in agriculture. We produce single crop which is often rice and rest of the period engaged in different tasks which can help us earn some money. We need money to buy salt, oil and tobacco which is bartered even with some rice.

Having very simple living styles and meagre demands the women realize the need of education but compromise with the prevailing condition of non-availability of minimal necessities. The other vital factors being historical background of the location, religious influence, the work context, competency, flexibility, inspiration and exposure towards various situations *viz.*, internal and external nature etc., contribute to the situational analysis as well as scope of occupational preference and strategic thought most desirable can be opted. The practical lessons learnt by the women by means of trial and error are not inferior to any characteristic needed for selecting the life choices.

- We are twelve children. Ours was a joint family with agriculture as prime occupation. We are not versatile in any skills nor very good in education. We produce rice and have some livestock. We speak only one language and we are comfortable by being engaged in these village jobs. There is nothing special about us.
- We are five girls and three boys. My mother runs a small grocery shop in the village. We are not highly educated but I am engaged as a domestic help which is a roaring profession in Shillong. Several young

women are engaged in this profession and we support ourselves and our families.

- I am engaged in private job as a labourer. Sometimes I have to look after the entire shop. I too prefer to have an own shop but my financial condition does not permit it. I don't have skills to run a business nor to expect a good job.
- We are engaged in second hand goods and this is reasonably good market for clothes and furniture. We don't have regular shops except pavements where we are still paying market tax. There is good demand for these goods even in the villages.
- We have a brown bread making unit and recently we expanded to chow-making of our own. We supply chow as per the order. There are too many chow makers in the urban areas and no one eats this in villages. The market is limited to urban areas.
- I am a civil engineer by profession. Engaged in the construction works in the Capital City of Shillong. I anticipate limited market but as of now it is still a good market. The construction works are massive especially in government sector which procure ample job opportunities. I prefer to be in Shillong as I have some family responsibilities. My husband is a non-tribal and stays in Pune.
- Shillong is the best place to live. I strongly believe as I consider it as my home. I prefer to do any job which enable to retain me in Shillong rather being sent on promotion elsewhere. I like being with my own people.

General Women's Perceptions

One can understand the minimal needs and expectations, strong preferences towards the group concept, non-contributing and simplistic occupational backgrounds, lack of ambition, aggressiveness, concept of large family, feminine contribution and familial expectations, ethnic enforcements on living style patterns, locational and promotional effect, developmental concepts etc., to a large extent have impact on their occupational decisions yet they to some extent realize the presence or absence of these contributors, search for alternatives, compromise their living systems, prefer to be selective in the limited available options and overcoming the rigidities in some suitable form.

Irrespective of sentiments exhibited by the women towards the sacred forests, traditional living styles, craze for urban life, resource dependencies, living preferences and partnerships, clan promotion, religious dependencies, meeting parental and familial expectations and self-dependencies etc., are few typical but very strong feelings expressed which have their impact on the occupational preference. In order to have an in-depth understanding of women's preferences towards issues associated to women in the situational context depict the following perspectives :

Table 4.1 : Category-I : General Women's Perceptions

Code	*Statement Detail*	*Response*
GW-1.1	The life preference of tribal women towards leading to honourable position	
	• Comfortable	(08.2%)
	• Responsible	(12.0%)
	• Conditional	(22.2%)
	• Rigid	(38.6%)
GW-1.2	Women's prominence in family decision-making	
	• Totally and partially agreeable	(22.3%)
	• Totally and practically disagreeable	(57.6%)
GW-1.3	Women's occupation represent as a symbol of class consciousness	
	• Applicable in general	(21.1%)
	• Applicable in few cases	(20.1%)
	• Applicable in other cases	(40.0%)
GW-1.4	Family issues need to be consensus rather than gender dominance	
	• Practically in all families	(22.2%)
	• Practically in few households	(60.1%)

(contd.)

Code	*Statement Detail*	*Response*
GW-1.5	Social mobility is minimal among matured women	
	• Reluctant to change	(23.1%)
	• Too old to move	(19.8%)
	• Find it impossible	(37.1%)
GW-1.6	Education deprive women to follow the tradition of supporting the family as	
	• She ignore domestic front	(08.0%)
	• Prefer to be mobile	(12.9%)
	• No cultural value preference given	(18.4%)
	• Tend to resettle and become culture-centric	(38.5%)
GW-1.7	Women are competent to do occupation on conditional basis	
	• Knowledgeable	(08.2%)
	• Educated	(13.1%)
	• Exposed to working in general	(21.0%)
	• Trained in specific work	(37.8%)
GW-1.8	Nature has created women to be submissive to man	
	• Totally and partially agree	(23.9%)
	• Totally and partially disagree	(56.7%)
GW-1.9	Women prefer to do stereo-typed duties only due to limited opportunities	
	• When opportunities are few	(09.0%)
	• When deprived of all jobs	(13.5%)
	• When creative environment is missing	(20.5%)
	• When there is no alternative	(37.3%)
GW-1.10	Women have a limited outlook over towards macro social issues	
	• No opportunity situation	(09.9%)
	• When she cannot understand complicated issues	(15.2%)
	• She is above politics	(19.3%)
	• She is restricted to family	(36.1%)
	• Disagree with the statement	(19.5%)

Category-I depicted the concepts of tradition, feminine competencies, social issues, stereo-typed preferences, gender dominance, social mobility etc., with response in percentages. The status revealed the family-centrism, reluctancies towards mobility, external involvement and cultural emphasis etc., proved to be prominent (see Annexure 4.1).

The category-II over general women's perceptions reveal the following :

Table 4.2 : Category-II : General Women's Perceptions

Code	*Detail*	*Response*
GW-2.1	Women's preferences towards making investments	
	• Short-term	(07.0%)
	• Long-term	(10.0%)
	• No willingness to investment	(13.1%)
GW-2.2	Foresightedness restricted to decision	
	• Making	(07.6%)
	• Implementation	(09.6%)
	• Support	(14.1%)
GW-2.3	Occupational decision limit wraps into the future of marriage	
	• Agree	(16.0%)
	• Disagree	(39.7%)
GW-2.4	Marriage and motherhood is no significant end of women's career	
	• Agree	(15.7%)
	• Disagree	(39.2%)
GW-2.5	Return to work after the temporary break from occupation arises due to personal liability	
	• Agree	(15.7%)
	• Disagree	(39.0%)
GW-2.6	Situation witnessed only provoke thought perceival	
	• Wholly and partially true	(37.9%)
	• Untrue	(46.9%)
GW-2.7	Femininity as constituted within the constructive age negate achievement in occupational decision	
	• Agree	(16.2%)
	• Disagree	(37.9%)
GW-2.8	Sub-cultural differences are prominent among young women	
	• Prominent	(16.0%)
	• Lenient	(38.6%)
	• Rigid	(14.7%)
GW-2.9	What comprises typical determinant of women	
	• Character and values	(07.8%)
	• Brightness in work	(09.1%)
	• Sociability	(13.8%)
	• Language	(25.1%)
	• Home background	(13.5%)
GW-2.10	Women conventionally takes interest in occupations branded	
	• Feminine	(16.0%)
	• Masculine	(37.6%)
	• Neutral	(15.4%)

The influence of non-occupational factors refer to the experience, conceptual framework, attitude, self-deterministic situations, predictability, occupational preference forms, criticalities etc., enables to measure the yardsticks developed and implemented in occupational terms (see Annexure 4.2).

Table 4.3 : Category-III : Women's Perceptions

Code	*Statement*	*Response*	
		Positive	*Negative*
GW-3.1 •	Women tend to care more for tradition and culture than men	(16.5%)	(38.2%)
GW-3.2 •	Women promote self-centric perception	(15.9%)	(40.0%)
GW-3.3 •	Older women hold more influence on culture than young women	(16.3%)	(40.1%)
GW-3.4 •	Occupational mobility suits men more than women	(15.9%)	(37.9%)
GW-3.5 •	Being clan promoter the women are considered as a privileged class	(18.4%)	(36.2%)
GW-3.6 •	Service flexibility is more in women	(16.3%)	(37.2%)
GW-3.7 •	Women's efficiency is split between family and occupation	(18.1%)	(37.2%)
GW-3.8 •	Fear of social isolation is common only to rural women	(18.4%)	(35.5%)
GW-3.9 •	Women's behaviour is totally unpredictable	(16.8%)	(38.0%)
GW-3.10•	Women are family specific rather than work-specific	(18.5%)	(34.8%)
GW-3.11•	Women prefer part-time jobs rather than full time occupations	(17.0%)	(37.6%)
GW-3.12•	Competency in hi-level skills help enable women to learn gainful occupation	(18.3%)	(37.8%)
GW-3.13•	Skill stereo-typing keeps women in safe place	(18.0%)	(37.1%)
GW-3.14•	Women hold responsibility at par with men	(17.2%)	(36.9%)
GW-3.15•	Gender inequality in the social segment affects the women more than man	(19.7%)	(35.4%)
GW-3.16•	Life cycle stages of women make big differences in labour market	(18.4%)	(36.9%)
GW-3.17•	Do you consider that the tribal lifestyle patterns of women are too primitive	(18.9%)	(37.5%)
GW-3.18•	The ethnic determinants are rigid on women's political participation	(17.6%)	(37.6%)
GW-3.19•	The internal social distances create the heterogeneous women group	(16.7%)	(39.4%)
GW-3.20•	The community approach has been supporting the tribal women	(16.0%)	(40.0%)

The marriage, motherhood, nurturing the family, homemaking, closed attitude of small and isolated locations, lack of comprehensive understanding, incompetence, predictability and complexity in selection procedures etc., were revealed as personalized decisive-effects both at individual and clan level.

The preferences in orientations towards tradition, culture, mobility, clan promotion, service offer, social isolation, concept of unpredictable behaviour, stereotyping preference, gender inequalities, life cycle stages, lifestyle patterns, social distances and community approach etc., seemed to be the socio-maintenance that have a bearing on their work indications (Annexure 4.3).

Further the occupational concept is also exerted by the supplementary effects *viz.*, total volume of the occupational scope, occupational capabilities, weighted occupations, occupations for livelihood—for supportive services, occupational access, channel and remarkable adaptation of the occupation, deviation and continuity of occupations etc., matter much before taking appropriate decision.

Business Women

Engaged in the multiple business activities of variable dimensions, situations and conceptual forms, the women are backed by various reasons *viz.*, family business, partnering, entering into contractual agreements, trading etc. The following self-reporting questionnaire enables to focus on women-orientations on business issues :

Table 4.4 : Business Women

Code	*Statement Detail*	*Urban*	*Rural*
Bs.1	Nature of the business		
	(i) Manufacturing :	09.5%	20.6%
	(ii) Small time trading	23.9%	08.7%
	(iii) Large scale retailing	48.0%	42.4%
	(iv) Wholesaling	18.3%	28.1%

(contd.)

Code	Statement Detail	Urban	Rural
Bs.2	Inspiration drawn to be in the business		
	(i) family in business	09.7%	18.8%
	(ii) self-initiation	25.6%	09.5%
	(iii) undergone training and acquired	49.4%	41.2%
	(iv) did business studies	15.1%	30.3%
Bs.3	Women's role-consideration in undertaking the activities		
	(i) Can do low level activities	05.7%	20.9%
	(ii) Can perform complex activities	19.1%	09.7%
	(iii) Business decisions only by consultation	42.3%	38.6%
	(iv) Biased in specific areas	32.7%	30.6%
Bs.4	The self-sustained status of the women		
	(i) Above average	23.1%	23.5%
	(ii) Average	46.1%	39.8%
	(iii) Below average	30.8%	36.5%
Bs.5	Implicit or explicit level of dependency over		
	(i) Self	04.8%	18.5%
	(ii) Spouse	17.6%	05.0%
	(iii) Both	46.2%	46.0%
	(iv) Employed personnel	31.2%	30.3%
Bs.6	Credit of growth assignment		
	(i) self-skills	04.8%	19.4%
	(ii) external financial assistance	19.4%	08.2%
	(iii) institutional support	46.1%	40.1%
	(iv) locational advantage	35.0%	32.1%
Bs.7	Ease in initiation of business		
	(i) Self-competency	05.1%	23.0%
	(ii) Government support	16.3%	05.1%
	(iii) Financial grant to boost business	12.6%	27.0%
	(iv) By means of self-help group	35.0%	33.3%
	(v) Tookover the existing business	19.1%	03.1%
Bs.8	Business scenario and environment		
	(i) Very limited	06.8%	18.8%
	(ii) Very high	18.0%	07.6%
	(iii) Scope only in some areas	30.6%	20.4%
	(iv) Partially within and partially outside state	34.4%	33.0%
	(v) Internal business activities and external control	08.1%	09.0%
Bs.9	Skills needed in the business		
	(i) Communication skills	04.0%	19.1%
	(ii) Analytical skills	18.6%	07.9%
	(iii) Persuasive skills	45.0%	40.7%
	(iv) Managerial skills	32.1%	32.1%
Bs.10	Locational positivities favouring business		
	(i) Communication	05.3%	18.5%
	(ii) Physical infrastructure	18.8%	07.1%
	(iii) Markets	42.4%	41.5%
	(iv) Knowledge	33.3%	32.7%

(contd.)

Code	*Statement Detail*	*Urban*	*Rural*
Bs.11	Managerial effectiveness of business women		
	(i) < 20yrs	06.0%	17.6%
	(ii) >20 yrs and < 30 yrs	17.7%	06.1%
	(iii) >30 yrs and < 40 yrs	42.6%	41.2%
	(iv) > 40 years	33.5%	34.8%
Bs.12	Nature of business activity		
	(i) Only single	24.2%	18.8%
	(ii) Multi-tasking	39.6%	49.8%
	(iii) Seasonal	36.1%	31.2%
Bs.13	Level of business operations preferred		
	(i) Within Rural	05.7%	18.2%
	(ii) Urban	18.8%	08.5%
	(iii) Both in rural and urban	45.0%	39.2%\
	(iv) State Capital	30.3%	33.9%
Bs.14	Gender influence over business		
	(i) Skewed towards high	27.1%	25.9%
	(ii) Average	42.1%	46.0%
	(iii) Skewed towards low	30.6%	28.0%
Bs.15	Business threats count on women's business		
	(i) Social	07.4%	20.9%
	(ii) Ethnical	15.6%	07.6%
	(iii) Democratic	47.3%	42.7%
	(iv) Physiological	29.5%	28.6%
Bs.16	Contributories of business promotion		
	(i) Language skills	08.0%	21.2%
	(ii) Market status	17.1%	06.1%
	(iii) Value additions	47.0%	43.0%
	(iv) Interactive skills	27.7%	29.4%
Bs.17	Factors influence women's business involvement		
	(i) Child rearing	08.8%	22.4%
	(ii) Health factors	16.5%	06.4%
	(iii) Deficiency of skills	48.4%	42.7%
	(iv) Lack of information	26.2%	28.3%
Bs.18	Status of business in income diversification		
	(i) Sole occupation	25.1%	21.5%
	(ii) Part-time occupation	48.4%	09.1%
	(iii) Contingent source	26.2%	38.3%
Bs.19	Extent of which the social supportive measures boost women into business		
	(i) Preferred favourability	26.7%	17.9%
	(ii) Neutrality	47.6%	46.9%
	(iii) Unfavourable	25.6%	35.1%
Bs.20	Level of business migrations preferred by women		
	(i) Since inception	08.3%	17.1%
	(ii) Growth oriented	18.3%	36.2%
	(iii) Export oriented	27.4%	46.6%

* Difference in percentages suggest non-response

Women in Service

The urban women definitely have potential options in terms of education, modernization, living styles, time preferences, ambitious and leveraging between the family and work orientations. They are more flexible, independent, mobile and career oriented rather than being dedicated wholly to the families. The proportion of preferences layer several issues associated to the social levels, peer groups, intriguing influences and decision-making approaches seemed to be variant (Annexure 4.4).

The following are few areas which try to describe the personal, occupational and contextual framework valued by these potential and dynamic segments :

Table 4.5 : Women in Service

Code	*Statement Detail*	*Urban*	*Rural*
Wsr-1	I am competent to perform better than what I do here	29.2%	24.7%
Wsr-2	I won't mind going anywhere if I am offered a better job than this	18.0%	23.8%
Wsr-3	I give equal emphasis to rural and urban life styles	27.9%	23.3%
Wsr-4	Work is basically to earn money and I am satisfied with my income from this job	29.0%	23.0%
Wsr-5	I am a good planner and invest in potential sources	29.8%	24.1%
Wsr-6	My family is my first and foremost priority	28.8%	25.9%
Wsr-7	I believe in today and not in tomorrow	29.3%	27.1%
Wsr-8	One should not be money-minded in life	30.2%	21.5%
Wsr-9	I am engaged in social service activities	32.0%	23.5%
Wsr-10	I spend my time mostly with my family members	33.0%	22.4%
Wsr-11	I am not an ambitious person, you see	25.4%	20.9%
Wsr-12	The occupation I am in is my choice and I enjoy it	30.9%	22.7%
Wsr-13	I am engaged in second job as income from one job always falls short	33.6%	23.5%
Wsr-14	I find my job boring and monotonous	18.6%	19.4%
Wsr-15	I like venturing into new occupations	19.6%	20.0%
Wsr-16	I am lucky to get this position as I consider myself talented	31.5%	18.8%

(contd.)

Code	Statement Detail	Urban	Rural
Wsr-17	Had I been a man my life would have been much better	33.0%	18.5%
Wsr-18	My view points are always different from my family members	31.1%	17.6%
Wsr-19	These are the days of inflation and a family needs more and more money	26.7%	21.8%
Wsr-20	Education has no relation to get engaged in income generation	27.3%	23.3%
Wsr-21	Only unskilled people prefer to be selective about occupations	24.3%	21.2%
Wsr-22	I am in this job as most of my family members are engaged in this occupation	25.7%	19.7%
Wsr-23	The social image of the person is dependent on the occupation you do.	25.4%	16.2%
Wsr-24	Community and ethnicity has nothing to do with the occupational selection	25.0%	20.0%
Wsr-25	Occupations need not be based on gender differences	27.5%	25.3%
Wsr-26	The children from service families tend to opt service occupation	29.2%	24.1%
Wsr-27	I don't believe in gender discrimination in occupations	28.8%	24.0%
Wsr-28	I sacrifice promotion in my job if it is offered outside the state	27.9%	22.7%
Wsr-29	I am in this job because of my parental decision	29.0%	21.2%
Wsr-30	I lost my best opportunities in jobs as I always gave importance to my family	29.8%	24.4%
Wsr-31	I prefer to increase my educational qualifications if I get incentives in my job	28.9%	25.6%
Wsr-32	My job reflects my social status	29.3%	26.5%
Wsr-33	Except me, all my family members are engaged in different occupation	30.2%	24.4%
Wsr-34	I recommend the same job to my children	32.0%	26.8%
Wsr-35	Career guidance to a large extent help the females to decide on their occupations	33.0%	25.3%
Wsr-36	Which capital is important for women to earn a decent life style?		
	(i) Human	15.7%	04.1%
	(ii) Social	09.6%	20.3%
	(iii) Natural	41.5%	58.9%
	(iv) Financial	32.9%	12.9%
Wsr-37	Transformation in ethnic structure is based on		
	(i) Liberal status of women	18.1%	03.5%
	(ii) Institutional support towards developmental activities	12.7%	24.4%
	(iii) External changes *viz.*, market systems	37.8%	09.4%
	(iv) Internal forces *viz.*, population growth and scarcity of resources	31.1%	36.2%

(contd.)

Code	Statement Detail	Urban	Rural
Wsr-38	The ideal use of natural resources should be for		
	(i) Value addition	21.1%	28.0%
	(ii) For self-consumption	12.4%	11.2%
	(iii) Exchange with necessities	33.8%	60.1%
Wsr-39	The occupational patterns can be influenced by		
	(i) Migration	17.6%	28.0%
	(ii) Development of infrastructure	11.5%	09.4%
	(iii) Partnering with external forces	33.5%	34.2%
	(iv) Government involvement	33.1%	25.6%
Wsr-40	In order to cope up with occupational pressure what is appropriate?		
	(i) Self-help approach	19.0%	21.6%
	(ii) Promotion of service sector	11.2%	11.2%
	(iii) Boost governmental support	36.6%	33.3%
	(iv) Train local bodies	31.0%	31.5%

Self-Prescription of Lifestyle Models

The variation in the perceivable status, parental and peer group influence, exposure and futuristic understanding which enable the urban women i.e., women in service segment to be definite about the educational, gender-based and parental involvement in molding the life decisions. For several, their illustrations towards value systems are glorified ever since early stages of life which defines the value of money, preference towards status, power, recognition and achievement etc., enabled them to be suggestive in terms of the status, valuations of community, ethnicity, traditional values and concepts associated to the self and self-development. The priorities towards dependency factors portrayed the (i) resource-based, (ii) skill-based, (iii) money or economic criteria, (iv) Ethnic or cultural criteria or religious dominance or career orientations and (v) spouse or familial interests in association to the occupational engagements.

The sacrifice of the preferences in order to arrive occupation or the priority preference by sacrificing occupation is a matter to be decided. The initial opinionalities framed enable to define the occupational role may prove to continue to be dominant factors such as community, religion and family tend to remain so in the later stages but it depends on the status provided to them while deciding the new occupations, occupational alternatives and choices, futuristic concept, changing priorities towards the economic and non-economic valuations, growth orientations etc., which enable the women to alter the occupational preferences. The internal factors seemed to be the contributories but the external factors like NGOs, religion, career guidance from external sources, exposure and ambitious growth orientation towards decent lifestyles, preferences towards ethnic transformations, altering views of utilizing the natural resources and proximate or even distant reasons of occupational pressures, preferences etc., are the prominent reasons in deciding the occupational preferences.

Occupational General View

The women's occupational view in general with respect to their involvement and influence is persevered in the following table :

Table 4.6 : General Occupational View

Code	*Statement Detail*	*Urban*	*Rural*
OGw-1	Women's Commitment cannot be expected in quantum of work	29.6%	35.0%
OGw-2	Participation of women to the occupational spectrum is insignificant	26.8%	32.7%
OGw-3	Occupational options vary according to gender and proximity to towns and settlements	28.7%	32.4%
OGw-4	Segments with meagre income only opt for multiple incomes	29.2%	33.2%
OGw-5	Natural resources should support only the state exchequer	28.4%	32.5%
OGw-6	There is no use preserving natural resources when we remain hungry	26.4%	31.7%
OGw-7	Modern day youth need more skills for a gainful employment	28.6%	34.2%
OGw-8	Older generations cannot cope up with the rapidity of change	29.2%	33.3%
OGw-9	There is no gender discrimination in occupations and every job has its dignity	29.8%	34.4%
OGw-10	Only manipulative people get prestigious jobs	28.8%	35.9%
OGw-11	Job security should be primary consideration of the job	28.2%	33.9%
OGw-12	Life in the modern times is full of uncertainties	31.0%	34.8%
OGw-13	Good education is a necessity to everyone	27.8%	31.1%
OGw-14	Good education is too expensive and there is no guarantee of getting a good job	27.3%	33.8%

(contd.)

Code	*Statement Detail*	*Urban*	*Rural*
OGw-15	Distance should not be a determinant when good job is in offer	29.4%	35.5%
OGw-16	Preference to stay my community people	28.9%	32.0%
OGw-17	Shifting to new jobs provide new opportunities	28.4%	32.9%
OGw-18	Believe in long-term relations rather than personal benefits	28.2%	32.8%
OGw-19	Merged decisions with peer groups decisions	31.0%	34.1%
OGw-20	Critical view over accepting traditional practices	27.7%	33.0%
OGw-21	Today's women are empowered women	26.7%	30.3%
OGw-22	Occupational reservations on the criteria of gender	32.6%	22.3%
OGw-23	The beginnings were small but struggled their way	35.2%	37.1%
OGw-24	Nothing will change with my single decision	34.9%	29.9%
OGw-25	Our past experience pathway for the future	37.6%	32.5%
OGw-26	Elder's guidance is always desirable in our life decisions	33.0%	28.2%
OGw-27	I need facilities and I don't mind shifting to outskirts of the city	38.2%	31.3%
OGw-28	I prefer to stay near workplace but it is very expensive	35.2%	31.9%
OGw-29	Sheer experience provide the inside outs of occupation	35.6%	30.1%
OGw-30	I am not a kind to be satisfied with single occupation	36.2%	31.7%
OGw-31	Training helps sharpening skills in occupation	32.8%	29.1%
OGw-32	Hands on experience are more important than mere counselling	35.3%	31.4%
OGw-33	It is appropriate to change according to the times	37.1%	33.0%
OGw-34	Modern occupational trends unfortunately progressing towards corruption and inefficiency	33.8%	31.6%
OGw-35	Balanced behaviour remains undeterred even in most crises conditions	31.4%	32.9%
OGw-36	I thought several times that I should resign from here	33.3%	31.7%
OGw-37	The opportunities are marginalized but there is ample scope for improvement	35.5%	32.0%
OGw-38	Job market has reached saturation. Nothing can be done	34.1%	33.2%
OGw-39	Dual career and multiple careers overcome occupational compromise to a large extent	32.4%	32.1%
OGw-40	Low profile lifestyle can reduce the occupational anxiety	30.7%	31.2%
OGw-41	Mostly it is lack of confidence make people indecisive about occupational shift.	19.3%	34.3%
OGw-42	Occupational relocation is being restricted to urban areas	24.4%	33.4%

Occupational Specific View

The positioning of women in occupational preference base is perked in specific view with respect to their variable situations, capacities and social stances in the following (see Annexure 4.5).

Table 4.7 : Specific Occupational View

Code	*Statement Detail*	*Positive*	*Negative*
Osp-1	Childcare is the exclusive responsibility of women	41.5%	26.6%
Osp-2	The level of women's status cannot be described by the level of progressiveness of society	40.7%	28.0%
Osp-3	Variations in skills lead to varying occupational preferences in rural and urban areas	41.2%	28.1%
Osp-4	Rural environment is looked down upon by urbanites	42.2%	29.8%
Osp-5	Being micro participants natural resources are our source of livelihood	41.2%	29.8%
Osp-6	It is the responsibility of the government to create employment to us	39.2%	29.5%
Osp-7	Youngsters are better decision-makers about their occupations	41.5%	29.9%
Osp-8	Recently our youth adopting lifestyles which are not suitable to us	42.6%	26.8%
Osp-9	Occupational satisfaction is more important to determine the occupational prestige	42.4%	28.9%
Osp-10	Earning more money is the criteria of good job	43.6%	22.7%
Osp-11	My priorities are towards my family than my job	42.4%	27.9%
Osp-12	Good jobs need big struggle. They are reserved only for few	44.9%	28.2%
Osp-13	Had I been more educated I would have been in much better position	40.3%	28.5%
Osp-14	Our meagre income forced us to earn rather than to study	41.3%	29.0%
Osp-15	Occupational scope gets widened in urban areas than rural	43.0%	28.9%
Osp-16	Retaining one's own identity is important in life. My family culture and tradition are important to me	41.2%	28.4%
Osp-17	Building up career has important bearing on social recognition	41.8%	29.8%
Osp-18	Only inefficient people talk about job shift	41.5%	29.0%

(contd.)

Code	*Statement Detail*	*Positive*	*Negative*
Osp-19	We are all engaged in community development and we draw different strength, you see	44.5%	30.1%
Osp-20	The globalization will ultimately change these rural practices	41.5%	29.6%
Osp-21	Women's role is always appreciated in different forms	39.5%	29.6%
Osp-22	Government should introduce more women oriented developmental schemes	40.8%	31.2%
Osp-23	Forming self-help groups is the most successful concept	43.6%	31.5%
Osp-24	Our status depends on our individual calibre and dedication but not by being a fraction to it	43.6%	29.1%
Osp-25	I always made trial and error before taking best decision	48.3%	34.1%
Osp-26	Career guidance programme helped me in deciding about my job	42.6%	36.0%
Osp-27	Ultimately rural areas are the best places to settle	48.0%	37.8%
Osp-28	Rural areas are good only for a change but not for settling	46.5%	37.5%
Osp-29	My ambition enabled me to be successful in very short span	45.8%	36.4%
Osp-30	There is no one in this field except me	47.9%	37.9%
Osp-31	There is no age limit for learning process	43.8%	35.2%
Osp-32	Youngsters learn thing faster than their previous generations	47.6%	34.5%
Osp-33	My core values towards my occupation remained intact.	49.2%	36.0%
Osp-34	I get upset if things go against me	45.8%	34.9%
Osp-35	There were adjustment problems but I managed them	47.2%	34.0%
Osp-36	Allied occupations also are substantially contributing towards occupational inefficiencies	46.1%	33.4%
Osp-37	Integrated developments prove to be contributory in creating new realities	48.0%	33.0%
Osp-38	There is no hope of improving the occupational status in near future	47.2%	32.0%
Osp-39	Multiple occupations contributing towards income diversification need to be encouraged	44.7%	32.1%
Osp-40	Continuous assistance from external bodies alone can cope up with crisis conditions	43.3%	31.0%

(See Annexure 4.6).

More applicable reasons being :

- **Personal initiatives and performance competency** : The initializations contributing towards life situations have their beginnings in several unnamed forms which consciously or subconsciously contribute to the overall growth of personality factors which have their roots in the self-development of performance competencies.
- **Preferences towards occupational mobility** : The strong occupational standing which define the attributes of occupation and occupational choices most desirable are competent to provide the needed satisfaction goals or in association to the preferences or priorities other than the occupation.
- **Leveraging occupational and non-occupational lifestyles (rural vs. urban) :** The tribals being secluded and are being considered as having priorities other than the occupation i.e., the non-occupational preferences need to be influenced by the occupational decisions or otherwise. Therefore, it is important to perk into the occupational framework based on the preference load as per the non-occupational patterns.
- **Provoking occupational saturation :** Depends on the work priorities and what is occupation to them in the context of life what role does the occupation really matters or even the occupational contribution in the wholesomeness of life patterns etc. determines the occupational saturations not because of occupation but due to the overall satisfaction arrived due to the content of non-occupational factors
- **Occupational monotony** : A rare feeling if defines the lack of change in the occupational situation its concentrated feeling develop only when the occupation is only source of earning and the context is irrevocable. This situation is different to having multiple income preferences which is more common than having monotony among ethnic groups.

- **Venturing into new occupations** : Not very significant but the creative concept has been arriving due to the unsuppressed desire towards settling in the region but growth-orientations are still in their infancies.

Situational Analysis

An overall analysis about the business women define the level and extent of business operations engaged and it is quite a common site that the women take massive initiative to enter into the micro business behind which the survival motive is prominent. Each woman within her resources and expertise decide the kind of occupation to be selected and each of such occupation is being continued for limited time. The women who arrive from extended families make a partial effort of contributing and it is not that the occupation has to literally meet the needs of family. It is apparent that each member in the family contributes to the extent possible and simple living styles enable to assure that the meagre incomes earned make it partial fulfilment. Each family is often kept with multiple occupational sources and for majority a single occupation is not really a need gratifier of the entire family. This concept relaxes the women who earn and at the end of the day/period provide them sufficient to take the minimal necessities needed in the family besides meeting the small-time luxuries such as tobacco, betel nut and betel leaf, meat or dry fish for supper. In urban, the context is regular and continuous but in rural segments it is mostly and prominently the weekly markets which are held once in 4 days a big market day and a small market day. The big market day has a prominence of too many visitors including the urban clientele but the later has very few clients restricted to neighbouring villages.

The occupational centricism has different flavours as in urban areas as the urbanization is still limited and hardly there is any city or urbanized environment prominently visible. The markets provide ethnic look and concept of urbanization still seemed to be in infant stage. The facility, standards, concepts and approaches etc., do contribute towards ethnicity and the privatization implied due to the clan and community domination. The general infrastructure is meagre with its environment having no planning and the informalities dominate the scene. The occupational association enables to depict a disproportionate outlook of ethnic power and dominance glorifying the tribal image rather than a cosmo effect. The ethnic events such as ceremonies, community gatherings, sport and religious events, cultural and ethnic living styles and general code of conduct which reflect the tribal rigidities determine the occupational perception not totally professional but have more than a normal ethnic perseverance. Irrespective of the occupational status the ethnicity predominantly dominates as to the prejudices, favouritisms, ethnic-synchronizations, language and religious barriers and the feeling of being identified as branded ethnic identities are prominently felt.

Sum Up

The **occupational reflections** define that the variation aroused due to the urban, rural, the locational circumstances, the occupational.promotional factors or occupational proneness of the location and the occupational perceptions developed in the region as an internal or external factors, have the primary reflections. The women's self and developmental efforts, progression, opportunities and realizations define the self-initiations of women which is purely individual. The grasp towards situations and familial contributions, environmental factors etc., determine the group-based influences, and the ethnic norms which suggest the typical thinking and attitude formulations over the issues, the thought processes, the weighted priorities, the occupation in totalities, the occupational compositions, the occupational role contribution in the women's life, the role of non-occupational priorities preferred by the women and the level of occupational contentment defined etc. The most proximate reasons of determining the occupational patterns for **Congruency Model** are given below :

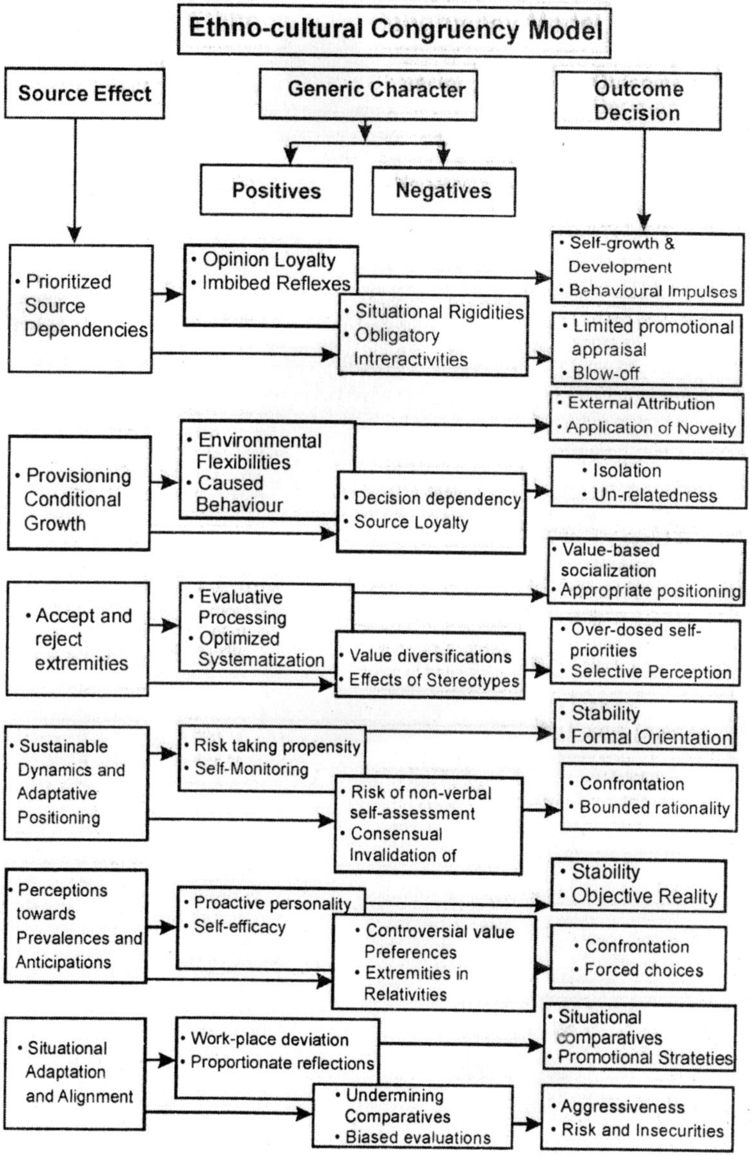

Ethno-cultural Congruency Model
Source Effect
Generic Character
Outcome Decision
Positives
Negatives
• Prioritized Source Dependencies
• Opinion Loyalty
• Imbibed Reflexes
• Situational Rigidities
• Obligatory Intreractivities
• Self-growth & Development
• Behavioural Impulses
• Limited promotional appraisal
• Blow-off
• Provisioning Conditional Growth
• Environmental Flexibilities
• Caused Behaviour
• Decision dependency
• Source Loyalty
• External Attribution
• Application of Novelty
• Isolation
• Un-relatedness
• Accept and reject extremities
• Evaluative Processing
• Optimized Systematization
• Value diversifications
• Effects of Stereotypes
• Value-based socialization
• Appropriate positioning
• Over-dosed self-priorities
• Selective Perception
• Sustainable Dynamics and Adaptative Positioning
• Risk taking propensity
• Self-Monitoring
• Risk of non-verbal self-assessment
• Consensual Invalidation of
• Stability
• Formal Orientation
• Confrontation
• Bounded rationality
• Perceptions towards Prevalences and Anticipations
• Proactive personality
• Self-efficacy
• Controversial value Preferences
• Extremities in Relativities
• Stability
• Objective Reality
• Confrontation
• Forced choices
• Situational Adaptation and Alignment
• Work-place deviation
• Proportionate reflections
• Undermining Comparatives
• Biased evaluations
• Situational comparatives
• Promotional Stratetics
• Aggressiveness
• Risk and Insecurities

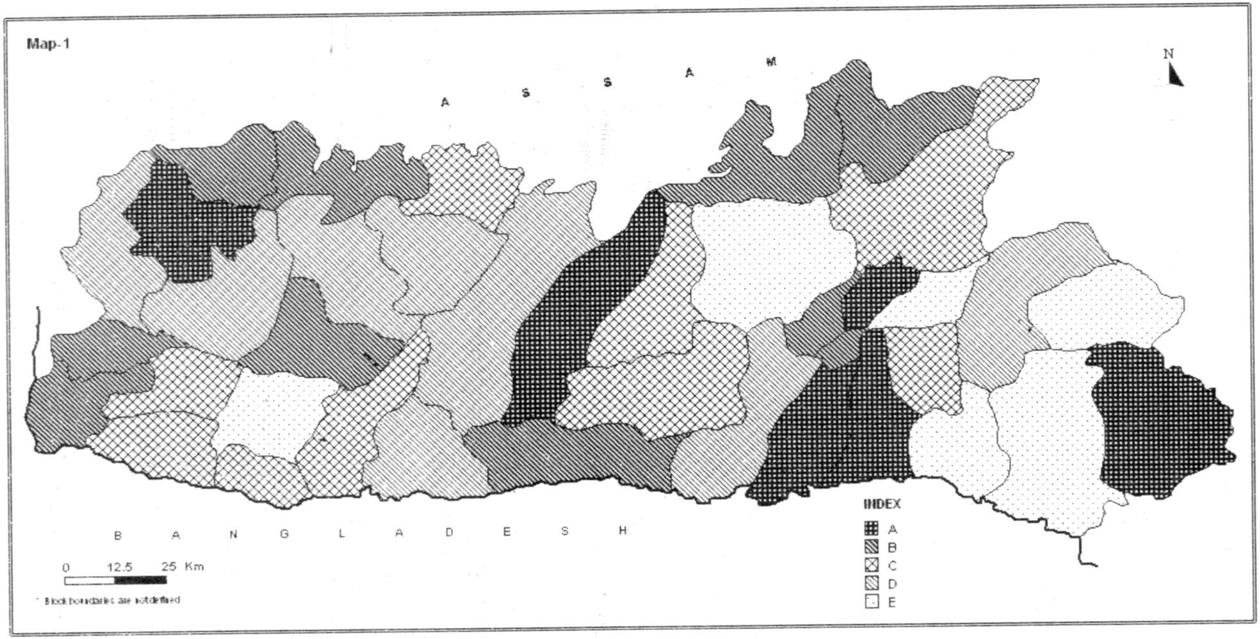

Map-1 : Occupational Stretch and Direction (Rural)

* **Index Detail: A** : Occupational closeness and ethnic professionalism; **B** : Micro Occupational Perspectives (entrepreneurial); **C** : Ethnic Perspective; **D** : Leveraging Performance Patterns; **E** : Resource Possession

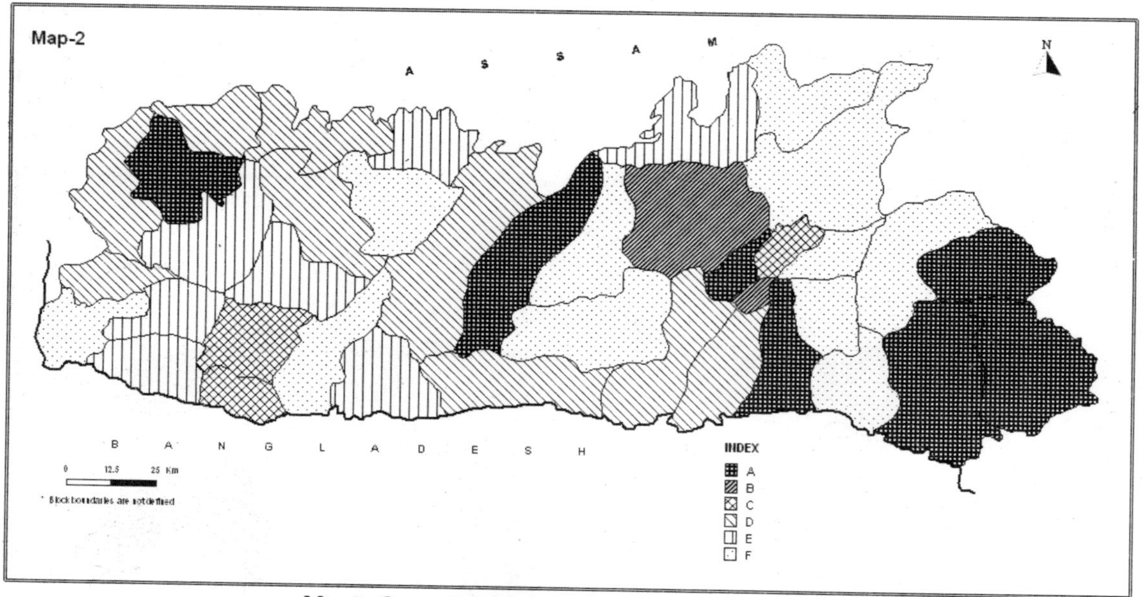

Map-2 : Occupational Serve and Subserve Criteria (Rural)

Index Detail : A: Major influencer :Internalities; Minor influencers: Social Supportives; Externalities; Mutualities; Isolates ; Informality; **B**: Major influencer : Socio Supportives; Minor influencers: Internalities; Externalities; Mutualities; Isolates ; Informality; **C:** Major influencer :Externalities; Minor influencers: Internalities; Social Supportives; Mutualities; Isolates ; Informality; **D:** Major influencer :Mutualities; Minor influencers: Internalities; Social Supportives; Externalities; Isolates ; Informality; **E**: Major influencer :Isolates; Minor influencers: Internalities; Social Supportives; Externalities; Mutualities; Informality; **F:** Major influencer :Informality Minor influencers: Internalities; Social Supportives; Externalities; Mutualities; Isolates ;

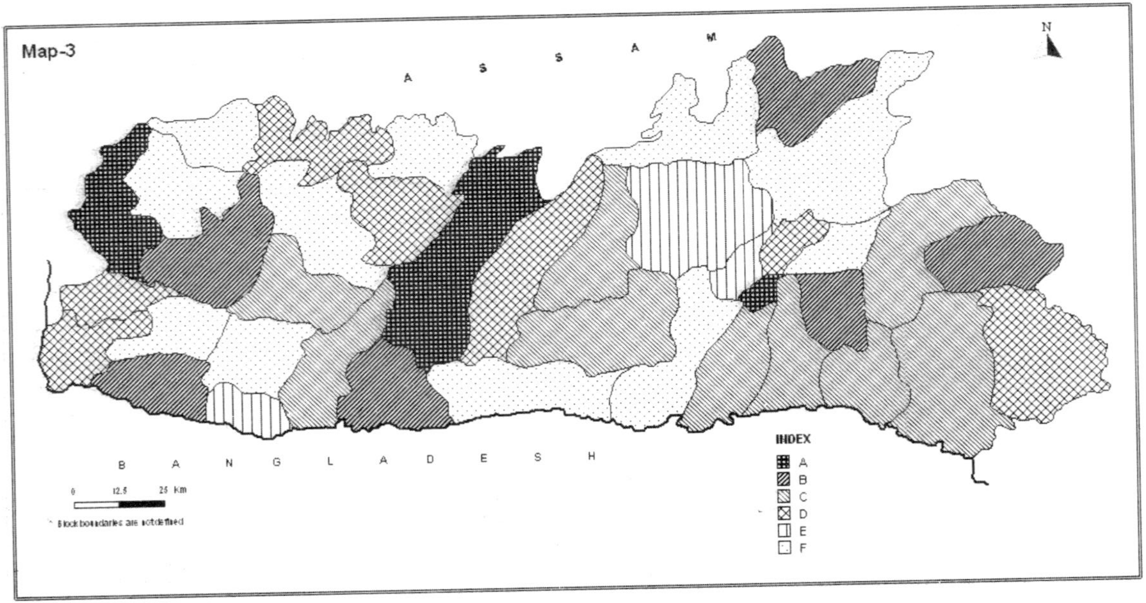

Map-3 : Occupational Decision-Consequence (Rural)

Index Detail : A: Context appropriation in occupational segregation-Intensity of localized complexities consequencing occupational stereotyping; **B:** Usage of local capacity in income diversification-Micro participation and occupational stretch; **C:** High magnitude of resource dependencies-Occupational preference discrepancies and counter urbanization; **D:** Focus over occupational radius-Drives based on external causes with internal effects; **E:** Self-centricism and feminine volatilities-Anticipating decision consequences of occupational spectrum; **F:** Anticipating decision consequences of occupational spectrum-Life cycle stages and activated occupational dynamism

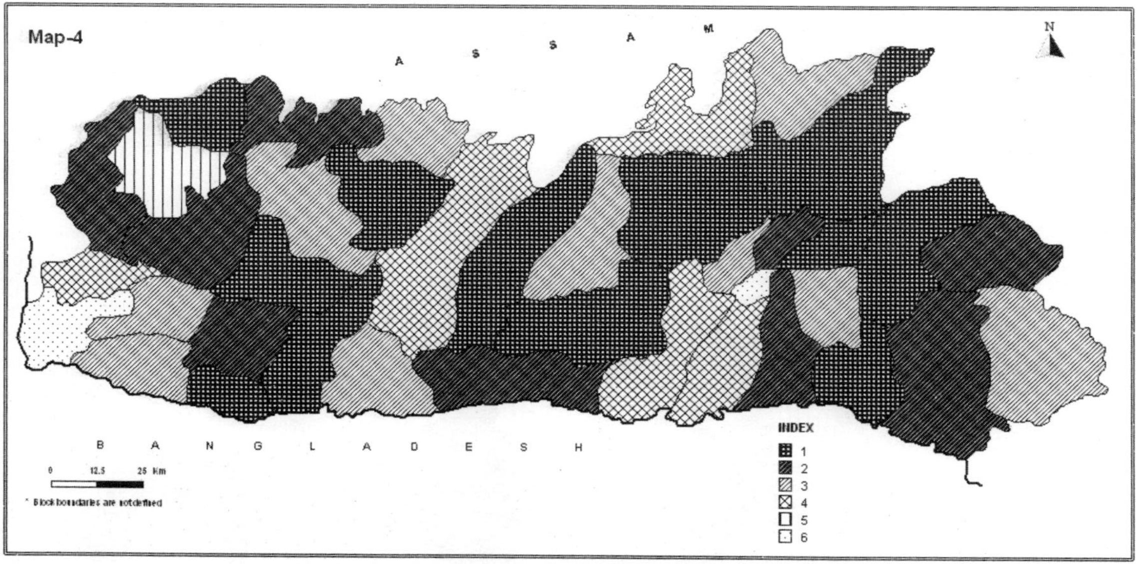

Map-4 : Coordinated Occupational Inclinations (Rural)

Index Detail : 1. Behavioural reactions based on conceptual and objective criteria-At convenience socio-cultural norms-Compromised inadequacies; **2.** Leveraging transformational attributes-Composite and comprehensive preferences-Adaptabilities and advocations;**3**. Extent of Limitedness in decision domain-Lifestyle profiles-Mobility and migration-Allied (non-occupational) contributions; **4**. Occupational selectivities-Positivities in relation to opportunities and facilities-Intrigue into occupational compatibilities and preference discrepancies; **5**. Situational response: Occupational adequacies-Ethnic professionalism-Occupational insights and commitment: **6**. Marginalized perseverances-Access to the dependency-proven condition-Impact of socio-cultural reconciliations

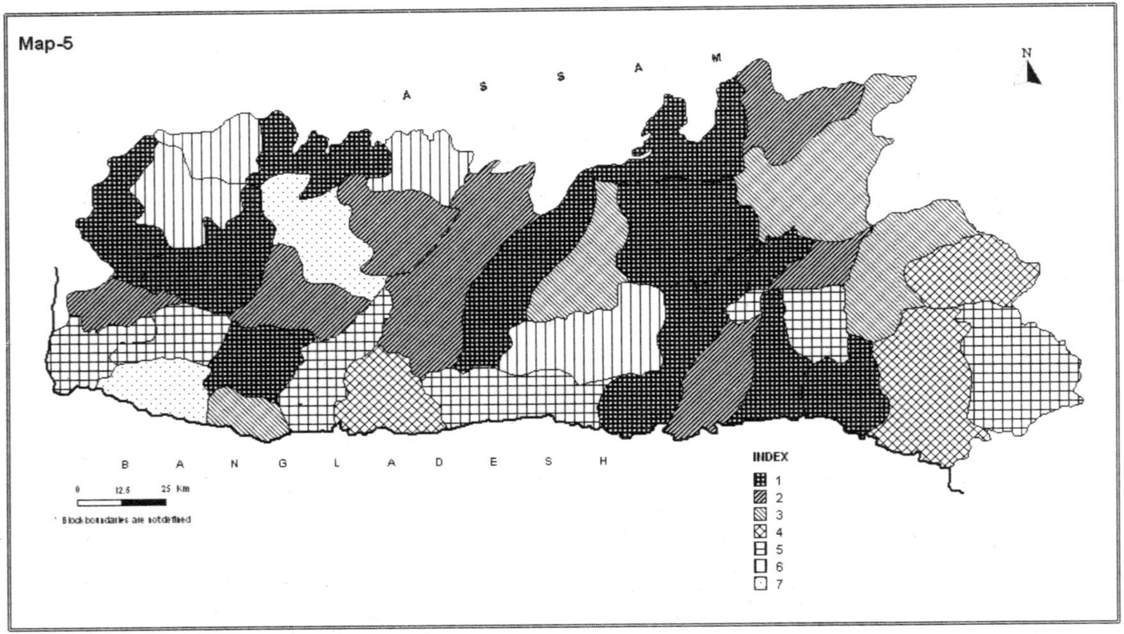

Map-5 : Occupational Self-direction (Rural)

Index Detail : 1. Level of Interactivities and Connectivities; **2.** Level of Permissiveness, Compromises and Cope up; **3.** Level of Value Perception Discrimination; **4.** Level of Behavioural Rigidities; **5.** Level of Opportunistic Situations in Familiar and Non-familiar Conditions; **6.** Level of Disproportionate Perseverance towards Need Gratification; **7.** Level of Associative Tendencies Influenced by Subsequent effect/s of Decision

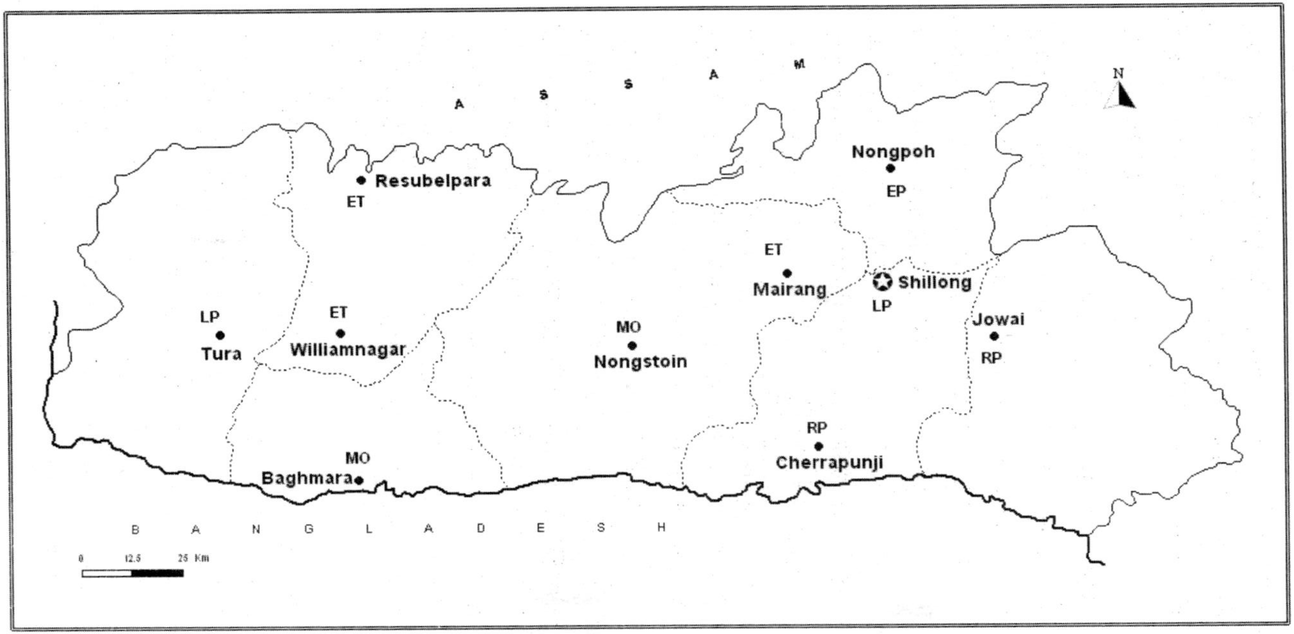

Map-6 : Occupational Stretch and Direction (Urban)

Index Detail: **EP:** Occupational closeness and ethnic professionalism; **MO:** Micro Occupational Perspectives (entrepreneurial); **ET:** Ethnic Perspective; **LP:** Leveraging Performance Patterns; **RP:** Resource Possession

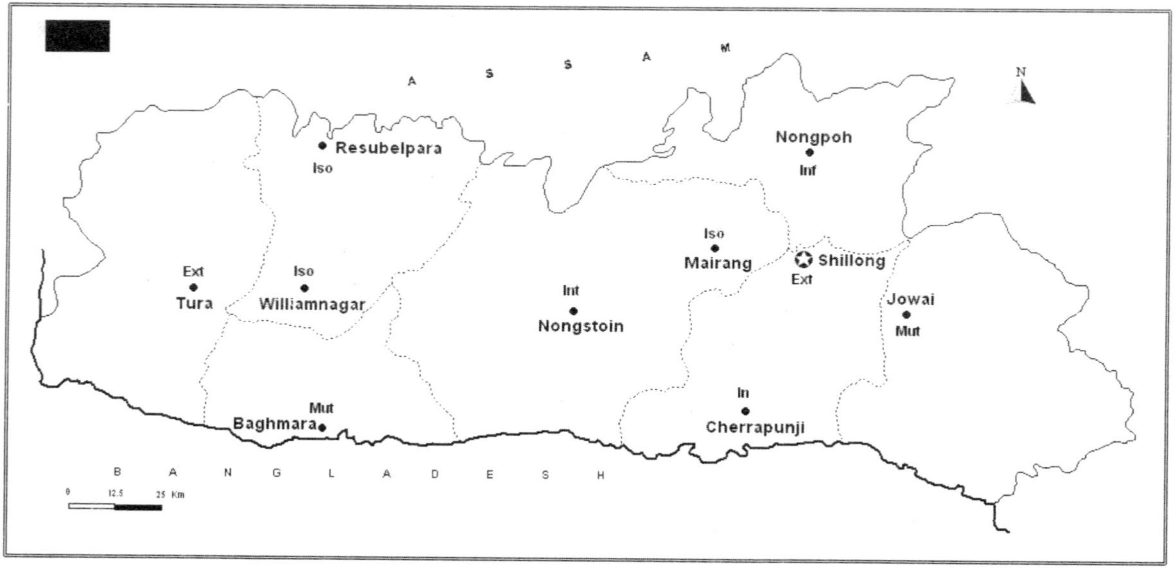

Map-7 : Occupational Serve and Sub-serve Criteria (Urban)

Index Detail : In: Major influencer :Internalities; Minor influencers: Social Supportives; Externalities; Mutualities; Isolates ; Informality; **Ss**: Major influencer :Socio-Supportives; Minor influencers: Internalities; Externalities; Mutualities; Isolates ; Informality; **Ex:** Major influencer :Externalities; Minor influencers: Internalities; Social Supportives; Mutualities; Isolates ; Informality; **Mu:** Major influencer : Mutualities; Minor influencers: Internalities; Social Supportives; Externalities; Isolates; Informality; **Iso:** Major influencer :Isolates; Minor influencers: Internalities; Social Supportives; Externalities; Mutualities; Informality; **Inf:** Major influencer :Informality Minor influencers: Internalities; Social Supportives; Externalities; Mutualities; Isolates.

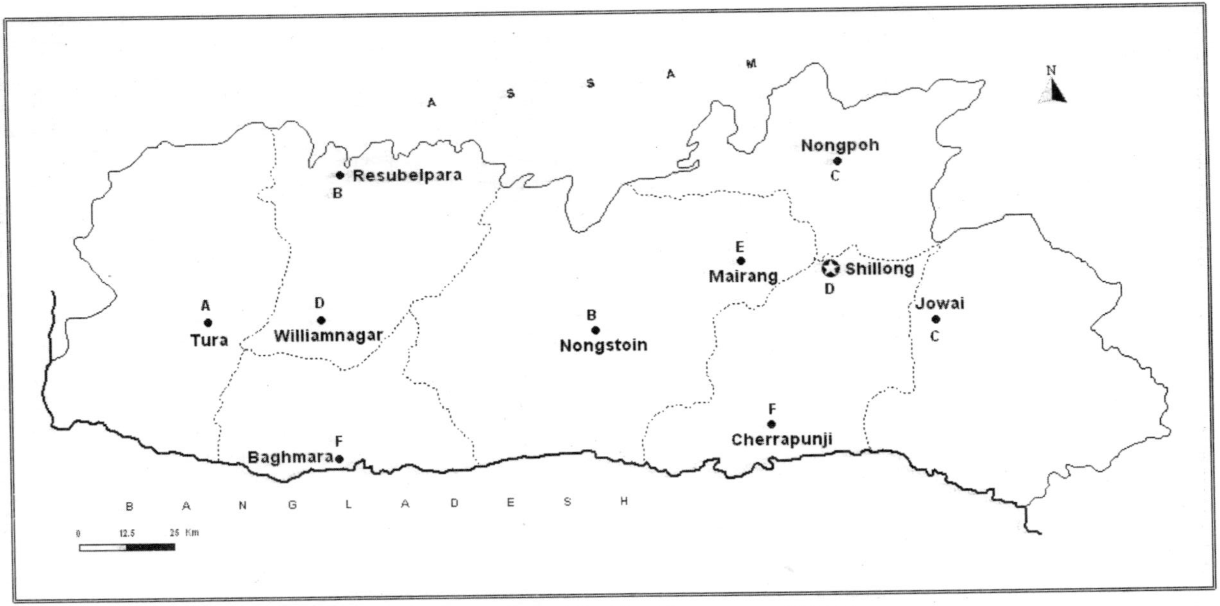

Map-8 : Occupational Decision-Consequence (Urban)

Index Detail : A: Context appropriation in occupational segregation-Intensity of localized complexities consequencing occupational stereo-typing; **B:** Usage of local capacity in income diversification-Micro participation and occupational stretch; **C:** High magnitude of resource dependencies-Occupational preference discrepancies and counter urbanization; **D:** Focus over occupational radius-Drives based on external causes with internal effects; **E:** Self-centricism and feminine volatilities-Anticipating decision consequences of occupational spectrum; **F:** Anticipating decision consequences of occupational spectrum-Life cycle stages and activated occupational dynamism

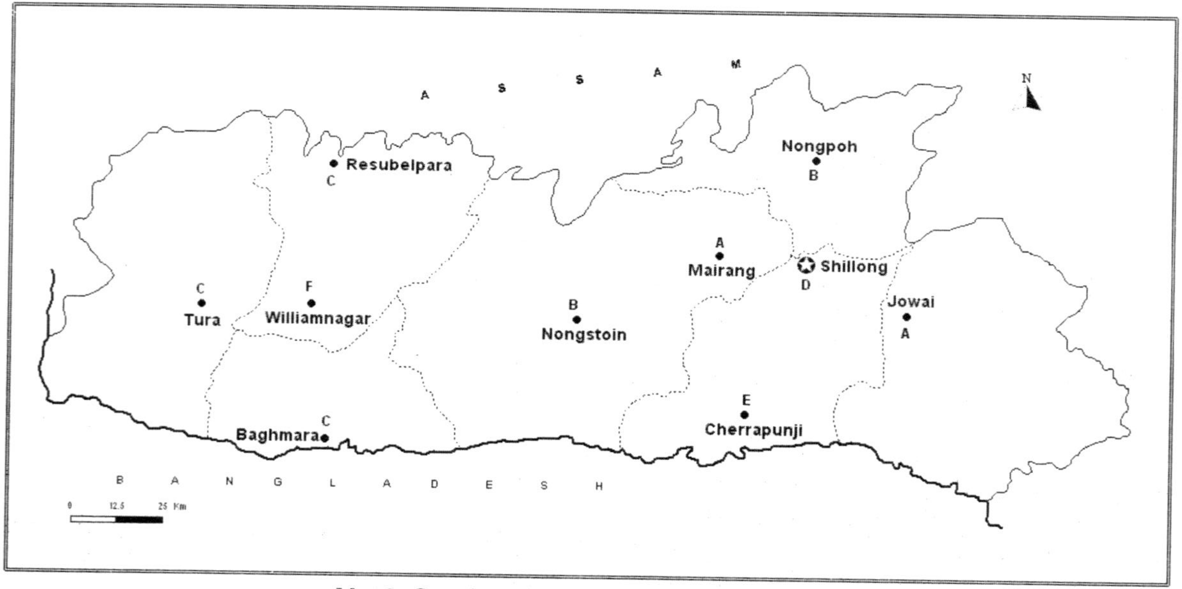

Map-9 : Co-ordinated Occupational Inclinations (Urban)

Index Detail : A. Behavioural reactions based on conceptual and objective criteria-At convenience socio-cultural norms-Compromised inadequacies; **B.** Leveraging transformational attributes-Composite and comprehensive preferences-Adaptabilities and advocations; **C**. Extent of Limitedness in decision domain-Lifestyle profiles-Mobility and migration-Allied (non-occupational) contributions; **D**. Occupational selectivities-Positivities in relation to opportunities and facilities-Intrigue into occupational compatibilities and preference discrepancies; **E**. Situational response: Occupational adequacies-Ethnic professionalism-Occupational insights and commitment; **F**. Marginalized perseverances-Access to the dependency-proven condition-Impact of socio-cultural reconciliations .

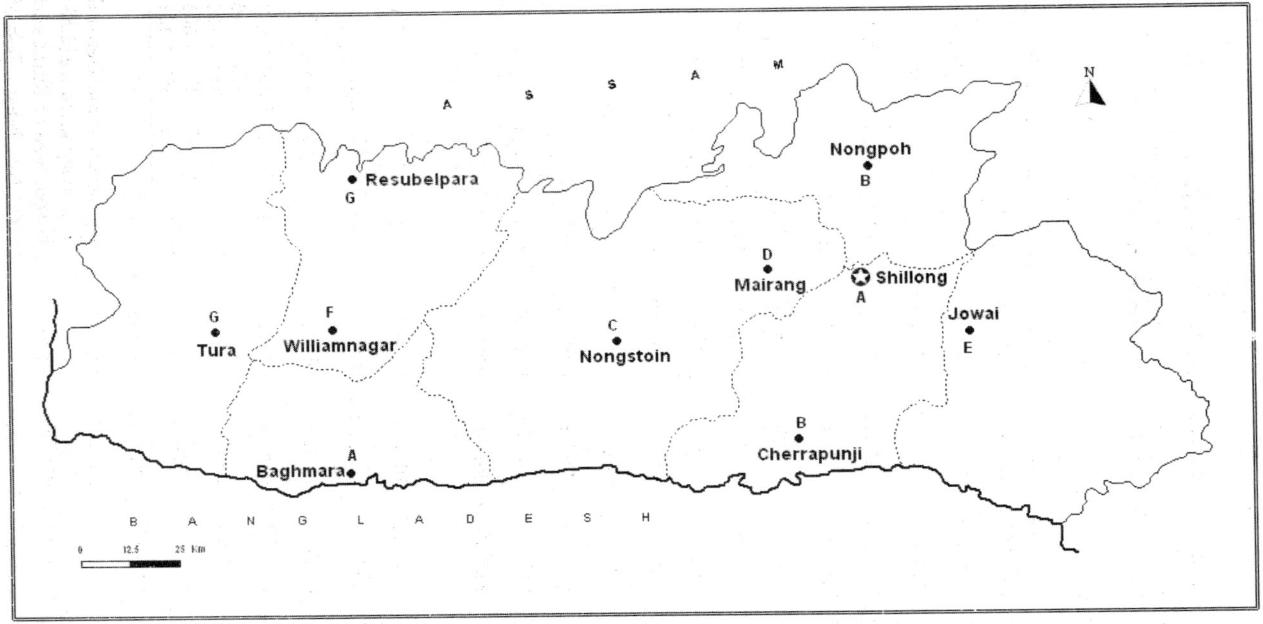

Map-10 : Occupational Self-direction (Urban)

Index Detail : **A**. Level of Interactivities and Connectivities; **B**. Level of Permissiveness, Compromises and Cope up; **C**. Level of Value Perception Discrimination; **D**. Level of Behavioural Rigidities; **E.** Level of Opportunistic Situations in Familiar and Non-familiar Conditions; **F**. Level of Disproportionate Perseverance towards Need Gratification; **G**. Level of Associative Tendencies Influenced by Subsequent effect/s of Decision.

Annexure 4.1 : Urban *vs.* Rural Women's General view

Urban		*Rural*	*M1*	*M2*	*t-value*	*N1*	*N2*	*SD1*	*SD2*	*F-ratio*
UOccG1	vs	ROccG1	3.956	3.313	16.672	1715	1898	0.901	1.346	2.228
UOccG2	vs	ROccG2	3.396	3.328	17.153	1715	1898	0.926	1.352	2.129
UOccG3	vs	ROccG3	3.948	3.330	16.161	1715	1898	0.918	1.321	2.072
UOccG4	vs	ROccG4	3.957	3.319	16.265	1715	1898	0.952	1.349	2.010
UOccG5	vs	ROccG5	3.966	3.332	16.284	1715	1898	0.937	1.343	2.053
UOccG6	vs	ROccG6	4.019	3.393	16.111	1715	1898	0.915	1.356	2.198
UOccG7	vs	ROccG7	3.971	3.315	16.980	1715	1898	0.916	1.345	2.152
UOccG8	vs	ROccG8	3.949	3.307	16.356	1715	1898	0.957	1.349	1.989
UOccG9	vs	ROccG9	3.951	3.306	16.545	1715	1898	0.932	1.349	2.094
UOccG10	vs	ROccG10	3.969	3.265	17.802	1715	1898	0.948	1.368	2.080
UOccG11	vs	ROccG11	3.970	3.288	17.339	1715	1898	0.940	1.362	2.099
UOccG12	vs	ROccG12	3.922	3.263	16.715	1715	1898	0.965	1.351	1.958
UOccG13	vs	ROccG13	3.956	3.361	15.458	1715	1898	0.939	1.320	1.973
UOccG14	vs	ROccG14	4.004	3.316	17.501	1715	1898	0.925	1.370	2.197
UOccG15	vs	ROccG15	3.984	3.300	17.327	1715	1898	0.927	1.377	2.208
UOccG16	vs	ROccG16	3.955	3.351	15.523	1715	1898	0.950	1.333	1.969
UOccG17	vs	ROccG17	3.974	3.328	16.519	1715	1898	0.943	1.349	2.047
UOccG18	vs	ROccG18	3.979	3.330	16.635	1715	1898	0.940	1.347	2.055
UOccG19	vs	ROccG19	3.918	3.274	16.388	1715	1898	0.970	1.342	1.915
UOccG20	vs	ROccG20	4.001	3.328	16.982	1715	1898	0.946	1.372	2.103
UOccG21	vs	ROccG21	3.986	3.370	15.841	1715	1898	0.944	1.338	2.008
UOccG22	vs	ROccG22	3.816	3.389	11.363	1715	1898	0.989	1.238	1.566
UOccG23	vs	ROccG23	3.788	3.327	12.266	1715	1898	0.990	1.238	1.562
UOccG24	vs	ROccG24	3.816	3.352	12.136	1715	1898	1.005	1.259	1.570
UOccG25	vs	ROccG25	3.788	3.266	13.164	1715	1898	1.056	1.298	1.510
UOccG26	vs	ROccG26	3.856	3.398	11.833	1715	1898	1.022	1.276	1.560
UOccG27	vs	ROccG27	3.754	3.279	12.091	1715	1898	1.057	1.280	1.466
UOccG28	vs	ROccG28	3.837	3.284	13.804	1715	1898	1.050	1.324	1.590
UOccG29	vs	ROccG29	3.784	3.296	12.536	1715	1898	1.038	1.278	1.516
UOccG30	vs	ROccG30	3.809	3.276	13.268	1715	1898	1.069	1.318	1.519
UOccG31	vs	ROccG31	3.83	3.34	12.81	1715	1898	1.028	1.275	1.537
UOccG32	vs	ROccG32	3.80	3.25	14.01	1715	1898	1.040	1.288	1.535
UOccG33	vs	ROccG33	3.79	3.23	14.05	1715	1898	1.051	1.304	1.540
UOccG34	vs	ROccG34	3.85	3.28	14.41	1715	1898	1.026	1.312	1.637
UOccG35	vs	ROccG35	3.90	3.22	16.91	1715	1898	1.030	1.350	1.721
UOccG36	vs	ROccG36	3.83	3.25	14.72	1715	1898	1.026	1.309	1.629
UOccG37	vs	ROccG37	3.78	3.24	13.97	1715	1898	1.038	1.275	1.509
UOccG38	vs	ROccG38	3.83	3.24	15.19	1715	1898	1.011	1.310	1.680
UOccG39	vs	ROccG39	3.87	3.29	14.59	1715	1898	0.998	1.319	1.746
UOccG40	vs	ROccG40	3.90	3.32	14.75	1715	1898	0.981	1.314	1.796
UOccG41	vs	ROccG41	3.66	3.14	12.50	1715	1898	1.118	1.372	1.508
UOccG42	vs	ROccG42	3.47	3.18	6.76	1715	1898	1.271	1.350	1.129

(*Note* : "t"-test of significance with df 3611).

U Occ : Urban Occupational General view; R Occ : Rural Occupational General view; M1 and M2 : Means of Urban and Rural; 1% level of significance (2.58) and 5% level of significance (1.96); N1 and N2 : Sample Size of Rural and Urban; (SD1 and SD2 : Standard Deviation of N1 and N2; F-test : Test of variability.

Annexure 4.2 : Rural *vs.* Urban Special View

Rural	*Urban*	*M1*	*M2*	*t-value*	*dt*	*N1*	*N2*	*SD1*	*SD2*	*F-ratio*
ROccsp1 vs.	UOccsp 1	3.243	3.601	-9.628	3611	1898	1715	1.206	1.005	1.440
ROccsp2 vs.	UOccsp 2	3.159	3.601	-12.045	3611	1898	1715	1.182	1.005	1.383
ROccsp3 vs.	UOccsp 3	3.156	3.601	-11.953	3611	1898	1715	1.208	1.005	1.445
ROccsp4 vs.	UOccsp 4	3.144	3.601	-12.193	3611	1898	1715	1.222	1.005	1.479
ROccsp5 vs.	UOccsp 5	3.136	3.601	-12.453	3611	1898	1715	1.212	1.005	1.455
ROccsp6 vs.	UOccsp 6	3.138	3.601	-12.643	3611	1898	1715	1.178	1.005	1.374
ROccsp7 vs.	UOccsp 7	3.222	3.601	-10.242	3611	1898	1715	1.197	1.005	1.418
ROccsp8 vs.	UOccsp 8	3.151	3.601	-12.057	3611	1898	1715	1.212	1.005	1.455
ROccsp9 vs.	UOccsp 9	3.202	3.601	-10.698	3611	1898	1715	1.213	1.005	1.456
ROccsp10 vs.	UOccsp 10	3.186	3.601	-11.147	3611	1898	1715	1.208	1.005	1.445
ROccsp11 vs.	UOccsp 11	3.165	3.601	-11.740	3611	1898	1715	1.201	1.005	1.429
ROccsp12 vs.	UOccsp 12	3.180	3.601	-11.154	3611	1898	1715	1.237	1.005	1.514
ROccsp13 vs.	UOccsp 13	3.117	3.601	-13.062	3611	1898	1715	1.197	1.005	1.419
ROccsp14 vs.	UOccsp 14	3.170	3.601	-11.641	3611	1898	1715	1.197	1.005	1.417
ROccsp15 vs.	UOccsp 15	3.226	3.601	-10.060	3611	1898	1715	1.213	1.005	1.457
ROccsp16 vs.	UOccsp 16	3.129	3.601	-12.646	3611	1898	1715	1.213	1.005	1.457
ROccsp17 vs.	UOccsp 17	3.150	3.601	-12.156	3611	1898	1715	1.203	1.005	1.433
ROccsp18 vs.	UOccsp 18	3.132	3.601	-12.523	3611	1898	1715	1.221	1.005	1.476
ROccsp19 vs.	UOccsp 19	3.151	3.601	-11.844	3611	1898	1715	1.247	1.005	1.540
ROccsp20 vs.	UOccsp 20	3.116	3.601	-12.977	3611	1898	1715	1.216	1.005	1.465
ROccsp21 vs.	UOccsp 21	3.055	3.601	-14.693	3611	1898	1715	1.204	1.005	1.435
ROccsp22 vs.	UOccsp 22	2.963	3.601	-16.504	3611	1898	1715	1.285	1.005	1.634
ROccsp23 vs.	UOccsp 23	2.995	3.601	-15.345	3611	1898	1715	1.325	1.005	1.738
ROccsp24 vs.	UOccsp 24	2.989	3.601	-15.454	3611	1898	1715	1.332	1.005	1.756
ROccsp25 vs.	UOccsp 25	2.988	3.601	-15.145	3611	1898	1715	1.374	1.005	1.870
ROccsp26 vs.	UOccsp 26	2.934	3.601	-17.118	3611	1898	1715	1.300	1.005	1.674
ROccsp27 vs.	UOccsp 27	2.960	3.601	-15.901	3611	1898	1715	1.368	1.005	1.852
ROccsp28 vs.	UOccsp 28	2.977	3.601	-15.735	3611	1898	1715	1.335	1.005	1.764
ROccsp29 vs.	UOccsp 29	2.950	3.601	-16.425	3611	1898	1715	1.332	1.005	1.756
ROccsp30 vs.	UOccsp 30	2.961	3.601	-16.062	3611	1898	1715	1.344	1.005	1.788
ROccsp31 vs.	UOccsp 31	2.962	3.601	-16.418	3611	1898	1715	1.297	1.005	1.664
ROccsp32 vs.	UOccsp 32	2.985	3.601	-15.604	3611	1898	1715	1.324	1.005	1.737
ROccsp33 vs.	UOccsp 33	3.002	3.601	-14.933	3611	1898	1715	1.357	1.005	1.823
ROccsp34 vs.	UOccsp 34	3.001	3.601	-15.318	3611	1898	1715	1.309	1.005	1.697
ROccsp35 vs.	UOccsp 35	3.013	3.601	-15.182	3611	1898	1715	1.288	1.005	1.643
ROccsp36 vs.	UOccsp 36	3.009	3.601	-15.210	3611	1898	1715	1.295	1.005	1.660
ROccsp37 vs.	UOccsp 37	2.999	3.601	-15.262	3611	1898	1715	1.324	1.005	1.735
ROccsp38 vs.	UOccsp 38	3.071	3.601	-13.598	3611	1898	1715	1.301	1.005	1.675
ROccsp39 vs.	UOccsp 39	3.065	3.601	-13.936	3611	1898	1715	1.272	1.005	1.601
ROccsp40 vs.	UOccsp 40	3.072	3.601	-13.964	3611	1898	1715	1.242	1.005	1.528

(*Note* : "t"-test of significance with df 3611).
U Occ : Urban Occupational General view; R Occ : Rural Occupational General view; M1 and M2 : Means of Urban and Rural; 1% level of significance (2.58) and 5% level of significance (1.96); N1 and N2 : Sample Size of Rural and Urban; (SD 1 and SD2 : Standard Deviation of N1 and N2; F-test : Test of variability.

Annexure 4.3 : Rural *vs.* Urban Business

Rural	*Urban*	*M1*	*M2*	*t-valu©e*	*df*	*P*	*N1*	*N2*	*SD1*	*SD2*	*F-ratio*
UBs 1 vs.	RBs 1	3.75	3.92	2.78	996	0.01	659	339	0.86	1.01	1.38
UBs2 vs.	RBs 2	3.70	3.94	3.82	996	0.00	659	339	0.84	1.05	1.55
UBs3 vs.	RBs 3	4.02	3.91	1.74	996	Insig	659	339	0.87	1.07	1.54
UBs4 vs.	RBs 4	4.03	3.95	1.31	996	Insig	659	339	0.83	1.07	1.67
UBs5 vs.	RBs 5	4.04	3.88	2.60	996	0.01	659	339	0.83	1.04	1.59
UBs6 vs.	RBs 6	4.00	3.85	2.52	996	0.01	659	339	0.83	1.08	1.70
UBs7 vs.	RBs 7	4.07	3.81	3.94	996	0.00	659	339	0.86	1.13	1.71
UBs8 vs.	RBs 8	4.03	3.88	2.36	996	0.02	659	339	0.89	1.07	1.44
UBs9 vs.	RBs 9	4.05	3.86	3.19	996	0.00	659	339	0.82	1.07	1.72
UBs10 vs.	RBs 10	4.04	3.88	2.48	996	1%	659	339	0.86	1.06	1.54
UBs11 vs.	RBs 11	4.04	3.93	1.66	996	Insig	659	339	0.87	1.06	1.48
UBs12 vs.	RBs 12	4.08	3.87	3.51*	996	HS	659	339	0.84	1.06	1.60
UBs13 vs.	RBs 13	4.00	3.89	1.80	996	Insig	659	339	0.85	1.07	1.59
UBs14 vs.	RBs 14	3.961	3.844	1.859	996	Insig	659	339	0.89	1.02	1.31
UBs15 vs.	RBs 15	3.991	3.791	3.178	996	1%	659	339	0.86	1.07	1.54
UBs16 vs.	RBs 16	3.945	3.808	2.155	996	5%	659	339	0.87	1.08	1.52
UBs17 vs.	RBs 17	3.927	3.770	2.455	996	5%	659	339	0.88	1.09	1.54
UBs18 vs.	RBs 18	3.930	3.788	2.185	996	5%	659	339	0.90	1.10	1.49
UBs19 vs.	RBs 19	3.91	3.917	-0.110	996	Insig	659	339	0.86	1.06	1.51
UBs20 vs.	RBs 20	3.924	4.115	-2.994	996	5%	659	339	0.88	1.07	1.46
UBs21 vs.	RBs 21	3.91	3.965	-0.841	996	Insig	659	339	0.87	1.11	1.63
UBs22 vs.	RBs 22	3.927	4.068	-2.239	996	5%	659	339	0.87	1.05	1.44
UBs23 vs.	RBs 23	3.907	3.906	0.028	996	Insig	659	339	0.87	1.12	1.64
UBs24 vs.	RBs 24	3.874	4.062	-2.990	996	1%	659	339	0.86	1.07	1.56
UBs25 vs.	RBs 25	3.868	4.018	-2.241	996	5%	659	339	0.90	1.15	1.61

(*Note* : "t "-test of significance with df 3611).
U Occ : Urban Occupational General view; R Occ : Rural Occupational General view; M1 and M2 : Means of Urban and Rural; 1% level of significance (2.58) and 5% level of significance (1.96); N1 and N2 : Sample Size of Rural and Urban; (SD 1 and SD2 : Standard Deviation of N1 and N2; F-test : Test of variability.

Annexure 4.4: Rural and Urban Services View

Rural		*Urban*	*M1*	*M2*	*t-value*	*P*	*N1*	*N2*	*SD1*	*SD2*	*F-ratio*
USr 1	vs.	RSr 1	3.822	3.591	3.435	1%	940	337	1.051	1.096	1.087
USr 2	vs.	RSr 2	3.863	3.629	3.402	1%	940	337	1.055	1.153	1.194
USr 3	vs.	RSr 3	3.857	3.647	3.119	1%	940	337	1.043	1.119	1.152
USr 4	vs.	RSr 4	3.847	3.588	3.770	1%	940	337	1.066	1.128	1.119
USr 5	vs.	RSr 5	3.821	3.576	3.495	1%	940	337	1.07	1.186	1.211
USr 6	vs.	RSr 6	3.856	3.608	3.551	1%	940	337	1.053	1.223	1.348
USr 7	vs.	RSr 7	3.835	3.552	3.975	1%	940	337	1.086	1.217	1.255
USr 8	vs.	RSr 8	3.844	3.504	4.817	1%	940	337	1.057	1.242	1.379
USr 9	vs.	RSr 9	3.796	3.682	1.655	Insig	940	337	1.068	1.106	1.073
USr 10	vs.	RSr 10	3.760	3.644	1.648	Insig	940	337	1.090	1.146	1.105
USr 11	vs.	RSr 11	3.918	3.626	4.421	0%	940	337	1.025	1.081	1.113
USr 12	vs.	RSr 12	3.820	3.691	1.888	6%	940	337	1.066	1.099	1.064
USr 13	vs.	RSr 13	3.779	3.650	1.836	Insig	940	337	1.119	1.067	1.100
USr 14	vs.	RSr 14	3.863	3.682	2.633	1%	940	337	1.066	1.111	1.087
USr 15	vs.	RSr 15	3.817	3.804	0.186	Insig	940	337	1.074	1.141	1.128
USr 16	vs.	RSr 16	3.789	3.772	0.260	Insig	940	337	1.072	1.109	1.071
USr 17	vs.	RSr 17	3.778	3.777	0.003	Insig	940	337	1.095	1.089	1.012
USr 18	vs.	RSr 18	3.837	3.807	0.441	Insig	940	337	1.082	1.056	1.051
USr 19	vs.	RSr 19	3.933	3.774	2.386	2%	940	337	1.042	1.059	1.034
USr 20	vs.	RSr 20	3.873	3.647	3.315	0%	940	337	1.082	1.059	1.044
USr 21	vs.	RSr 21	3.936	3.629	4.512	0%	940	337	1.070	1.078	1.016
USr 22	vs.	RSr 22	3.890	3.650	3.521	0%	940	337	1.087	1.045	1.083
USr 23	vs.	RSr 23	3.896	3.682	3.162	0%	940	337	1.077	1.019	1.117
USr 24	vs.	RSr 24	3.949	3.757	2.898	0%	940	337	1.064	0.988	1.160
USr 25	vs.	RSr 25	3.914	3.688	3.275	0%	940	337	1.099	1.041	1.114
USr 26	vs.	RSr 26	3.822	3.582	3.556	0%	940	337	1.051	1.107	1.110
USr 27	vs.	RSr 27	3.862	3.638	3.257	0%	940	337	1.055	1.152	1.191
USr 28	vs.	RSr 28	3.857	3.626	3.419	0%	940	337	1.043	1.127	1.169
USr 29	vs.	RSr 29	3.847	3.602	3.590	0%	940	337	1.066	1.089	1.043
USr 30	vs.	RSr 30	3.821	3.674	2.152	3%	940	337	1.077	1.091	1.026
USr 31	vs.	RSr 31	3.856	3.614	3.482	0%	940	337	1.053	1.205	1.309
USr 32	vs.	RSr 32	3.835	3.579	3.618	0%	940	337	1.086	1.198	1.217
USr 33	vs.	RSr 33	3.844	3.543	4.334	0%	940	337	1.057	1.185	1.255
USr 34	vs.	RSr 34	3.796	3.582	3.037	0%	940	337	1.068	1.222	1.310
USr 35	vs.	RSr 35	3.760	3.546	2.983	0%	940	337	1.090	1.227	1.266
USr 36	vs.	RSr 36	3.918	3.537	5.611	0%	940	337	1.025	1.185	1.336
USr 37	vs.	RSr 37	3.820	3.593	3.245	0%	940	337	1.066	1.192	1.251
USr 38	vs.	RSr 38	3.779	3.472	4.224	0%	940	337	1.119	1.213	1.174
USr 39	vs.	RSr 39	3.863	3.564	4.254	0%	940	337	1.066	1.214	1.296
USr 40	vs.	RSr 40	3.817	3.671	2.047	4%	940	337	1.074	1.261	1.380

(*Note* : "t"-test of significance with df 3611).

U Occ : Urban Occupational General view; R Occ : Rural Occupational General view; M1 and M2 : Means of Urban and Rural; 1% level of significance (2.58) and 5% level of significance (1.96); N1 and N2 : Sample Size of Rural and Urban; (SD 1 and SD2 : Standard Deviation of N1 and N2; F-test : Test of variability.

Annexure 4.5 : Rural vs. Urban Ocupational General View

Rural		*Urban*	*M1*	*M2*	*t-value*	*P*	*N1*	*N2*	*SD1*	*SD2*	*F-ratio*
ROccsp1	vs.	UOccsp1	3.243	3.586	-9.077	3611	1898	1715	1.206	1.050	1.319
ROccsp2	vs.	UOccsp2	3.159	3.586	-11.442	3611	1898	1715	1.182	1.050	1.266
ROccsp3	vs.	UOccsp3	3.156	3.586	-11.363	3611	1898	1715	1.208	1.050	1.324
ROccsp4	vs.	UOccsp4	3.144	3.586	-11.604	3611	1898	1715	1.222	1.050	1.355
ROccsp5	vs.	UOccsp5	3.136	3.586	-11.855	3611	1898	1715	1.212	1.050	1.333
ROccsp6	vs.	UOccsp6	3.138	3.586	-12.028	3611	1898	1715	1.178	1.050	1.259
ROccsp7	vs.	UOccsp7	3.222	3.586	-9.677	3611	1898	1715	1.197	1.050	1.299
ROccsp8	vs.	UOccsp8	3.151	3.586	-11.466	3611	1898	1715	1.212	1.050	1.333
ROccsp9	vs.	UOccsp9	3.202	3.586	-10.130	3611	1898	1715	1.213	1.050	1.334
ROccsp10	vs.	UOccsp10	3.186	3.586	-10.570	3611	1898	1715	1.208	1.050	1.324
ROccsp11	vs.	UOccsp11	3.165	3.586	-11.151	3611	1898	1715	1.201	1.050	1.309
ROccsp12	vs.	UOccsp12	3.180	3.586	-10.588	3611	1898	1715	1.237	1.050	1.387
ROccsp13	vs.	UOccsp13	3.117	3.586	-12.448	3611	1898	1715	1.197	1.050	1.300
ROccsp14	vs.	UOccsp14	3.170	3.586	-11.051	3611	1898	1715	1.197	1.050	1.298
ROccsp15	vs.	UOccsp15	3.226	3.586	-9.503	3611	1898	1715	1.213	1.050	1.334
ROccsp16	vs.	UOccsp16	3.129	3.586	-12.045	3611	1898	1715	1.213	1.050	1.334
ROccsp17	vs.	UOccsp17	3.150	3.586	--11.560	3611	1898	1715	1.203	1.050	1.312
ROccsp18	vs.	UOccsp18	3.132	3.586	-11.928	3611	1898	1715	1.221	1.050	1.352
ROccsp19	vs.	UOccsp19	3.151	3.586	-11.271	3611	1898	1715	1.247	1.050	1.411
ROccsp20	vs.	UOccsp20	3.116	3.586	-12.372	3611	1898	1715	1.216	1.050	1.342
ROccsp21	vs.	UOccsp21	3.055	3.586	-14.053	3611	1898	1715	1.204	1.050	1.314
ROccsp22	vs.	UOccsp22	2.963	3.586	-15.870	3611	1898	1715	1.285	1.050	1.496
ROccsp23	vs.	UOccsp23	2.995	3.586	-14.746	3611	1898	1715	1.325	1.050	1.592
ROccsp24	vs.	UOccsp24	2.989	3.586	-14.856	3611	1898	1715	1.332	1.050	1.609
ROccsp25	vs.	UOccsp25	2.988	3.586	-14.569	3611	1898	1715	1.374	1.050	1.713
ROccsp26	vs.	UOccsp26	2.934	3.571	-16.097	3611	1898	1715	1.300	1.053	1.525
ROccsp27	vs.	UOccsp27	2.960	3.586	-15.311	3611	1898	1715	1.368	1.050	1.697
ROccsp28	vs.	UOccsp28	2.977	3.586	-15.134	361	1898	1715	1.335	1.050	1.616
ROccsp29	vs.	UOccsp29	2.950	3.586	-15.812	3611	1898	1715	1.332	1.050	1.609
ROccsp30	vs.	UOccsp30	2.961	3.586	-15.459	3611	1898	1715	1.344	1.050	1.638
ROccsp31	vs.	UOccsp31	2.962	3.586	-15.791	3611	1898	1715	1.297	1.050	1.525
ROccsp32	vs.	UOccsp32	2.985	3.586	-15.001	3611	1898	1715	1.324	1.050	1.591
ROccsp33	vs.	UOccsp33	3.002	3.586	-14.353	3611	1898	1715	1.357	1.050	1.670
ROccsp34	vs.	UOccsp34	3.001	3.586	-14.713	3611	1898	1715	1.309	1.050	1.555
ROccsp35	vs.	UOccsp35	3.013	3.586	-14.570	3611	1898	1715	1.288	1.050	1.505
ROccsp36	vs.	UOccsp36	3.009	3.586	-14.601	3611	1898	1715	1.295	1.050	1.521
ROccsp37	vs.	UOccsp37	2.999	3.586	-14.664	3611	1898	1715	1.324	1.050	1.589
ROccsp38	vs.	UOccsp38	3.071	3.586	-13.017	3611	1898	1715	1.301	1.050	1.535
ROccsp39	vs.	UOccsp39	3.065	3.586	-13.337	3611	1898	1715	1.272	1.050	1.467
ROccsp40	vs.	UOccsp40	3.072	3.586	-13.353	3611	1898	1715	1.242	1.050	1.399

(*Note* : "t"-test of significance with df 3611).

U Occ : Urban Occupational General view; R Occ : Rural Occupational General view; M1 and M2 : Means of Urban and Rural; 1% level of significance (2.58) and 5% level of significance (1.96); N1 and N2 : Sample Size of Rural and Urban; (SD 1 and SD2 : Standard Deviation of N1 and N2; F-test : Test of variability.

Annexure 4.6 : Rural vs. Urban Occupational Specific View

Rural		*Urban*	*M1*	*M2*	*t-value*	*P*	*N1*	*N2*	*SD1*	*SD2*	*F-ratio*
ROccsp1	vs.	UOccsp1	3.243	3.504	-6.833	3611	1898	1715	1.206	1.081	1.244
ROccsp2	vs.	UOccsp2	3.159	3.504	-9.142	3611	1898	1715	1.182	1.081	1.194
ROccsp3	vs.	UOccsp3	3.156	3.504	-9.095	3611	1898	1715	1.208	1.081	1.248
ROccsp4	vs.	UOccsp4	3.144	3.504	-9.349	3611	1898	1715	1.222	1.081	1.277
ROccsp5	vs.	UOccsp5	3.136	3.504	-9.586	3611	1898	1715	1.212	1.081	1.256
ROccsp6	vs.	UOccsp6	3.138	3.504	-9.716	3611	1898	1715	1.178	1.081	1.187
ROccsp7	vs.	UOccsp7	3.222	3.504	-7.416	3611	1898	1715	1.197	1.081	1.225
ROccsp8	vs.	UOccsp8	3.151	3.504	-9.202	3611	1898	1715	1.212	1.081	1.256
ROccsp9	vs.	UOccsp9	3.202	3.504	-7.882	3611	1898	1715	1.213	1.081	1.257
ROccsp10	vs.	UOccsp10	3.186	3.504	-8.311	3611	1898	1715	1.208	1.081	1.248
ROccsp11	vs.	UOccsp11	3.165	3.504	-8.877	3611	1898	1715	1.201	1.081	1.234
ROccsp12	vs.	UOccsp12	3.180	3.504	-8.361	3611	1898	1715	1.237	1.081	1.308
ROccsp13	vs.	UOccsp13	3.117	3.504	-10.153	3611	1898	1715	1.197	1.081	1.225
ROccsp14	vs.	UOccsp14	3.170	3.504	-8.773	3611	1898	1715	1.197	1.081	1.224
ROccsp15	vs.	UOccsp15	3.226	3.504	-7.263	3611	1898	1715	1.213	1.081	1.258
ROccsp16	vs.	UOccsp16	3.129	3.504	-9.774	3611	1898	1715	1.213	1.081	1.258
ROccsp17	vs.	UOccsp17	3.150	3.504	-9.284	3611	1898	1715	1.203	1.081	1.237
ROccsp18	vs.	UOccsp18	3.132	3.504	-9.668	3611	1898	1715	1.221	1.081	1.275
ROccsp19	vs.	UOccsp19	3.151	3.504	-9.048	3611	1898	1715	1.247	1.081	1.330
ROccsp20	vs.	UOccsp20	3.116	3.504	-10.101	3611	1898	1715	1.216	1.081	1.265
ROccsp21	vs.	UOccsp21	3.055	3.504	-11.747	3611	1898	1715	1.204	1.081	1.239
ROccsp22	vs.	UOccsp22	2.963	3.504	-13.637	3611	1898	1715	1.285	1.081	1.411
ROccsp23	vs.	UOccsp23	2.995	3.504	-12.571	3611	1898	1715	1.325	1.081	1.501
ROccsp24	vs.	UOccsp24	2.989	3.504	-12.687	3611	1898	1715	1.332	1.081	1.517
ROccsp25	vs.	UOccsp25	2.988	3.504	-12.449	3611	1898	1715	1.374	1.081	1.615
ROccsp26	vs.	UOccsp26	2.934	3.504	-14.259	3611	1898	1715	1.300	1.081	1.446
ROccsp27	vs.	UOccsp27	2.960	3.504	-13.177	3611	1898	1715	1.368	1.081	1.600
ROccsp28	vs.	UOccsp28	2.977	3.504	-12.966	3611	1898	1715	1.335	1.081	1.524
ROccsp29	vs.	UOccsp29	2.950	3.504	-13.633	3611	1898	1715	1.332	1.081	1.517
ROccsp30	vs.	UOccsp30	2.961	3.504	-13.298	3611	1898	1715	1.344	1.081	1.545
ROccsp31	vs.	UOccsp31	2.962	3.504	-13.572	3611	1898	1715	1.297	1.081	1.437
ROccsp32	vs.	UOccsp32	2.985	3.504	-12.823	3611	1898	1715	1.324	1.081	1.500
ROccsp33	vs.	UOccsp33	3.002	3.504	-12.217	3611	1898	1715	1.357	1.081	1.575
ROccsp34	vs.	UOccsp34	3.001	3.504	-12.521	3611	1898	1715	1.309	1.081	1.466
ROccsp35	vs.	UOccsp35	3.013	3.504	-12.356	3611	1898	1715	1.288	1.081	1.419
ROccsp36	vs.	UOccsp36	3.009	3.504	-12.395	3611	1898	1715	1.295	1.081	1.434
ROccsp37	vs.	UOccsp37	2.999	3.504	-12.488	3611	1898	1715	1.324	1.081	1.498
ROccsp38	vs.	UOccsp38	3.071	3.504	-10.834	3611	1898	1715	1.301	1.081	1.447
ROccsp39	vs.	UOccsp39	3.065	3.504	-11.119	3611	1898	1715	1.272	1.081	1.383
ROccsp40	vs.	UOccsp40	3.072	3.504	-11.100	3611	1898	1715	1.242	1.081	1.319

(*Note* : "t"-test of significance with df 3611).

U Occ : Urban Occupational General view; R Occ : Rural Occupational General view; M1 and M2 : Means of Urban and Rural; 1% level of significance (2.58) and 5% level of significance (1.96); N1 and N2 : Sample Size of Rural and Urban; (SD 1 and SD2 : Standard Deviation of N1 and N2; F-test : Test of variability.

5

Unchartered Compositions and Reconciliations : Coping Social Decelerations
(A case of spinster segment of Meghalaya)

Introduction

The social transformations are a natural phenomenon to the extent of the change-impact seemed to stimulate social segments—it is equally important to understand its spread over the concerning dominant-level/s affected by the impending change. The social acceptability, willingness and social inclinations towards accepting the innovative situations help determining the change impact over given segments. However, the societal reactions represent direct or phased acceptances depending on which the change is promulgated on its resource competencies including human. The highly interactive societies react positively due to their adaptive and flexible provocations but the situations remain different in segments which need persuasion and insist on closed character. The extent of preparedness is dependent on societal decisional-rapport with externalities as to the situational-effects by means of reciprocal dependencies.

The social segments reasoning unique attributes and compositions opt for secluded approaches, views and acceptances due to the reasons of identity preservations, inhibitions and anticipated complicacies in adaptabilities both in prevailing and innovative situations. The ethnic structure present distinct patterns, socio-behavioural dynamics and ethnic reflexes pose an understanding enabling the people-resource to contribute under conditional environment. The ethnic rigidities imbibed as such by the society from intrinsic reason/s promote a limited outlook towards developmental issues as against the growth measures which cannot be made comparable to the extent of growth evidenced in these land-locked conditions.

Ethnicity : Issues, Associations and Appraisals

Effect of Matriliny and Matriarchal Systems

Viewing matriliny as ethno-cultural concept and as a prerogative the social angle question its status as developmental allocator. The concept with potential heredity-base attribute to the gender privilege in terms of shared responsibilities and involvements assigned to fair sex. Emphasizing gender divide, the masculine involvement at source for decision-making and allocation in least prominent and feminine's seek (Boeri and Pissarides., ed., 2005) towards more contributory issues such as resource-access, finances, cultural norms and traditions have been the prerogatives enabled advantage to women providing a natural power towards families and clan.

Decisions associated to identify masculine tasks hold men's responsibility but several are defined beyond gender *viz.*, resource usage, clan survival and protection, the external interactivities etc., value no gender discrimination including developmental issues (Crompton and Harris, 1998) and rest of the domains taken care by women irrespective of their vitality. The decision criteria over the challenging issues and matters associated to community, clan and their cultural component are the men's privilege. The societal description exhibit a wrap-up of ethno-cultural spirit which develops :

- Subjugated insights constantly influenced by perceptional discrimination,
- Overload of the regulatory means irrespective of the issue-concern, and

- Selective preferences which are aligned to the temperament and ethnicity.

Coping with Rigidities

Placidly expressive in continuum range the tribal rigidities can be perceived to be wrapped over their personality, familial and community/societal levels. Focusing over externalities characterized by uncontrollables *viz.,* the external participations, interactivities, market conditions, trade effects and syndicated domineering forces paved their way into the system are too quick to react for such "external change conditions". These interactivities have not been able to claim any specific structure but depict the changes by means of "self-understanding" inclusive of the hype or limitations associated.

Further it :

- exhibits community behaviour with underneath fear of loss of identity followed by external threats by unfortified reasons.
- perceives at convenience behaviour, cultural norms and superficial system progressions and insignificant ethnic loyalty and genuineness in preservative of in-depth values, efforts due to perceived individuality and understand culture in one's own terms.
- understands the stability of women in managing the concept of socio-cultural insecurities and at the same time creating more stability in the traditional norms having long-term repercussions *viz.,* playing dominant role by representing the supportive concept overcoming the insecurity of race promotion.

The current research case concentrate on "spinster", the tribal unmarried women representing sizable population created a trend by them and are significantly distinguishable as vital segment. Developing as a parallel but non-ignorable cluster they share similar ethnic characteristics of matriliny, inheritance of socio-cultural norms *viz.,* responsibility towards family and clan members, maintenance of tradition, customs and practices etc., creating a self-prominence due to their contributory and participatory means.

The well acceptable cultural purview offer decision autonomy to the women who by custom are honoured in their priestly position and placement. Theoretically, the women's image is signified by the feminine role-responsibilities, congruency in customs and commitment towards the well-being of the tribal-cum-clan cult and insists on the reinforcement and adaptive thought process. The system congruency highlight the (i) youngest daughter, (ii) daughters other than the youngest daughter and the oldest female member of the family who possesses unquestionable authority in promoting and maintaining clan-based orientations consistently or optionally supported by male participation in different positions.

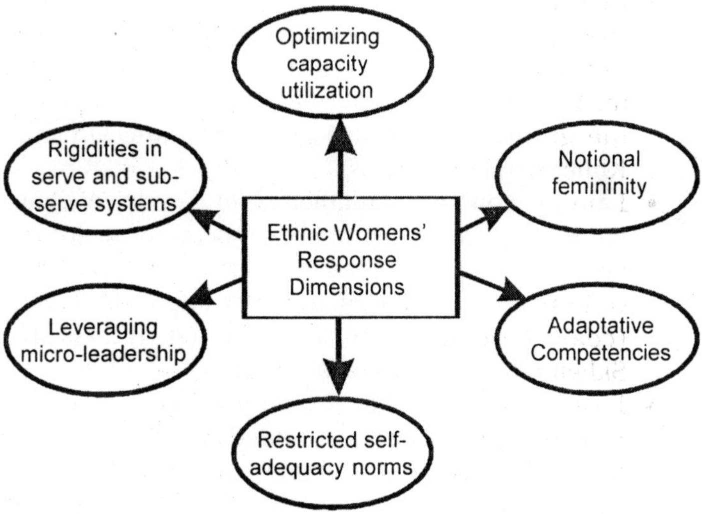

Model : Feminine Response Dimensions

The prominent reasons towards opting the spinstership by women are personal decisions arisen over the casualties in relationships of close/family members, over and under expectations from relationships, religious, health factors, non-availability of ideal suitors etc. Here are the few briefs over the familial and self-occupational decisions made by spinsters.

The respondents' self-descriptive reflections suggest the following :

- I am one of the twelve children to my mother. Her first four children are from my previous father. Even though we are borne from two different fathers, we all grew in the same environment. I took to service to cope up with the family expenditure. (A Khasi from Lapalang, Pynursla, E.K. Hills)
- I decided not to marry due to our family condition. Being a catholic I continued my studies taking help from Church. I took to an early job to support my family and now became a nun. (A Khasi from Nongdiat, Mawkyrwat, W.K. Hills)
- I could not simply think of my marriage as I had to look after my grandmother and aunts (maternal). I lost my mother at an early age and it is they who brought me up. I entered into business as it's my turn to repay the gratitude. (A Jaintia from Shiliang Umshong, Khliehriat, Jaintia Hills).
- I am the youngest daughter of my family. We have a large extended family of six aunts out of which three never married, one separated and one divorced. I share collective responsibility and look after both business (coal) and agricultural farm. (A Jaintia from Skhenpyrsit, Amlarem, Jaintia Hills)
- I am a school teacher. I have three sisters who got married to non-tribals and settled outside the state. We have house and land property which need to be taken care. I never thought of marriage as I consider that I am too much engaged in social and religious activities. (A Garo from Snal Dajreng, Songsak, E.G. Hills)
- I am engaged as a member in non-governmental organization. We are always on travel due to the nature of our work. My schedules are too busy and I am a rheumatic patient since childhood. My fragile health

does not permit me to think about marriage and I prefer to look after my nieces and nephews. (A Khasi from Siltham, Mawkynrew, East Khasi Hills)

- I was previously working in New Delhi. After my father expired, my mother wanted me to stay with her. I resigned my job as I feel comfortable being in home state. I will search for some job here itself. I won't mind drawing less salary than what I was drawing earlier. (A Garo from Silki Rongsibogre, Chokpot, South Garo Hills)
- My mother never minded for living together arrangement. We are three children born from three different fathers and none of them continued with us. I have no faith in the institution of marriage. I run a retail shop for my living and prefer to stay alone. (A Garo in Shillong from Shipragre, Betasingh, W.G. Hills)

The conjugal relations are outside the jurisdiction of clan or community authority and are privileged as purely personal. The result of such advancements waivering with complexities and uncertainties inclined to expand the range of expectations enabling to overload the relations. The factor of non-stability in marital character is most prominently evidenced in both Khasi and Jaintia tribes but less significant among Garo community. This is due to the Church's influence in personal life decisions.

The marriage literally offers no significant change in the current life of the women as a means of social or emotional security. Custom-wise the husband after marriage proceed to settle with wife in her house. On women the concept of marriage is added responsibility as after marriage the spouse leaves his parental house and shifts to wife's house.

The consequences are : Independent women find marriage a source for multi-expectation fulfiller barring the source significance as being a relation for clan-promotion. For majority of the women clan promotion is the vital criteria and in several contexts this fulfilment of the criteria need not necessarily be from husband. The resultant situations' being high flexibilities in the relationships beyond the parameters of marriage transforms into conjugal extremities enable them to be short-lived, followed by innumerable and at-convenience relationships attending to elementary needs has become the fact of the life of majority of the women. Lack of appropriate understanding and definiteness in relationships with due responsibilities made it a bizarre system disadvantageous both for women and men.

Inference of Women's Image

The ethno-cultural decision supportiveness enabled them to be independent since childhood, learn the basics of future responsibilities and made them very strong. The role significance and role responsibility is prominently vigilant even among young women who accept the facts of life and the living systems enable them to accept the trend without opposition. This situation led to the positivities ignoring the personal context depict alternative range of temperamental status highlight women as highly independent, growth-oriented, aggressive, ambitious, domineering, self-decision making and hard working and at the same time gullible, rigid, indecisive, group-conscious, and highly reactive etc.

The Socio-environmental Character

The characterization of women can be viewed to be much to their persona but the choice options towards skills, knowledge/ information, interactivities with external situations etc., are minimal forcing them towards resource-based dependencies for their survival. The tribal norms possess direct access of the precious natural resources which permit indiscriminate use of these to meet their survival needs. Of presence, the possession of these vast deposits of resources and lack of understanding towards the capital usage of these by the most enterprising women segment who are the micro entrepreneurs subserving the ethnic norms and leading a dualistic life of autonomy at the lower layers of society cannot raise beyond a limit due to the same reasons of ethnicity as it sealed their future growth and development. It is a passing situation of temporariness providing merely a solution of survival.

If the concept of tradition is referred differently by perceivable groups at individual levels its reference seemed to be distorted and is applicable to limited outlook. The casualisation, disproportionate interventions by influence groups, lack of supportive stimulants, special inapplicabilities etc., have been hovering the ethnic character into more compromising and adaptative forms.

Survival-based Informalities

The outlook of ethnic-fulfilment has been thoroughly misrepresented as the situation clashes occur in the context of survival. A negativism has been significantly been adopted as a system which is seen as a submerged family-character. The system bearing its dependent title on the specific characters of drawing the structural changes defining re-compositions of acculture, intensified vulnerabilities and replacements of individualism in place of community concept and a new social divide based on behaviouralism is more visibly expressed in terms of availability of opportunities.

The self-review questionnaires framed with 42 statements for general and 40 statements for specific perceptions towards the occupational understanding to be measured by using 5-point Likert's scaling. The respondent selection is restricted to spinsters, who are unmarried women is done using convenience sampling. The initial sample was however 350, the non-response and partial response reduced the sample size to 224. The sample takes into concern the rural and urban respondents from 7 districts of Meghalaya.

The highlights of overall respondent-detail of the chosen sample for the case are as follows :

- *Age-wise representations* : (i) 26-35 yrs—26.3 per cent, (ii) 36-45 yrs—22.8 per cent, and (iii) 46-60 yrs—21 per cent and 20.5 per cent are < 25 yrs.

- *Education-wise representations* : (i) 31.3 per cent are graduates; (ii) 27.7 per cent are > class 12th and < Degree; (iii) 12.1 per cent are >10th class and <12th class.
- *Self-occupation details* : 78.1 per cent have more than one occupation; 17.4 per cent are in Government service with asset backing, 26.1 per cent in farming out of which 19.3 per cent are also engaged in business, 13.8 per cent are in private service; and 10.3 per cent in multiple businesses.

The response from the respondent's spouse for general occupational perception reveals the district-wise response is given in Chart No. 5.1 for both rural and urban.

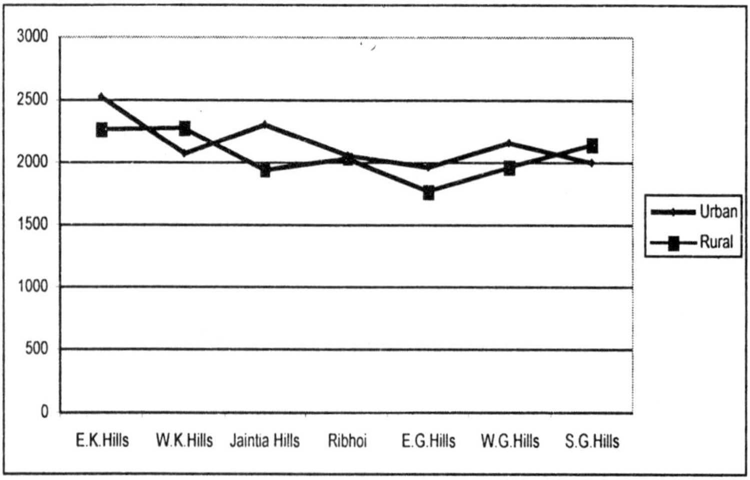

Chart 5.1 : Perceptions on Occupational trends : General (rural and urban)

The statistical techniques used for this purpose are regression analysis, analysis of variance, chi-square and t-tests of significance. Based on the criteria 18 statements are found most responsive. They are :

Table 5.1 : Perceptions on Occupational Trends : General

S. No.	*Statement (Perceptions on Occupational Trends : General)*	*"t"-Values*
1.	• No.3 : Option Variation based on gender and proximity to urban	-2.042
2.	• No.5 : Natural resources should support the state exchequer	1.884
3.	• No.7 : Modern youth need more skills for a gainful occupation	2.111
4.	• No.8 : Pace of coping ability of older generation with modern times is significantly less	1.944
5.	• No.9 : No gender-based discrimination in occupation; every job has its dignity	1.133
6.	• No.11 : Prestigious jobs can be arrived only by manipulation	2.337
7.	• No.12 : Life in modern times is full of uncertainties	1.164
8.	• No.14 : Good education is too expensive and it cannot assure a good job	3.028
9.	• No.15 : Distance should not be a determinant when good job is in offer	2.850
10.	• No.19 : Decision-preference towards settling in native place	1.959
11.	• No.24 : Self-declaration towards low self-esteem	1.273
12.	• No.25 : Past experiences providing the pathway for future	1.493
13.	• No.28 : Cost comparatives towards facility options	1.580
14.	• No.30 : Preference towards multiple occupational pre-occupation	1.074
15.	• No.33 : Non-resistance towards the change components	-1.015
16.	• No.35 : Modern occupational trends unfortunately progressing towards corruption and inefficiency	1.237
17.	• No.38 : Opportunities are marginalized but there is ample scope for improvement	1.620
18.	• No.40 : Dual career and multiple career overcome occupational compromise to a large extent	-1.076

The **Occupational General Perceptions** based on age criteria revealed high significant statements using Chi-square test revealed *viz.*, (a) that distance should not be the criteria when good job is in offer; (b) Modern occupational trends unfortunately progressing towards corruption and inefficiency; and (c) It is appropriate to change according to the times.

Using the specific perceptions Pearson Correlation's identified eight statements as most significant : An inter-statement preference variation dependent and independent status of the perceivables is also sought. The **dependent statement** is "Natural resources as the source of livelihood to micro participants".

Dependent Variable : Being micro participants natural resources are our source of livelihood.

Table 5.2 : Occupational Specific Perceptions : Independent Variables

S. No.	*Statement (Perceptions on Occupational Trends : Specific)*	*Significance*
1.	• No.06 : Responsibility of the Government to create employment to micro-participants	0.430
2.	• No.04 : Look down attitude of urbanites over ruralities	0.342
3.	• No.09 : Supremacy of occupational satisfaction as a determinant to occupational prestige	0.288
4.	• No.03 : Parity towards skill-diversities lead to occupational preference urban/rural areas	0.280
5.	• No.07 : Witnessing enhanced decision-competence of youth over their occupational priorities	0.263
6.	• No.02 : The level of Women's status and level of progressiveness of society are not mutually dependent	0.239
7.	• No.08 : Recent youth lifestyle adaptations remain as exclusive privilege and cannot be uniformly adaptable	0.237
8.	• No.26 : Career guidance programme enabled ease in occupational decision approach	0.154

Table 5.3 : Model Summary

Model	*R*	*R Square*	*Adjusted R Square*	*Std. Error of the Estimate*
1	.549(a)	.301	.282	.93699

a Predictors : (Constant), SPE08, SPE03, SPE09, SPE02, SPE04, SPE06

The Analysis of Variance (ANOVA) is

Model		*Sum of Squares*	*Df*	*Mean Square*	*F*	*Sig.*
1	Regression	82.040	6	13.673	15.574	.000(a)
	Residual	190.514	217	.878		
	Total	272.554	223			

a Predictors : (Constant), SPE08, SPE03, SPE09, SPE02, SPE04, SPE06

The regression coefficients reveal of the total sample of respondents suggest

$$Y = .210 + .276X_1 + .177X_2 + .114X_3 + .095X_4 + .139X_5 + .141X_6$$

Using the same dependent variables the tests of significance (t-test) reveal :

- Responsibility of the Government to encourage micro-participation : (4.034)
- Rural environment is looked down by urbanites : (2.834)
- The level of women's status cannot be described by the level of progressiveness of society : (2.440)
- Recently the youth adopting lifestyles which are not suitable to adopt : (2.288)
- Occupational satisfaction is more important to determine the occupational prestige : (1.867)
- Variations in skills lead to varying occupations preferences in rural and urban areas : (1.504)

* Figures in the parenthesis ( ) are the "t" values

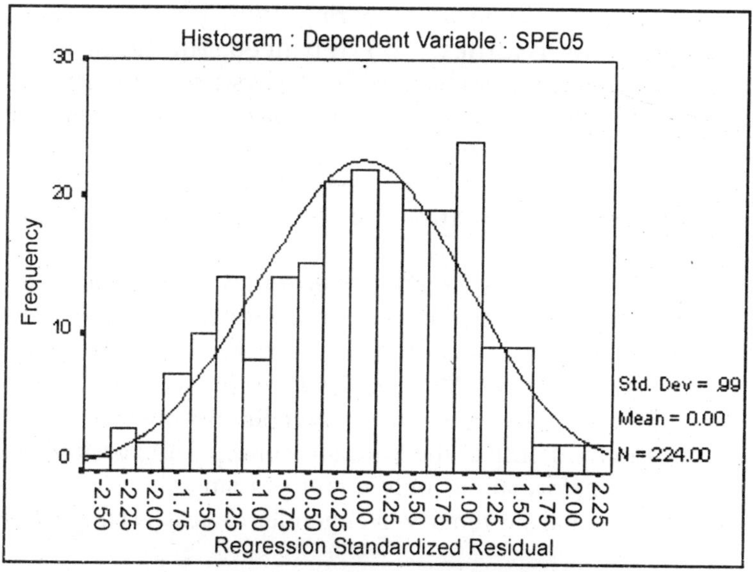

Chart 5.2 : Spinsters' Occupational Response

These statements' representations are shown by means of histogram depicting nearly significant and reasonably significant variables.

Analysis

The domain of influence perceived in the questionnaire attend to the respondent's self and self-appraisal over the involvement and influence status under different occupational situations as layer-I. The issues of immediate influence and impact conditions are responsible to the current status held by the respondents form as layer-II. A larger perception about the macro-effect of the issues relevant to women, trends and factors of uncontrollable influence are taken care as layer-III.

The respondents feedback depicted continuum range of significance skewed to high significance (*) to significant domain representations are : (i) occupational options, (ii) resource utilities and exploitation, (iii) need of basic tools for acquiring good occupation, (iv) mobility*, (v) macro derivatives over micro issues, (vi) community concept, (vii) preferences in decision-sharing, (viii) rational attitude proximate to realities, (ix) felt-need for adaptative transformations as per change*, (x) the system loopholes and their predominance in a system progressions*, (xi) undeterred balanced behaviour under crises, (xii) opportunities get marginalized in wider growth environment, and (xiii) low profile lifestyle adaptations can reduce the occupational anxiety.

The specific view attend to selectivities of the issue based high significance over the issues relevant to the dependent factor of resource-based dependencies and its inter-connectivities (Bevan, M. *et al.* 2001) with the independent variable *viz.*, (i) preference towards the current need gratification rather than the futuristic concept, (ii) possibilities of status transformations only under pressing circumstances, (iii) occupational supremacy over gender issues, (iv) impact of

(*) are considered highly significant and rest are nearly significant.

urbanization and self-status on occupational decisions, (v) the women's insignificant role-contribution towards occupational advancedness, and (vi) inter-generational gaps and coping efforts with occupational change.

The consequences stand to female prerogatives (as to the firm beliefs and understanding developed by women which eventually was adopted as their lifestyle) enabling them to prefer :

- Participating in major issues under micro approaches :

  Implication : The women's status as unmarried is not very different to married women who remain single, separated and divorced and maintain temporary living in relations. The personal, ethnical and socio-cultural ideologies to a large extent had their impact on the preference or priority rating of occupational decisions as each occupational decision is merely a part of their life decision.

- Adaptation of new casualisation in family concepts nurtured as future norms in children :

  Implication : Adoptation of spinsterhood does not really make the women live in total man-free domain as the masculine involvement in the form of maternal uncle, brothers, headman, religious leaders etc., have their impact on the decision-roles.

- The docile development and dominance of feminine cult is being syndicated with new role specifications forming current generic-culture.

  Implication : It is, therefore, evidenced that the persistent socio-cultural and ethnic norms tormented the male image to insignificance that seemed to be more tamed than what they ought to be. The performance based role-dominance seemed to be simplistic but is influenced by :

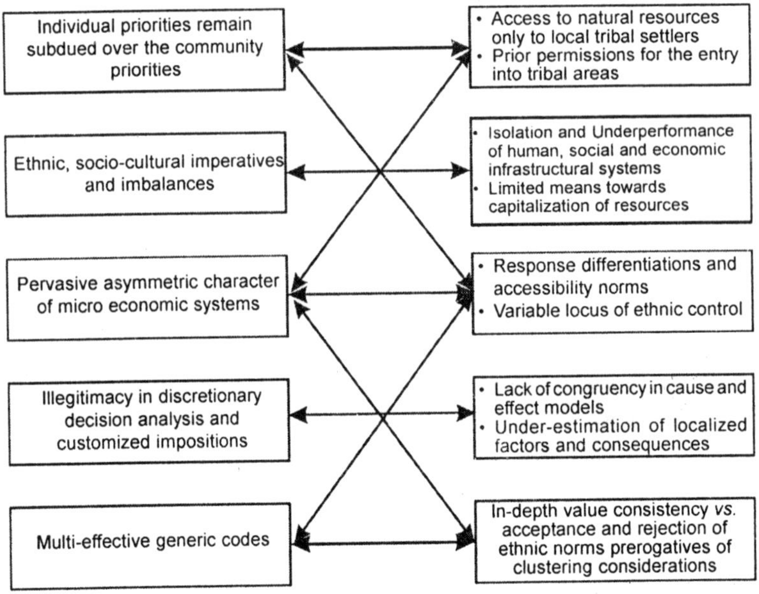

Figure 5.1 : Model of Ethnic—Imperatives

Occupational Repercussions

(a) Personal level : The spinster propagated in a closed economy and resource-based dependencies enable to reflect diversified behaviour. At personal level the traditional values did not hold well as to their age, education and income preference due to the alternative situational adaptations. The major demarcations in the service spectrum at individual level is observant at urban level is extremely limited and vast avenues are apparent in rural economies. The resource-based attractions are prominent which allure not only the rural but also the urban and several women find it easy to own the land from community, hire or lease the resource or even work on daily wage enable to earn to her content. There is no poverty felt as the women by culture or situation are robust enough to face the life realities from the training given by family environment and accept the positive and negative characters of the cult in equitable form.

(b) Family level : The extended matrilineal family is prominently a tradition still surviving in its minimal or macro forms enabling the old and young members share the single roof. The environment promotes a division of labour especially in farming and retail business where the entire family shares various responsibilities. Family planning is no concept to be admitted here as the tribals prefer in the philosophy of having as many children to support the familial needs at various levels. These extended complex structures in return have very humble living styles (e.g., of having just white rice with red tea as breakfast) have minimum aspirations towards life and are not aggressively ambitious towards enhancing the lifestyles. The leisure time is most preferred which is spent on music, fishing and community or religious activities. Absence of external communication simply creates an isolated environment and the tribal groups are literally not aware of the facts of happening world. In rural areas the families prefer to be engaged in occupation limited to meet the elementary needs and prefer to have some money to buy the essential items like oil, salt, tobacco, clothes etc. The role of spinster is not much distinctive from the rest of the members of the family.

(c) Clan/community level : Each tribe takes the pride of their identity by self-character on the dress code, language spoken and localized living patterns. The clan-based prerogatives of asset disbursement enable the community members to be provided with elementary (nominal) necessities. Barring few norms as to the utilization of these community assets the clan leadership is not felt keen in providing any fundamental facilities needed for living. The spinsters who are part of the system depending on their age who gain qualifications of education and are competent to move to urban areas or initiate business etc., remain a purely self-decision. The clan enable to promote activities associated to religion, clan promotion and cultural retention etc., are some which imbibe the women to view the clan as a whole and to be responsive towards the clan promotion. The concept is quite pre-dominant irrespective of the urban or rural condition. If family welfare is solely the responsibility of women the tribal women at large in all sections of the state firmly believe in extended family promotion (for the growth and survival of clan) and the spinster community uses their self-skills in supplementing the family requirements in this "angle of priority".

Occupational determinants : The Spinsters' Orientation

Their outlook definitely offer a contributory trend towards the familial and ethnic perceptions where the self-capacities to partial extent have been glorified and result mostly in government and quasi-government service/s, professional occupations, occupations in private sector and vast majority in micro retailing seemed to be of utmost supportive. The layering is multiple and involvement range create "leverage continuum" as per one's own means.

The decision-preference towards the micro participation is based on the historical, familial, and behavioural means and congruent approach forming the norm. The positioning of spinster in the occupational spectrum as such satisfied minimal norms as the role-character has literally not added to the occupational segment. The spinsters didn't seem to be aggressively inclined towards occupations. The status and prestige measures too have no direct relation with their women-hood status and in most of the cases the decision of being a spinster remained as independent character ignoring the occupational-accommodations.

In this reference the **positivities** represent promoting independent outlook, silent contributors towards the cultural enforcements and micro participants as social and human capital in a closed system. The concept of micro-entrepreneurship is an imbibed quality naturally acquired by spinsters can be regarded as surrogate promoters and loyalists of the system. They add to the advantage of ethnic promotion and the entire force can be channelled towards multiple dimensions for the growth and development of tribal segments.

Whereas the **negativities** are subconscious acceptances of ethnic norms, unilateral decisions based on culture-imposed natural responsibilities, inseparable and rigid mindset towards reciprocal contributions to the society. It created a system of informality and self-imposition which in majority of cases a sacrifice towards uplifting the family's financial condition and to procure supportives for nurturing the descendents.

The trend seemed to be equally prominent in new generation as to this micro segment indicate clan-based characters and compositions opt to remain secluded for different reasons. It is quite natural that a micro component of the society still accept and each of these indicate unique character and compositions opt to remain in secluded environments for different reasons. It is the people-segments and their approach, views and acceptances result in cultural preservations, loss of identity and inhibitions associated towards adaptabilities and fear for newness etc.

The socio-behavioural dynamics of spinster segment represent the crux of its response-character of change especially in reflective situations manoeuvring the already prevailing subdued competencies and subjugated insights towards developmental issues. The ethnic segmental effects at large depict behavioural representations based on their validity, judgment and acceptances which prove aligned to the conditions of homogeneity in attitudinal and response situations. However, the element of unpredictability persists with reference to the transformations at large exhibit the consequences on the criteria to the extent to which the situations accommodate to be receptive. Can it be accepted that such resistance be associated with societies' own intrinsic reasons compromise over a total non-rejection create unique and distinct prototypical specifications?

Meghalaya, symbolized by matrilineal social segment—evidence the symptoms of a closed economy with strong ethical and cultural wrap-up implies discrimination as to its value systems and living-styles. The component of meagreness is evidenced in every sphere as the top-layers of its socio-cultural hierarchy are overloaded with the so-called saviours of the ethnic component and preservation of tradition. The cultural-prerogatives posit each female as valuable contributor *viz.*, as clan and community promoter unilaterally in feminine dimension including the spinster segment and more importantly to nurture and support the vast family liabilities. The socio-feminine vulnerabilities remain as a felt-need insist on enforced preservation of ethnicity providing an option of willingness to the extent it is at-convenient ethno-cultural adaptations for "selectively privileged" segments. Presenting a decelerating environment in multiple spheres its unconditional but volatile survival strategies adopt non-formal survival outlook and approaches cannot remain exception as to their contribution/s. It is observed that the individual priorities remain subordinated to the societal in the case of underprivileged and at grassroots level/s. An overall deficit condition posing a threat to the very survival as the teeming masses which fail to understand the concept of socio-human capitalization and resultant utilities with a purpose of value creativity and coping survival strategies. The ethnic understanding towards developmental equilibrium question the extent of sacrifice/compromise of distinct character as compared to those developmental definitions recommended by externalities creating a wide perceptional gap. The general development cannot be turned to be a reality especially when their current dependencies are the external supportive measures rather than building internal competencies. The investigation observes the mounting pressure on unplanned consumption of available capital resources leading to non-functional, non-performing and non-contributory behaviour. Absence of value-added component at any given level which has not been able to do justice about the developmental capabilities are the very sources to underwrite the transformation of the society.

Sum Up

The research case made a modest attempt to understand the spinster stances in the tribal segment in its occupational preference context identified the dire need of strategic approaches marking the decelerating status of these remote ethnic groups due to their self-imposed living style policy framework believes development as an assignable external condition rather than an internal aspiration. The ethno-social typicalities present a character of "expectedness" which are being built over "survival-based compromises" viz., cultural sacrifices, accepting cross cultural relationships, living together family patterns, religious conversions, external over dependencies etc. The external supportives perceive the developmental status in self-defined and prescriptive forms rather than the making a more adaptative styles of prototypical forms. Absence of minimal living conditions present a living rigidity associated with deprivedness enabled static mindset far to neither perceive proper self-direction nor even accept the developmental design aimed by donor institutions which effort to bring the ethnic groups at par with other developed segments. The societal vitalities totally stand on trivial platforms and burden of growth is being perceived with conditioned frameworks lack appropriate priority and understanding. The entire system await for a proper direction which is mutually acceptable aiming towards paradigm shift enabling them to understand the path of growth the entire community inclusive of spinster segment have to opt for.

Picture 1 : Production for Self-Consumption: Primary Concern

Picture 2 : Struggle for Existence: A Jaintia from Nartiang

Picture 3 : Smoked Spices in Garo Household: Secured for Furture Sale

Picture 4 : Quest for Information: Khasi Women reading Newspaper

Picture 5 : A Typical Pigmy Market Cluster

Picture 6 : Concentric Market Systems: Limited Radius

Picture 7 : Ethnic Trends in Petty Marketing

Picture 8 : Jaintia Woman selling Dhoop Lakd

Picture 9 : Khasi Women selling Coal, Fruits and Betel Nut

Picture 10 : Age no bar: Work Preferences by Khasi Women

Picture 11 : Itinerary on Sale in Tura: Hardships and Livelihood Decisions

Picture 12 : Woman selling Second-hand Cloths: Roaring Business

Picture 13 : Mega Market with Micro-trends: Domestic Women's Market

Picture 14 : Family Business: Third Generation Continuity

Picture 15 : Tobacco on Sale: Jaintia Entrepreneur

Picture 16 : Retail Shop with Ethnic Mark: Neighbourhood Facility

6

Aspirants' Occupational Perceptions : An Appraisal

The Xers viz., Gen X, the seamless teen community—the future brand ambassadors and representatives who are today's splurgingly youthful and sparkling aspirants of social constructs deemed to be positioned in multiple roles when it comes to their own individual selves, families and at large to be components of radiant society. The teen-segment of current day unlike the previous generation have resource and information access, open to the advanced technologies and being the prime target of aspiring mass of individuals of modern commercial hub and business focus. A large majority of them imbibe the generic living style/standards from their parents and rest depends on the apparent exposure towards adopted blend of unabashed hype and emerging redispositions of connectivities and increased burgeoning of independent thinking and in-turn nurturing singular values. The convergent effect is equally felt in ado-context in its pursuit towards communication, technology and application having a direct or surrogate impact over the quantum of preparedness exhibited by youth formula prospectives.

Majority of them naturally import the typicalities of the ado-nature and character forming a vital fill-up group even in the subdued economies. The current transformational needs supposedly catering them with all-delightful environment where a natural phenomena develops and remain at par with ado appeal demonstrated elsewhere in the other parts of the country. A self-confessed, price-insensitive, frenzied lot and lucre too have been put for assessment over their developmental issues and their association with the occupational preparedness. A coping up situation which enable them to be identified as significant decision-makers within applicable context having the same influencing factors reflecting over their persona and are typical *viz.*, familial, social, cultural and the most non-ignorable and apparent global trends, rapidity in gratification and added value-consciousness enable to create a need towards the gamut of re-defining multi-system options sought by them also include occupational dimension.

The Meghalayan youth too present an outstretched behaviour which is hierarchical of the tribal effect and perceive their general preferences, stimulations, decision accuracies, risk-orientations, capacities etc., which have a bearing on their overall personality factors. The study enables to understand the ado-group with their temperamental effect, their adaptation models in a more complex and multilateral effects, synchronizations of tradition and modern versions currently creating high-sensitive external and internal behavioural change patterns. The effect of transformations can be felt from micro to macro effects with appropriate understanding gained by the youth within their parameters that need to be understood as to their views and value determinants addressing the modern trend/s.

Several research studies have been undertaken over the adolescent (ado)-segment/s in their individual and integrated approach, situational image reception and discrimination, the altering nodes of ado-perspectives, structural impediments, barriers and challenges etc., depict the impact on the value concepts, decision-making, level of influence and involvement etc., associated to given situations. Several studies are also done on their temperamental status such as self-personification, workholism, authoritarian, introversion, adaptability etc.

Considering the household arena as a complex structure and every member of the family exert some influence, which may go in degrees the persona-in-approach is the imbibed quality arrived from this source. Each family member may strongly believe that he/she exert a great deal of influence in some decision and a little in others independent of their influence of other family members (Bernard). The current case draws the parameters of its study to the adolescent segment to all seven districts of Meghalaya. Referred as Khasi Iing the Khasi Uxorilocal Family (Grudon) is a Khasi residential composition, which is a matrilineal extended family, comprises wife, husband, their children, wife's unmarried sisters and brothers including widowed, separated or divorced and other members belonging to the clan. The tribe presents both an outstanding and remarkable cultural practices which can be highlighted are :

- Adoption of matriliny or matriarchate cultural form, create the prominence of being identified by mother's title.
- Inheritance of family property to the youngest daughter i.e., ka kadduh make her to hold highest priestly office in economic, cultural and social aspects.
- Females other than ka kadduh, are treated as "non-heiress" and move out of their "natal Iing" i.e., the parental house, after their marriages to initiate the establishment of "new Iing" or neo-local family.
- Inheritance of ancestral property by the youngest daughter or ka kadduh with synchronized responsibility along with her maternal uncle(s) exercise the financial management within the household.

The uxorilocal family i.e., extended family can be considered as a household unit comprises any combination of members within itself and provide a scope for conceptual and methodological problems varying from the individual decisions to the group decisions or *vice versa.* As its customary tendency to adopt a mechanism of matrilineal inheritance which periodically define the parameters of "vertical expansion patterns" of tribal families, a substantial number of occupational decisions made by families deemed to reflex an asymmetrical distribution of influence over its family members.

The focus of current research is on the respondents who are young adolescent (Beckert, Troy E., 2008) women, assumed to present themselves as an appropriate unit of analysis in the occupational decision. The teenagers make their individual decisions independent of the influence of others and at the same time reflect their perceptions over preferences of family members and their relative importance on their own (adolescent's) decisions. As the behaviour of individuals is independent of the influence of others the current research observes :

- To understand the general background this has been making a ground to influence the thought process in association with its internal and external conditions.
- The impact of environmental conditions which enable the ado-segment to draw their future occupational framework and preferences.
- To estimate the extent to which the decision freedom is felt and the influencing factors decide over the priorities of ado-groups.

Review of the Literature

The earlier works over the influence of adolescents were on inter-relationships of family members, role of adolescents, teen's perceptions, measurement patterns and variations in behaviour. Research on single mothers of early adolescents (Beckert Troy E., 2008), socialization on leisure-time activities examined the importance and impact of peer groups, family and community (Arnon, Sara, 2008), effects of service participation, friendship networks, family support on developmental outcomes (Ngai, Steven Sek-yum, 2008) and influence of family communication structure (Chang, Wei-Lung, 2008; Satya Y., 2002) researched on the role patterns and degree of influence presented by an ado in uxorilocal family is different from a nuclear family due to the existence and involvement of several family members in decision-making. The earlier efforts were made by Foxman over adolescent's influence in decision-making. Her research attempted that ado tend to overrate their own influence relative to parent's ratings etc.

Objectives of the Study

Flexibility in the family role structure introduces an extensive participation among all family members. It results in growing involvement towards household responsibility and several major or minor decision-making. The central research objective is to characterize the perceived influence relationships of ado's in the family role structure :

- To understand the role significance of the ado group in the given environment.
- To identify their relative involvement with regard to occupational decision by the families.
- To find out the impact of their education, financial independence and knowledge preferences which tend to reflect the occupational priorities.

Hypotheses of the Study

The adolescent behaviour is assumed of having substantial influence in family decision-making. Their role both as being influenced and influencers has considerable bearing over their opinion-formulations towards occupational views. The following hypotheses were set in this reference :

H_1 the adolescents possessing good educational background may relatively have inclined decisions with minimal conditions viz., mobility etc.

H_2 Considering economic independence as a vital contributor the ado-segment prefers it as a means of independent status rather than presuming it as supportive to the family.

H_3 the ado-segment's occupational preference is much dependent on the decisions imposed by the parents and peer groups.

H_4 irrespective of the competency, the ado-group succumb to parental occupational preference by giving due weightage to parental opinion rather than self-decision.

Research Design

The current study is an effort to understand the outline of the conceptual framework of ado-segmental occupational preference in the context of supportives and challenging situations. It also analyzes the general background, parental influence, self-perception and decision influence and effectives aiming towards building the occupational capacities and preference criteria.

Methodology

The study is a descriptive piece of research which has two phases. First phase involved with the development of suitable tools, namely the attitude scale to measure the attitude of ados towards role participation and second phase involved with the collection of data in order to test the hypotheses of the study.

Sample Size and Instruments used

The sample size is restricted to 210 respondents comprising both rural (116) and urban (94) respondents from all seven districts of Meghalaya. Self-assessment is made by means of questionnaires comprising 30 multi-option statements covering issues associated to the needs and requirements of the case chosen for the study.

Parameter of Sample

As the case study is based on the interpretation and analysis of the ado-group, the oral information and description of the factual data, the method being followed in preparing this case is empirical in its study, analytical and descriptive in its treatment.

Research Analysis

The most proximately influencing factors which enable to present their reflexes over the subserve system are :

- Familial environment in common context holds a supreme and predominant position as a most basic and fundamental need provider. Its supremacy can be claimed as being an non-competitive platform contributing in building proactive emotional stability, persistent dependency, social security etc., help developing the core personal traits of Xers (aspirants).
- Value dimensions are the instrumental opinion formulators define specific conduct of existence which is personally or socially preferred by ado-groups help determining ought and ought-not-to-be done in variant contexts.
- Developing generic code associated towards the societal, cultural and environmental factors etc. create a provision to define the relative assignment of cognitive and behavioural forms.
- Alignment in materialism is a complex phenomena associated to multitude of influences at individual or collective attributes based on priorities, decision effects and openness to experience etc. Issues related to the ado-opinion trends, positional stance, ado-role significance and status of mind and decision-capacities etc., under different situations.
- The respondents are teenage young women out of which (37.6%) are > 18 yrs, (31.9%) >17 - <18 yrs and (20 %) >16 and <17 yrs. (47.6%) have >3 and <6 brothers and sisters followed by (41.0%) having > 6 and < 9 brothers and sisters. 83.3 per cent of the respondents continue in the same place they hail from and the rest are migrated from other places. Educationally (34.8%)

are pursuing graduation and (27.6%) are < graduation. (61.9%) have not been engaged in any formally occupationally prone activity but (22.9%) are engaged in business which is family business in all cases. Similarly 8.1% of the teens are also engaged in farming activities in rural areas.

- An overall parental educational trend represented that the 28.1 per cent fathers and 41 per cent of mothers are < 10 class and fathers with 21.5 per cent and mothers with 18.1 per cent are graduates. Occupationally the 21.9 per cent of fathers are in government service, 31.4 per cent are in business and 27.6 per cent in private service. For mothers the characterization represent 27.6 per cent as housewives, 37.1 per cent engaged in business and 16.2 per cent are in government service. About being busy, 39 per cent of respondents stated that fathers are busy, 32.9 per cent said that both parents are busy and 28 per cent affirmed that mothers are busy.
- In urban more than 51 per cent of the respondents have no asset and 40 per cent have more than one asset at their possession and 8.6 per cent have only house property in urban area. The rural detail suggested that 39.5 per cent have no assets except house, 23.8 per cent have more than one asset and 16.2 per cent have assets both in urban and rural areas.

The categorical information which enabled to highlight the respondents' feedback over.

Fig. 6.1 : Ado-Segment's Self-reporting of Preferences

• Respondents' leisure time activities	28.6 per cent are engaged in more than one activity 27.6 per cent with friends 17.6 per cent watching TV 17.1 per cent engaged in nothing
• Declaring the self-role	31.8 per cent admitted being dependent; 31.9 per cent perform supportive services 31.9 per cent conveyed that they are responsible

(contd.)

• After their current studies they anticipate to anticipate	48.6 per cent search for job 15.2 per cent study further 15.2 per cent look after family business 13.8 per cent initiate own business
• Availability of good opportunities	30 per cent prefer to be in Shillong 26.7 per cent prefer any urban area 24.8 per cent prefer to go outside the state 18 per cent prefer to be engaged in rural areas
• Respondents describe themselves as	38.6 per cent as social; 36.7 per cent as hard working 24.8 per cent as volunteering
• Command in speaking different languages	76.2 per cent speak < 2 languages 21 per cent speak >2 and <3 languages
• Future plans after study	45.2 per cent ask parents 25.7 per cent said too early to think 17.1 per cent said that they do not know
• Prefer to earn	34.8 per cent due to insufficient family support 31.4 per cent admitted that their expenditure is too much 11.4 per cent said that they prefer to be independent
• Prefer not to earn	36.2 per cent says that their family do not allow it 29.0 per cent said they did not feel the necessity to earn 18.6 per cent said that they never thought of it 16.2 per cent said that they are still very young
• Self-skills	76.2 per cent admitted of not having any skills 23.8 per cent admitted of having communication skills
• Parental preference towards respondents	33.8 per cent prefer to go as per the prevailing trend 27.6 per cent prefer to be innovative 24.8 per cent to decide on their own 13.8 per cent insist on adopting the same profession as that of parents
• Good job refers to	37.1 per cent says the job available locally 33.3 per cent said good pay 23.8 per cent says job which offer prestige
• Consider parents as	30 per cent said their parents are most expecting 30 per cent said that the parents are liberal 21.9 per cent said that the parents are modern 17.6 per cent said that their parents are strict

(*contd.*)

• What they consider important	31 per cent said family is important 27.1 per cent said money is important 18.6 per cent said job is important 14.8 per cent said power is important
• Feeling towards requesting pocket money	37.1 per cent said guilt 29.5 per cent said of being embarrassed 18.6 per cent said that they feel shy 14.8 per cent said that they don't ask
• Spending the extra money earned	36.2 per cent said they give it in family 30 per cent said that they spend it on self 22.4 per cent revealed that they save it
• Interaction with parents	35.7 per cent meet parents everyday 34.3 per cent meet often 15.2 per cent said once in a while
• Respondents sharing emotions with	62.9 per cent with friends 20.0 per cent with brothers and sisters 12.4 per cent with parents
• Nature of respondent	36.7 per cent said they are reserved 30.5 per cent said they are isolated 26.7 per cent said that they are social in nature
• Concern towards tribal cult	32.4 per cent has much concern in their lives 29.0 per cent revealed tribal cult as more than their life 20.0 per cent consider it as part of their life 18.6 per cent says that all cultures are same
• Opinion of women over matrilineal cult	42.4 per cent says men and women are equals 28.6 per cent says that it need to be highly honoured 21.9 per cent says it is the supreme condition
• Opinion of women's role contribution	51.9 per cent says that there is no gender difference 25.7 per cent says women can perform better than man 21.9 per cent reveals that women's contribution is less
• Matriarchy enhance respondents' spirit towards	67.6 per cent says that family is vital 17.6 per cent says society is vital 14.3 per cent says clan is vital
• Traditional values over gender issues still hold importance	44.8 per cent says no value prominence 39.0 per cent says that women's contribution cannot be ignored 10.0 per cent says that the traditions need to be rewritten

Initiating with the parental general and specific background which forms the basis of living style patterns the ado-behaviour reflected a definite positiveness as to their innovation, being independent, self-thinking and expression irrespective of the location. The preferences towards earning/ non-earning too were explicit and confident. Majority of the parents have ideal relations with their offspring's and this is revealed in their interrelations which are more encouraging and supportive. But the parametric views developed as to their own self-capacities and coping up in different situations, reflexes expressed over the socio-cultural and ethnical barriers which have been still holding good on the decision criteria made by ado-groups.

Preferences towards local settlement, language deficiency, lack of developmental skills and limited outlook due to the non-exposure is vigilant. However, the positiveness as to the improvement in skills, eagerness to acquire more analytical tools of self-built is preferred. The anticipations reflect as to the progression of dependent and independent styles such as imitating friends adopting parents' decisions. Postponing (its too early to think) the current responsibilities and planning to do something innovative which later I can think as my profession is the maturity shown as to the appropriateness, creativity and innovation.

Financial Autonomy and Status

(a) **Earning Capacities** : The financial preference is the foremost has been revealed in repetitive form as to meeting their self-expenditure, the association of earning requirement due to the insufficient financial support from family, the good pay packet is the criteria of good job and the extra money earned is used for spending on self etc., insist that the teens have been facing insufficiency and aspire on owning funds even at the means of having additional effort. But they were not sure whether their parents permit such decision or not. Aspirations towards enhancing occupation-based competencies are vigilant but witnessed lack of direction.

(b) **The Family Orientation** : Family played a predominant role in the lives of teens. Associating themselves as the formal members of the family, they reveal their expression of being dependents, which show their dependent attitude by adopting the parental decision as theirs, but they are not able to decide as to the location which need to be preferred and the children of strict parents revealed that their extra money being given for family use than those of children of modern parents.

(c) **Orientation of Self** : Prominently reveal their natural immaturities still lurk around (my family does not allow me to earn), status of dependency and lack of self-standing (earning need never felt) and decision influence (prefer to do what my friends does) etc. The non-earning preference also prove (there is no necessity felt as to the earning) reveal decision influence by family situations followed by self-criticism and partial family fulfilment. Urban and rural perceptions depicted some variation yet the trend seems to be progressing towards similar direction viz., participation in family business and participation in farming activities.

In this context the situations pose :

- the interrelational and motivational insights are influencing the relational means maintained by ado-segment, and
- the preferable approaches seemed to be more pragmatic to be acceptable in both conventional and innovative ado-situations.

An understanding towards the ado-environmental description represented by situational positivities and negativities define the implied condition of the immediate surrounding interactive effect with which the teens share the most innate feelings. **(a)** The high vs. low performance effect, **(b)** the high *vs.* low predicted behaviour, and **(c)** the resulting in the most opted vs. least opted spaces which bring in the shape of ado-segment.

Fig. 6.2: Ado-segment Behavioural Compositions

High Performance Effect	*Vs.*	*Low Performance Effect*
• Construction Values • Optimistic attitudes • Self-assured likes • Confirmatory feelings • Goals and buoyant orientations		• High expectation with minimal resource contribution • Contingent and likelihood dependencies • Over-estimation and high-doses of aggressiveness • Flexibility in leveraged approaches
High Predicted Behaviour	*Vs.*	*Low Predicted Behaviour*
• High drive/s • Competencies • Positive motivation • Career planning • Self-monitoring		• Contradictions • Troubled environment • Low self-esteem • Refrain/restrain • Minimal radius of influence
Most Opted Spaces	*Vs.*	*Least Opted Spaces*
• Community tasks • Money as prime indicator • Preference for leisure time • Innovation and creativity		• Indefinite orientations • Assessment gaps • Lack of compatibility • Preference towards informality

An intrigue into the overall perspective of ado view point focuses on adolescents' general self-understanding, self-position in relation to the family and familial values, environment and competency, influences and interrelationships within and with community at large. The impositions which have been duly honoured or accepted (at times even rejected in creating a suitable ado-preferred environment) by the imbibed thought process. Nurturing style-adaptations, provisioning growth and development (by creating an individual and composite environment), promoting relational (adaptive and longstanding situations) are creating opportunities at individual level over teen segment's personal growth and development as well as their family situations.

Multiple reactions as to the self, familial, economic, social and cultural context are gainfully transforming the behavioural patterns of positioning oneself in family stances, meeting the family expectation/s, celebrating the freedom and bearing the conditional environment insisted on by family and family members.

Ado-group is constantly been under interaction with familial environment provisioning the opportunistic conditions to develop themselves with family, peer groups, social and cultural norms, and to a large extent they can accommodate or become adaptative to the innovative situations.

Freedom in Participation

An ideal understanding towards decision-making approaches and organizing discipline and promotional skill as well as the growing self which has been branching out as a new individual (still alienated with parents due to the feeling of guilt). Self-concern family concern peer group dynamics social stances, intrinsic values, emotional attachments suggestively define the purpose for which occupation is preferred.

Occupational Understanding

Enable them to provide financial autonomy, self-dignity in decision-making, recognition and prestige, self *vs.* family supporting mechanisms paving way for overcoming their crises conditions. The need to develop by means of self-acquired skills, looking at parental living styles and standards matching educational and employment opportunities. The occupational preferences influenced by parental, peer groups, social and cultural understanding enabled occupational preparedness by means of skill development, mobility and openness etc.

Analysis : An Occupational Viewpoint

Based on the general views expressed complacency as dependent-being, preference towards security and lack of interest in acquiring more skills the tribal youth preferred to be a part of their own culture. Seeking local employment, considerations towards tribal values the ado-segment presented :

- Wider understanding of the vitalities of the work life and the associated effort to be invested for gainful occupation.
- Felt-need towards the occupational preparedness initialized due to parental work experience and work situations, familial interactivities, preferences, lifestyle patterns, and behavioural impositions etc., which have their influence on the respondents' self.
- The peer group pressure, relatives and other influences of inter-personal relations too have their impact provisioned an ideal understanding of occupational necessities.
- The job values enable to establish a response-based approach which seemed to provide opportunities of further study, mobility, lucrative jobs elsewhere and the perceptions towards investment and saving of finance etc.
- The tribal ideologies have been given due weightage as it depicted positive understanding of the situation volunteering self-impositions in terms of dependencies, incapacities, and limitedness.
- The in-depth socio-cultural and ethnic environment seems to still playing vital on their decision-making as collectively 81.4 per cent of ados revealed strong tribal feelings, depicted the lack of interest towards occupation-based mobility and supportiveness.

However, the positional stance as to the concept of self-dignity can be observed over the dependent status and mixed feelings of guilt and embarrassment create a forced feeling of the money earning. Majority of the ado-segments understand the value of money and are keen in finding out the ways and means of earning it.

The cultural congruency model expresses the mapping of ado-segmental involvement with respect to its source effect (dependent and influencing); generic character (the fundamental and core value formulations) leading to the outcome decisions (opinions currently-in-value and prevalent).

Based on the informal expressions, observations and judgmental factors the ado-model reveal their positional framework in their positivities *vs.* negativities each having corresponding outcomes to the extent of their participational enthusiasm based on self-felt necessities.

The development of self can be witnessed as to sharing of one's own feelings with friends, positioning themselves as a part of family, clan and in society they belong to and inclination towards expressing their feelings of demands, needs and priorities strongly. Developing self-perception towards ethnic values, traditions and customs at individual level form a part of tribal culture *viz.*, matrilineal culture wrapping self-opinions about female contributions etc.

It is therefore understood that :

H_1 : The hypothesis stands true as to the effect of education seemed to be flexible and adaptable to situations. An educated youth tend to analyze, evaluate situations as well understand the *pros* and *cons* of situations prior decision-making is an applicable fact when preferred services but the occupational options which had no relevance seemed to be having meagre impact of education over their occupational decisions.

H_2 : The hypothesis stands partially true as to the occupational preference motive is self rather than the family. An outlook towards ado-justifications of situations as to being a vital philosophy still waiting to be matured and anticipate transformations the ideologies are surely useful as the reflections of the family orientations currently prevailing.

H_3 : The hypothesis seems to be partially true as to the influenced exerted by parents and peer groups but it can be implied in due course that the ado-transitions may depict innovative trends based on self-situations and experiences.

H_4 : The hypothesis is partially true as to the decision-dominance of the parents over the ado-decision seems to reflect the internal opinionalities, natural fears and insecurities experienced by the parents who are also a part of social system. However, the ado-groups have been experiencing an in-process or passing stage of life may chance their way in order to gain wider exposure that can influence their decision-making.

Implication of Respondents' Self in Ethical and Cultural Context

At micro level the occupational vitalities have already been felt in the Xers, however, they seemed to be not very clear in their perceptions. But as to the general understanding about the situational influences they are equally reactive, prefer. to be identified with self-dignity, aspire to be more qualified, to be self-dependent, promote their personal calibre, and present the symptoms of autonomy both in financial status and behaviour. Majority of them to be independent, creative and at the same time at micro view have been compatible towards the socio-cultural issues, maintain ethics, tradition and family values. They insisted on gender equalities, limitedness of cultural as a part of life and more sensibly appreciate the contribution of females. Several ados shown interest in family preferences, consideration towards family pressures etc. The researcher clearly views the compassionate trends which enabled them to be highly sensible, family-oriented and at the same time eager to create a place of their own by enhancing their current identities, present a positive trend and are passionate to adopt every means which help acquiring the newly imbibed status of occupational preference.

7

Analysis and Recommendations

Analysis : The Meghalayan ethnic tribes form socially and ethnically fragmented over the language and cultural factors into Khasis, Jaintias, Garos and Bhois. These ethnic groups have simple living philosophy; pleasure seeking and fun-loving groups prefer easy lifestyles. Money handling, lending and trading practices are alien to them. The typical tribal approach believes in today and hardly cares for future. These attitudes relieve them from deep understanding in life concepts, developing a strong social responsibility, rational approach towards resources and building systematic methodologies aiming progressive societies. The current research investigation over the "occupational selectivities and mapping" summarizes the outcomes as follows :

Out of the total 3613, the 1715 urban respondents 38.7 per cent are between 30-40 years group, 23.23 per cent are between 50-60 years and 20.6 per cent are between 20-30 years in rural and 41.5 per cent are between 30-40 years and 26.1 per cent between 50-60 years and 21.2 per cent are between 40-50 years age groups. The participatory trends didn't show wide differentiations based on age. The rural educated respondents represented 24.5 per cent for $<10^{th}$, 16.1 per cent for >10 - $<12^{th}$ and 11.6 per cent are graduates and 6.1 per cent are professionals whereas in urban 11.3 per cent undergraduates, 31.2 per cent are graduates and 7.9 per cent are post-graduates. The parental background did not show noteworthy variations education (with average ranging school level), mobility (preferred to remain in the place of birth else preferred to settle in capital), religion (mostly Christianity but some non-converts/no-religion adapts were prevalent) and occupational activities between urban and rural (urban preference arrive neutrality as a preferred domain only for elite public but rural with its resource base, interstate and international trading, commerce is more sought than urban for business-oriented, resource owners and regional power mongers). But it is noteworthy that 73 per cent of the respondents had single parent, 84 per cent of the respondents' mothers are engaged in occupation, 59 per cent of the respondents have been a part of family business since childhood, 72 per cent admitted that they entered into occupational condition without really feeling any need of having a preference towards occupation, 89 per cent of the families have multiple-businesses of various combinations which support the family needs, 46 per cent women shifted their occupations for first time, 23 per cent shifted several times out of which 8 per cent shifted due to self-reasons. 31 per cent of the women began their occupational career as early as less than 10 years.

Few strongest beliefs which have an impact on occupational effect :

- There was always a situation available to be engaged in some occupation when alternately one can sacrifice it for education, religious service, health issue of a senior member or looking after the dependents, a total lack of opportunities or lack of initiations (self or familial).
- Occupational need arises as any other occupational task and there appear innumerable "tasks" especially in rural which earn near cash or convertibles against occupations which are laborious and earn marginally. Majority of the girls have been observed to be versatile of being engaged in several occupations viz., piggery, selling vegetables, supply of tobacco, dry fish in rural and in urban support retail trade, sitting in shop, distribution of newspaper etc., as daily chores along with education.

- The work concept is a part of culture and irrespective of status, material possessions and need arousal etc., the tribal women prefer to work as matter of habit irrespective of the nature of job, decide on the criteria of self-potentiality form the preference rather than the selectivities attributed of occupation.
- Majority of the occupations form a part of family pool and contribute towards dimensional effect in totality i.e., multi-tasking rather than single event. The work cult is inherited in majority of the households with a continuum range of high involvement to low involvement especially in extended/large households with several members engaged in different occupations as per one's own choice to earn common livelihood source for family rather than self. This enable a part-responsibility to each member and similarity in trend is observed even in the representations made by the middle and youth segments presented characters beyond comparatives with any other systems functional elsewhere.

Temperamentally the women wrap around the women's persona, base associated with the weighted (complex) issues relative to environmental effects over occupational preferences, integrated approaches by means of orientations of survival, growth, insecurity and informality, the stunted ethical and cultural dimensions without parameters valuing the situations and accommodations are much beyond the perceptional limits of majority of the women's understanding. Keeping in view the general womens' status suggest a deliberate prescription of assignments, a major struggle over the *status quo* of traditional and modern positional role-competitives and aspirations felt play important as change determinants and variants. Much of the decision-making is still being the privilege of seniors who have been reconciling with modernities and traditional views. Revealing the culture as the strongest to fulfil the materialistic needs (community enforcements) one can notice the eagerness to be insured under the brand identity of being within the ethnic systems for several understandable reasons viz., the package of benefits assigned to the formal status. These identified prerogatives associated with compromise and even under criticism in several contexts yet prefer to retain with suitable dilutions.

The typical women in association coping with "prevailing context" as being positioned based on personal choice and to considerable extent situational favouritism has not depicted its effect or variance in terms of diversified role dimensions, participatory as well as reception trends and reactions towards external influences, prototypical understanding, supremacy of women over men with variable value systems and positivities etc., proved to be of minimal variation being rural or urban occupational trends. The "acceptable role" assignments by means of traditional and modern views "within" the women have pampered rigidities (reservations), flexibilities (adaptives), blame (controllables), frustrations (limitedness of choice), anticipations (personal incapacities) and expectations (self-deficiencies) etc. But the trend also reflect the open neglect due to the system manipulations by local administrative machinery, lack of authority and micro initiatives of intermediaries yielding insignificants, reluctance and lack of supportives. But these lacunas hardly have any impact over the faith and loyalty over communities or its preservators, lack of complacencies have not been implied towards any concrete sources, lack of complaint against or voice raise over the imperfections/inefficiencies of preliminaries and missing orientations. The cultural perpetuations have their significance in prescribing their impositions over the thinking processes, approach, language, dress code, beliefs and value systems but more importantly the social stances and group effect which has been prominently felt as being the undercurrent which has been witnessing resilience.

The generalized grasp and understanding of the investigation over the women reveal their dependencies over the knowledge, exposure and experience has not been taken appropriate shape to be used in the occupational decision sub-serving life decision context. The associative rigidities, expectations leading to variable reactions of silent compromises, alternative behaviour, aggressiveness and micro spread as per the "personal and situational" array reflecting, reacting and valuating into the assortment of totally unproducible to nominally producible structures. Accommodating new and innovative systems have been observed to be facing the practical adversaries contributing due to lack of appropriate understanding of the objective outlook, context, background, cultural insights and philosophies are not been estimated nor predicted due to lack of exposure. The overall valuation and understanding especially over the new methods and techniques cannot become instant-acceptables unless the context-suitability succeeds. A prototypical understanding is not able to provide the vision, strategy, practice which bear a need of new cope up with strange situations when the tribal segments accept tradition as part and parcel to be dominant over their current cultural stretch to accommodate these innovative ideologies in the context suitable to them. These advocations have been taking "at-convenient" shapes over the values prevalent (living styles), preference (situational) to realize (context) and to compare with applicabilities (analytical comparatives). A single sided view cannot encourage a totality in view of positives and negatives with equivalent measure or balance.

Occupational Relevancy

The imbibed work culture inherited by the women folk ensure the "quantum in utility terms" by adopting the conceptions of micro entrepreneurship, part-time preferences, leveraging work *vs.* non-work life compositions, organizing business and service skills shaped and structured as per the system requirements. The behaviour has been the result of impulsive notions, urges, instincts routing the women to face the critical consequences of life, to be self-supportive, to be responsible towards the individual and familial responsibilities and at large develop orientations towards the clan/community without reciprocal accommodations and recognition.

It is, however, questionable to the extent of which the variations of women being accommodating themselves to these transformations in totally new or familiarized situations. The social, ethno-cultural and psychographic dimensions have been collectively contributing towards a "synchronized" effect over creating a desirable environment. The supportive system is multi-dimensional and the women draw her strengths from more than one source and also from different angles of single source which is not otherwise possible when they prefer to settle in new situations without all these supportives. Each woman inherits priorities, accept and promote the occupational context and dimension to be used not only to the women in particular context but also as a part of family, clan and society make their roles multiple and especially in close-knit tribal segments.

Women are both cause and effect of the ethnic situations and the hierarchy of liabilities, responsibilities are being taken care but within the "understandable and synchronized" effects. Each woman witnessed of being pampering trivial and insignificant living conditions aiming conditional fulfilment, enabling applicable status (to be one amongst of the tribe, cult and culture) holds the responsibility of providing bare minimum need for survival. Exposure to situations promote deeper understanding is missing fact especially among rural women segments which need to strive overcoming language, cultural alienations, lack of opponents knowledge and understanding which have been drastically hindering the growth orientations beyond the comfort zones. A typical rural household describe occupation by means of a gamut of services which fetch cash or cash equivalent considerations irrespective of size, structure, conversion effort and value determinants etc. In rural set up besides agriculture a typical household is equipped with a small patch of horticulture, broom, beetle nut and beetle leaf, some mushrooms, poultry, piggery, goatary, basket making, herbs resourcing ethnic medicines, orchids, rice, corn, spices, dry or smoked meat and honey etc., which can be sold for barter trade or can be converted into cash or near cash items with minimum effort on the weekly market days. Similarly the urban household which is supported by means of taxi, shop, trading and networking of facilities and services viz., ready-to-eat local products, bakery items, retailing and itineraries which keep the entire household (member/s especially women) in the process of occupation. The term occupation therefore to be understood that the involvement of the entire "relevant" group, segment or household being engaged to provide the task in its complete shape where each of the contributor irrespective of the size possessed to be responsible to its earning or can preferably occupy multiple tasks as per one's own capacity or interest. For women comes her responsibility as foremost priority and women are being engaged since childhood in multiple tasks both within and outside the household. It is observed that the women have depicted of having the calibre of organizing and administering multiple tasks at a given point of time with equal vigour, initiative, willingness to be reactive and sensuous to situations, search for opportunities, tolerance, adaptability and at the same time occupationally engaged (even without being a necessity) as for majority of tribal women work has become a necessity of life.

Decision Reflections

If employable condition is an ideal outcome representing too many priorities it should take into account the prominent and prevailing gaps viz., infrastructural deficiencies, limitedness in opportunities, the lackadaisical approaches in the system machinery and the ethnic lifestyle context, which enable to determine mutually inclusive or exclusive conditions. Disproportionate occupational portfolios have become the tribal trend merged with the informalities and personification of dimensions. The occupational character represents predominantly synchronized concepts which have been morphed functions as integrated units accommodating different (include non-occupational) needs and requirements. Provisioning the means-ends individually of members and collectively of family majority of women adopt multiple priorities associated with different occupational benevolences help in deeper understanding of the extent to which the dependencies can be promoted, diverted or even withdrawn.

Preference Towards the Priorities

The women revealed multiple considerations in adopting the styles as per the choice towards love life, marriage, cultural dominance, ethnic priorities and non-occupational role preferences *viz.*, entertainment, hobbies, social and familial engagements, religion and customs etc. The "personalized preferences" are important for self-centricism especially when the senior members holding decisions concerning implicit ethnic dominances, vitalities towards clan promotion, service flexibility, social isolation, unpredictability, family orientation, stereo-typing, internal and external social distances, rigidity, and inequalities in lifestyles. Various views have been presented as reflections (a) when occupation is formally accepted; (b) when the preference approaches seemed to be matching with the occupational situation; (c) occupational shift which was the result of conflicting status of events; (d) primitive occupational stances which have been accepted (compromises) or search for alternative (drives); expectations towards high aims, changing values and proneness for occupational decisions. The reactions for such situations (preparedness) witnessed by family, dependent/s liabilities, calibre building enabled to

- Application of restricted/extended preferences within subdued/highly conditional environment,
- Gaining knowledge and information to evaluate the available alternatives,
- Extended orientation and value prescription preferences, and
- Parity in terms of distinguishable character and narrowfied variations based on age, distance, location, investment and progressive outlook.

Applicability of Urbanalities vs. Ruralities

The State of Meghalaya comprises minimal urban and vast rural segments. But this does not in any form created discriminations in the dependency levels as both systems remained mutually dependencies in disproportionate forms under differentiated situations. The urban with its historical background has proved to be a vibrant domain for its lucrative character and potentialities viz., its positive climate, cosmo culture and prospective core servicing enabled it as sellers' paradise. Ample resource-base proved to be the most striking feature forms the most basic and most fundamental. The resource-basedness is the prominent character for both urbanites and ruralities for which the education, knowledge, language, information and also value determinants have become insignificant and the total economy has been directly, indirectly or even in hierarchical forms of social layering gain resource access as the noted and fundamental preference for the very survival the State's economy. The women's classification of status to a large extent based on their persona or personal calibre (arise due to the personal competencies) or due to the supportives provided by means of resources (acquired calibre). The self-impositions, ethnic identities and cultural enforcements etc., have variant reference as to the interactivities with other communities (inclusive of acculture behaviour), exposure to different cultural contexts and levels of understanding as well as perceptions developed towards work-prone issues. Irrespective of rural or urban, all women who claim to the custodians of tradition uniquely accept the prerogative of being clan promoters. These are the implied responsibilities which have been accepted as inevitable events, beliefs and statuses. The occupational consequences based on these beliefs enable them to be responsibility towards the "dependency overload" caused, created and nurtured. These natural consequences force women to compromise with stereotyped occupational consequences, meagre educational levels, and teenage conjugal attractions convenienced by culture accompanied by lack of responsibility and illegitimacy promoted a package of living styles which can be pampered or promoted. The ease in living, pleasure-loving and strain-free living styles cannot be accommodated without intervention enabled these areas as "culturally branded comfort zones" which air freedom and autonomy towards informality and unstructured promotion.

Overall Views Reflecting Occupational Ramifications

The research investigations reveal the identifications associated to the living environment which is ethically and culturally vibrant with an underlying concept of adaptability. The rigidity and adamancy are the external conditions where the women in particular is being branded by themselves with some unique identities but there are several compromises as to the leniency, multi-cultural behaviour and permissibility etc., which has been highly accepted in the life context. Keeping in view the geo-demographic and socio-cultural factors the women segments have adopted a typical behaviour which is equally reflected in their occupational choice spans. The ethnical influences and tribal norms which have assigned with the gender-based responsibilities have well become the system itself such as the maintenance of traditional values, community cult, homogeneous ethnic character and compositional framework of life trajectories etc. But the lacuna which fail to hold the sanctity of associated enforcements in the areas of marriage, concept of mutuality, to support the perceived aspirational levels and self-direction even if it has a larger impact over the dilution of the core values of the tribal belief systems. Few concepts such as community cult, group think, mutuality, nativity and value system towards work stratification and micro entrepreneurship etc., are some of the most acceptable views depicted by women.

The occupational reflectives based on the preferences/ prevalences within and external situations seemed to be in offer of some differences aroused due to the clan-cult beliefs, sect/ community, language etc., at base levels demarcated the women over their dress code, language, accent, food habits and work style patterns etc. But the prominent discriminative attributes *viz.*, massive resource-supportives of Jaintia women, work-preferred orientations with business progressions by Khasi women, micro-participation and work diversities of Garo women and small business dominance and micro entrepreneurship of Bhoi women visualize the work concept accompanied by resource-base supportives, empowered spirit of work participation need to be admitted as the fundamental character which can be highlighted among these tribal segments.

The research investigated the environmental character, positivities and dependencies of the women over the resource-base; external factors *viz.*, market conditionalities and reflectives, interconnectivities and dependencies, channel sources and co-habitation in controllable and uncontrollable forms have their diversified effects under different conditions. Even if it is considered feasible that being matrilineal the tribal women have not depicted for their supremacy towards anything unusual such as being more confident or bold but have been representing the typical cultural facets prescribed to womenhood. However, these tribal women present themselves as a kind with difference due to their leveraged situations with an impact of ethnic sensitivities, cultural imperatives, sprillover effects and deliberations of casuality and informality to a large extent have their impact on their day-to-day living styles and over their occupational conditions. It need to be an acceptable fact that the occupational suggestives demonstrated have not been depicted which is different of their belief system which is inclusive of manifestations overall conditions of selectivities with respect to the location, mobility, life styles, challenges, involvements and volatilities etc. These realistic conditions in which women's considerations are to be supported with well thoughtful strategies but restrict them being engaged into the workable conditions, within parameters of being selecting the survival choices but in reality has not been equipped with suitable tools such as knowledge, information, education, economic support or even the moral support. Despite being of possessing the massive micro-entrepreneurial, self-preparedness and initiatives, organizing multi-tasking and possible coordinations of semi and unstructural situations the self-imposed and contextual rigidities in correlation with opportunity-spectrum, the women of Meghalaya have not been able to grow beyond specific limit.

Towards Developmental Reflections

The concept of matriliny and matriarchy has its profound influence over its economy. The traditionally imbibed positional authority sanctions to the women enable them to hold a predominant role and the women's force seemed to be networked in all activities especially those of having influence over the very economic status. But women who arrived some plateau with or without using this prerogative doesn't seem to have been perturbed with the newly acquired status did not depict of being using their distinctive power which has been provided by the ethnic culture to them. A narrowfied perspective arrives as to their being satisfied with their feminine qualities and contributions to the family, to the clan—the most feminine contribution and justification is being understood as the clan promotion, nurturing the future generation, taking care of the older generation, being accepting the responsibility of the clan and community as well as the traditional norms to some extent possible. The directives prescribed in these references have been the living culture of the women folk. The major occupational pockets being the resource base in its raw condition, resources-based in its converted forms, markets, business channels, government and private jobs etc., seemed to be the derivatives of the proneness of the system sanctions.

The Perspectives towards Occupational Wrap-up

The "abundancy and generosity" in the rest of the systems merit highly selective gains leaving large masses struggle to acquire means-ends at-convenient forms. The ethnic core values remain unperturbed with these ground realities as the ethnic diversities by culture adopt self-centric attitudes have limited perceptions and understanding ignoring the visionary effects or system-prominences of overall effects. The occupational selectivities reveal stern rigidities as the new enforcements which have been the result of "permissible acceptances and acquisitions" of new ideologies. These prototyped understanding encourage limited participation and loose its sanctity and objective fulfilment. The ethical dynamism has been projecting adopted behaviour and at convenience approaches i.e., peri-stereotyped mechanisms by younger generation have been witnessing the overall determinants currently stretching the ethnical boundaries. The cultural erosion is also witnessed leading to catastrophic imbalances in social systems, promoting inconsistencies and extensive compromises at the cost of "potentialities" which seemed to draw new measures of shortages in the Progressive Mapping (PM). The ethically provided liberalization backed by the lack of responsibility and attempted casualisation even in the matters of developmental importance. The women's effort seemed to be too insignificant and is associated with lack of knowledge, understanding, information, association and disorganization leading to dire consequences. The clan promotion which has its own negative consequences in the long run lead to resource fragmentation and exhaust especially in the absence of any developmental measures, limitedness in exposure and rigidities towards progressive measures.

The research investigation reveals that the tribal women segments adopting a rare phenomenon of matrilineal extended family patterns, clan cult and traditional systems of segmentation with local chiefs under the supremacy of king. This created a generic formal and informal institutions parallelly run and have been indigenously monitoring the encapsulated social structures towards sustenance. The ethno-cultural pre-dominances display loose, undefined and volatile structures present internalities influenced by equally vibrant (within conditional frameworks) forces when compared with penetrating external factors. The systems co-exist but adopt a deliberate measure of individual stances, interact to the extent desirable and prefer to remain isolates rather than produce synergistic effect. The prevalence of micro and meso systems create a need to perceive broader analytical forms which permit structural change in "indigenous" form adopt absolute liberty at personal and rigidity at community levels. The occupational concept, being a dependent function to a large extent relies over the "informal" life styles adopted and preferred selectivities especially of women-based over the limited skills acquired by heredity or any preferable means. Local dependencies prefer occupations which satisfy the norms viz., ease in entry and exit choice, direct or indirect resource-dependency, micro-managerial and participatory trends, parity with family system pre-dominances, pigmy scale of operations etc. Accommodating women barring any criteria, these systems have been preferably labour intensive, adopt informality, perceive dichotomies of abundance and scarcity at common point of time. An incremental growth is not vertically significant but the growth consequences alarm the :

- Excess usage of natural resources lay excessive load over the resources.
- Segregated preferences have been skewed towards specific choices of occupations.
- Over-growth in the micro informal segment with minimal meso effect.
- Internal turbulences lead to system erosion and leniency enable the externalities to gain advantage.

The lacuna in growth can be anticipated as an end decision of the occupational abilities glorified within the peripheries of the state boundaries as the informal growth stemmed within the local limits is being nurtured demonstrate robustness by means of local adaptations. The demarcations between the rural and urban are not significant as the variations anticipated in the areas of education, mobility, living standards and the inclination/s towards ethic identities etc., are minimal except the temperament, cosmo trends and semi-urbanized adaptives (due to exposure), access to infrastructural amenities etc. In short, it is a partial environmental contribution which lay the difference. Occupationally the women's "likabilities" seemed to be adopting homogeny in the domain where spirit of oriented outlook has arrived parity in norms and systems, behavioural dynamism, organizational and entrepreneurial talents etc. The system interactivities viz., the technologies, present distinguished dimensions-based on the issues of involvement, penetration, impact and mutuality in the meso occupational influences have their reflections in micro systems. Each system has been domesticated with the conventional knowledge most applicable and tacit to the localized conditions. The occupational accommodation/s need to be restructured as per the prototypical contexts which does not warrant the non-adaptations of the assimilated external systems. The under-performers, non-cope ups, subsequent stage local stakeholders (women), opportunists, counter urban (Halliday, J. and M. Coombes, 1995; Champion, T. and G. Hugo, 2004) formal/informal segments seemed to be encouraging multi-dimensional stability *viz.*, preferences towards dual-base (both rural and urban); multi-tasking (part-involvement in associated and differentiated tasks); backward and forward integrations (in similar or dissimilar occupations); coordinating trial and error as micro portfolio occupational systems (combination of low and high risk occupations) and new modes of speculative occupations (permit least capital involvement associated with high risk) seemed to be few of their occupational solutions based on choice preference.

Due to manifold expansion of occupational rigidities with reference to the occupationally preferred comfort zones (within the state) the impact of informality attained an indispensable position. Each of the formal channels have been supported by several informal channels promote reciprocal dependency in the areas of communication to gain utility base, connectivities, intriguing for serve and subserve patterns aiming individual/clan/community-based occupational processes. The character of informality can well be understood in ethnic context as an assignment of micro-entrepreneurial characters imbibed by culture and is manifested by the womens' ideologies, treatments and perseverances towards system constituents. Majority of the informal adaptors have been educated in formal systems have explored the opportunity of infrastructural merits but those who have been contended in the informal structure are not opportune to be significantly merited.

The women's segregated views form a generic necessity articulated by ethnic professionalism, cultural definiteness prefer least aggressive occupations towards growth, communication, interaction, to be knowledgeably and accommodate align cultures. It is found that women, as stakeholders prefer to be dependent over both enforced and acquired capabilities transversed through ethno-cultural, socio-environmental and familial norms. The uncertainties associated enable them to accept or accommodate the situational complexities prefer differentiations even being accompanied at any given level. A typical woman in micro segment has too many layers of preferences, aspirations and assigned values as individual and as a part of clan/community and at large towards the society. These values are, however, volatile and few have arrived rigidities as being developed in the process of upbringing, operational in the nurturing forms, value assignments as per the social-determinations and prescriptions etc. The applicability of the implicit conditions much under the localized pressures witness the decisions to be "most acceptable" to the context rather than individual preference.

The vulnerabilities of stereotyping, seclusion, limited perspectives provide a comprehensive means of value, social, cultural and familial directions to be met simultaneously. The synergistic view of these variables composes a totality with an intriguing effect of mutuality over the occupational decision. The concept of clan promotion encouraged matrilineal extended families with wider spectrum of family relations under single roof and large family systems form another striking feature of combating the survival risks as the occupational participation remain as partial involvement and contribution encouraging new designs towards preference and selectivity systems. The work patterns are :

- Regular and continuous in order to cope up with routine demands of survival.
- To reduce the occupational risk which is disproportionately shared over by (micro and meso) occupational portfolios.
- Multi-activity occupational priorities are inclined with the women's living style adaptations and preferences.
- Typical parameters of age, education, gender, religion, location (include rural and urban), infrastructural support, proximity to opportunistic situations viz., resource ownership or access, mobility and micro input portfolios etc., have not been the factors seemed to be non-influencers of occupational preferences. However,

more fluid parameters *viz.*, flexibility, accommodation, adaptation, and capacity etc., seemed to be the fluid determinants of realistic situations.

Majority of the variations arise due to the scope of applicability in the context of individual, group/social result in the occupational flexibility. Besides these the occupational preference come into sight due to :

- Womens' exclusive reference towards survival and growth factors.
- Primary and secondary preferences towards accumulation of social, human and physical capital.
- At convenience systems of farm/non-farm, manufacturing/service, pigmy or itinerary occupations under the banner of micro enterprising/ entrepreneurialism promote constructs insist feasibility to be channelised towards potential occupational mechanisms.
- Locus of control over extensions of the familial processes, applications and adaptations of primitive systems form typical character for occupational proneness and choice.
- Prominence towards undue values to the traditionalism which has been hindering the progress of innovation and creativity. Learning from the conventional systems constituted as one of the prominent channels of communication with easy access of reference deemed to be inclined towards ease in occupational decision.
- Individual *vs.* clan preference to "informal familiarity" rather than formal unfamiliar systems have been creating choice-centric effect associated with leniencies.

Identifying the temperamental effect the informality is found the generic concept of women's life which only reflected in their occupational preference as it wrapped the entire thought process of the people at large of all segments enable to isolate themselves in specific behavioural climate, culture and workable patterns and practices of "ethical models" and formally approved procedures by culture or heredity only gain acceptance (in fact reverence). Ethnic rigidities overshadow the externalities with the purview of systems depict reluctance to understand the external context and emphasize their cultural reference. It is found that majority of the externalities have been tamed so as to elaborate their span of survival and to gain inspiration of innovatives which can be adaptable in tailor-made situations does not stand much to the merit of occupational proneness. The contemporary systems domestically put-to-use has their origins in the process of acquisition by trial and error form the articulated style reflected in their occupations. The group reflections have their presence felt in the process of hierarchically adopted ethnic adaptations navigating the womens' occupational needs. Surprisingly these are group-based rather than individual at micro level and *vice versa* in meso level.

The micro approach is being understood in its nuances as to aim the survival needs based on aspirations stand alone over unrefined/crude skills popularly adaptive in multi-tasking, prefer micro investments in micro physical assets (tools) restricted motivation towards growth and expansion and adapt simplicity in lifestyles (Hakim, C., 2000) including food, entertainment and habits or addictions etc. The individual approach of occupational preference is mostly done by intuition which is being understood as an ability of subconsciously valuing the individual and social scope and opportunity, option for diversification, command over the activity and complexity, supportive to meet the expectations and status with horizontal and vertical linkages and ease in entry and exit options etc. The micro "schematics" attend to the most basic needs and intimately monitor their basic decisions and commodification of efforts. Not all aspirations modelled in uniformity due to the impact of urbanization and much credit to its cosmo effect, its historical base (of British rule), its enforced interactivities with neighbouring states and channels extended to the interiors of north-east, its international access etc., comprise conglomerated structural effect in disproportionate forms.

These effects have a tremendous impact in the "occupational transformations" penetrating into ethnic heterogeneous system effects creating a massive micro economic scope of activities directly and indirectly been chosen for occupational preferences. The pettiness is prominent over the producible and service systems attracting pigmy but informal growth potentialities with total perfection. The co-existence had its influence over the integrated effects with underlying disintegrated effects reveal the striking contrast of cultural effects and occupational compromise to arrive the fruits of informality.

Besides the survival need the employable preferences are also based on the employable background/s, reasons of occupational continuity, preparedness towards learning new skills, cautiousness in the living styles and local knowledge supplements etc. The external changes aroused due to convergences to minute extent lay its impact in the localized systems but the system operators are still not sure as to the form or order of implementing as the adaptations have been still being retained as a choice, the status of primitiveness is still in its infancies and any change does not really make much impact and the definition of development in ethnic terms is totally different *viz.*, acquiring petty material needs rather than visualizing an integrated transformative policy structure. The change impact is prototypically applicable to be introduced as mere non-producible extensions rather than creating a congruent of inter-sectoral synergies to be glorified towards purposeful dimensions. The norms and feasibility of the informal structure/s remain lenient and socially contested value approaches adopting contemporaneous processes in organizational, socio-economic capital, political (including statutory), manufacturing, market and other influencing domains forming well-knitted networking components etc., however ignoring the balanced distribution norms. Operationalising the changes remain a Hercules task in the primitive informal systems have not arrived any sophistication indicate "too many interventions" to bring self-designed logical systems as they claim eventual possibilities leading to system imbalances even under perfect strategic conditions. The occupational spectrum need to be a (i) dynamic system (adopting both internal and external motivation), (ii) knowledge (to be applicable at micro and meso levels), (iii) proximity and access (formal acceptance and close understanding in applicable terms), (iv) promotives backed by [Pugh, C. (ed), (1996)] self-sustainability (at individual and institutional forms) and communication (for ideal inter-connectivities). The occupational conditions, therefore, are dependent over the agricultural and natural resource base with locally spread itinerary and pigmy options can be well referred as a resource-based system. The women's force remains independent to their administrative set up and the former have been left to fend for themselves under the localized environmental conditions with meagre interactivities between administrative systems and stakeholders. The proportion of non-formal is significantly high and its stance evidence a constant pressure over the state depends over the stake or benefit arrived. The women forcing their way by culture, by social sanctions or even as emerging force retain the authority of being conventional seemed to be vital has independent status, essentialities and autonomy leaving insignificant role in the matters of social importance. The concept of privatization, recognition, appreciation are to be contextually defined have not encouraged any generic transformations making a room for new occupational creatives. An overall occupational scenario reveals a closed approach conditioned by cultural and ethnic limits remain "individually constructive" rather than as state structure. The local administration precisely holds meagre role as it is being cornered to be a promoter rather than any other role. The Meghalayan occupational scenario within the women's preferences foster a conducive autonomous environment self-designed in the guise of informality adopts considerations randomly meeting the short-sighted prospects and adhere formal privatization. Its beyond-the-means of pigmy systems have been invariably understand the concept of long-term growth and persistent development aiming occupational means as any major structural change remain out of sight. As a system based on individually segmented components restrict its vision not beyond localized peripherals fail to perceive the global or convergent effects eventually pouring in into the ethnic system and there exist a dire need to anticipate a vision towards massive and impending changes arriving with their professional packages demand a paradigm shift.

Nuances of Occupational Ethics

The Meghalayan matriarchy embossed with cultural issues pertinent to customs, beliefs and attitudes empowered their living patterns inclusive of their occupational choices and preferences. Occupation as a significant decision equally evolved, nurtured and sighted as a significant priority of women under all conditions with its fuzzy over consistencies and volatile structures and view points. Suitability and form determinations over the priorities towards aspirations, living styles, ethnical effects display the fundamental ways of necessitating the optimum choice are dependent over the womens' (stakeholder's) choice. At individual capacity or as a part of clan women feel the necessities partly due to adverse physiological factors and partly due to administrative lethargy and neglect resulted in lack of both visionary and missionary leadership, direction, non-operational governance and practices, wider perceptional gaps, approaches and rigidities etc., as macro contributors effecting their positivities of hard work, ideal determination and even inabilities towards survival presenting an aspiration-driven behaviour. The prominency of women's attribution of being "individualism with independence" is populous character observed among majority of the women. They preferred of being promoted as a total non-homogenous group even while practicing ideal community concepts applicable in multi-layered situations. It is important to note that based "on chance" their socio-economic and status differences have primarily been arrived due to asset acquisition and dependencies networked in multi-lateral forms. In an environment offering frugal infrastructural means, hard to cope up conditions the lacunal in the women's domain is characterized with short-sighted vision, sub-minimal awareness, knowledge, information leading to irrelevant and irrational adaptations. These situations not being appropriately backed by causes of authenticity nor reasons encouraging degenerating cultural values, sub-optimal returns, short-term gains, lack of visionary and missionary approaches towards development.

The locational centricism and superfluous ethos have a major concern over occupational decision-analysis and the macro segmental effects pleateaued over the micro-entrepreneurial faculties over the workaholic trend is a matter of networked preferences of informality and itinerary. In the midst of equally important concepts of religion, clan promotion and ethnicity a display of resilience, legacy and simplicity display the wedged conceptual adaptations jettisoning the long term realizations. The internal environment has been layered with overloaded focus of variable administrative half-measures designed by local government, NGOs (recognized/unrecognized and domestic/foreign), student and service (formal *vs.* informal) organizations, religious bodies and the most vital of all i.e., the parallelly run traditional rulers of the land indeed result in "administrative overload". Each have been differentiated and segmented in their functionalities with disintegrated objective perceptions aiming the growth in self-directed form rather than integrated approaches. But the noteworthy aspect is the prevailing system with all its structural divisions, its nature, status, liabilities and felt-need towards community and society at large sharing fuzzy core values have neither shown any significant performance nor innovation as it concerns the state as a whole. However, it is quite remarkable to notice the women's focus over occupational engagements and inclination to be a potential supporter at familial level prove to be an outstanding factor which :

- enable the women to be engaged in some occupation or other having no permanency nor specific preference.
- determining the concept of self-sufficiency the women insist on being both self-standing and also to be

potential contributor in both occupational and non-occupational forms.

- occupation is viewed as natural as play and spectrum permit design, methods and competencies in synchronized forms aiming the circumstantial needs wrapped around the women.

An extensive readaptation of the traditional practices rather than engineering innovative new value-based mechanisms (competent to yield encouraging results) the system promotion is being at the mercy of "limited understanding" and encouraging traditional practices and values anticipating new results. Absence of accountability at every level leading to vitiating the ethno-cultural context leading to erosion of the well preserved values. The ethnic segment can no more function on the tag of relationships as the multi-situational effect has too many consequences. The worst of all is the clan promotion concept of "matrilineal mega families" can no more be taken with pride due to the changing philosophies manifesting new lifestyles and leveraging women's dynamism with the new survival and growth concepts articulated for current and future generic needs. But being identified as a "well protected" tribal segment the promotives stand as hindrance to guard against the risk, competition, deviation, coping up and exposure (towards communication) deprive the "needed learning" skills most desirable for the very concept of introducing acceptable forms of development else a system-collapse processing dynamic trends prove to be too serious as the survival/growth is based on unnatural means will not cope up sustainability. The differentiations create new brand identities based on new core values need to be promoted with new portfolio forms overcoming the personal and non-personal non-contributive forms.

Keeping in view the prevailing social machinery, there is a need to design prototypical strategies which can take into confidence the new structural drives being supportive to be identified and scaled may set the positional allocations. Ideal socio-developmental concepts by government/institutional levels initiated the regulatory, supervisory and promotional focus attend to the needs of occupational spectrum to be vibrant of being a balanced spread with values much to the adulation of women (real) entrepreneurs of the domain. A total system transparency need to be encouraged at each level so as to respond to the fair share of growth in the areas-of-priority has been understood appropriate by the natives. The behavioural drives currently viewed have not been system-based but of individual based with no/low concept towards occupational development and preference structure. The involvement displayed by women segments towards contributory trends at large to society and even community seemed to be elementary but the issues have been endlessly opined without drawing meaningful conclusions over the impact of democracy and its effects been under-utilized due to the under-capacities of the "non-competencies" of participant groups.

New developmental proposals need an innovative outlook and are encouraged either as system extensions (prevailing) with or without the sprillover effects remains variant to the new evolving systems encouraged most suitable to the contextual development. Each of the trial and error need to attend to the SWOT (strengths, weaknesses, opportunities and threats) of idealistic trends accepted *viz.*, the micro capacities and contributions, high participatory pigmy trends, base-level entrepreneurship, promotives of cult and culture dedication etc., been the prerogatives of the women segment for their excellent enigma competent in multifarious forms. However, the occupational persuasion leading to distinctive adaptative styles for those more loyal to traditional system, the pseudo system promoters, innovatives and creatives etc., could not justify and convert them into happening forms. Walking through the consequences it is more appropriate to perceive the systems based on majority encouraging them as a trendy to evolve multiple autonomous systems under the centralized legacy of sustainability. The situation also suggest

- discourage the occupations irrelevant of the times and are being out-of-date and non-contributory methods.

- to encourage persecution of ideal women managerial nodes which can link proper planning and policy making to create a difference in the circumstances.
- to boost hi-performance structuring applicable to absorb multiple insignificant systems and to reinforce new occupational-orientations.
- new role identifications of women's natural talent as being custodians of tradition and also are competent to be reformers, system administrators, defendants and visionary managers who are also the determiners of the future system dependencies or its extent based on the selection.

The possibilities of the presence/absence of eventualities in a determinable form need comprehensive designing based on clear understanding of system/s and sub-system/s, cultural and sub-cultural effects, structural and segmental choices based on understanding and risk appetite nurtured by women's groups to the desirable extent. The occupational choices have been identified as choices elegantly groomed in the gab with least leadership patterns of non-contributive forms ruling the most deserving and vibrant system components. The vitalities of tribal women being excellent micro entrepreneurial qualities, self-potentiality, individual growth in the midst of community classifications and performance driven high on ethnic, service and occupational practices. The energizing roles truly identified the necessities of current day yet backed by the basic amenities in-offer produce a stunning contrast. The situations have been provided with innumerable rational explanations articulating the values of the chosen forms of occupational preferences and the abilities to conceive and design the occupational alignment. But the underperformance is being identified in its fullest extent taking into the value concern and identifying the behaviour that deliver the value systems above gender terms. Most of the women are deliberately restricting their line of sight in values, culture, behaviour and on the other hand the occupational strategies target performance over the fuzzy consequences of wide noise.

The strategic system layering the occupational levels based on the system-culture and people in comparison to the leadership/coping ability, character, behaviour and the intent expressed in their operational performance need to be supported if a systematic occupational spectrum is advocated by means of careful mapping even if the system adopts a *diktat*—the public initially reluctance and resistence eventually accept it as a part of their social living styles. But these needs require careful and patient administrative strategies with a total understanding of the character, temperament, cultural preferences and the time limits etc. In fact, it should be the women's force to be in the portfolio of change, ensure the ways and means of the types the system promotes, value determinants and promotive thinking towards the specific dimensions (thoughts and interactions). These are influenced by power themes, experience and clan-based (segmented) leadership to look into the merged features of the culture-based occupational promotion towards diluting the rigid role peripherals at individual or clan levels having the full knowledge of the tasks and consequences. The community coordinators need to initiate clan/community-based developmental notions with due accountability, objectivity and relevent forms being adoptable in stable and consistent occupational contexts which arrived maturities and the subsequent inconsistent occupational environment need due manoeuvres in the internal system-reactions or of external influences resulting in the crisis (Tripp, A.M., 1992) arriving new promotional strategies with nuances to be encouraged by keeping the tribal mindset in view.

Clan/community-based leadership (Rang ba shnongs) on heredity or by election seemed to be non-stretchable in terms of larger vision, inviting change and focus on core competencies of the community. The new knowledge synchronizations over the prevailing basic styles merged with local possibilities enable to construct new horizons of micro development. A competent and performance-based developmental leadership can provide purposeful direction and decisions on behalf of the women's groups. These role-holders need to develop deeply internalized target systems which can conditionally/unconditionally align their approaches towards micro-strategies towards mega plans. They are peripheries of the traditional system who have not been owned responsibility. A transparent system will enable the clan leaders to develop and enhance their role responsibilities.

New occupational models to be made adaptable in the rigid and conditional spaces enable them to be adopting in the lines of images, opportunities and occupational share felt by the "participants" with proper perspectives and focus. Several situations have been viewed but no breakthrough intent with each decision-maker remains absent barring few distinguishable identities categorizing the risk-factors taking the resort of entrepreneurial approach. There is no surprise as the matrilineal extended families or the clans have been outgrowing their size in the guise of "conventional philosophy of clan promotion" leading into deep trouble as those have their impact over the resource ownership, distribution and need fulfilment and ultimately on occupational status. Despite the strong resource base, traditional leadership, cultural values and willingness to grow by the people the state is being identified as the most backward even among its neighbouring states (of north-east) as there seemed to be only limited hands to support the positivities and majority passing the buck, blame, fear suspicion and insecurity where the real innovation and creativity have become a myth. The questionable issues are the extent of commitment, sharing the situations of openness, encouraging trust, learning and accepting the need of change. The tribal women can well be marked as brand ambassadors of occupational load by compelling logic of self-initializations, proactive perspectives, as upgraders willing to reinvent the occupational fraternity towards overcoming the gender-based imbalances otherwise created by system relaxations and functionalities making it more to believe that these talented women have been promoting outstanding occupational situation.

But, one can notice that Meghalaya is in dire need of being certainly caught in its origins help to adopt the traditional practices which are outdated and are being adopted even when the outcome is negligible. No effort to diagnose its real strengths today jettisoning those traditional practices as deterrents to change which pose a big challenge ahead as its systems and processes have the change but also its individual values and behaviours (Change in all context). Its bottom line is being under terrible neglect as there is a need to introduce multiple-effective measures at both short and long-term for its survival. Being accommodated in frugalities the women groups have been compromising with severe bottlenecks *viz.*, illiteracy, the tougher life conditions, unlimited responsibilities, poor communication and interaction and with poor determinations majority of the women still await for mystical power to be into operation that the possibilities of new leadership to perform miracles so as to begin with new hopeful and vibrant (unknown) future.

The rub-off effects of the prevailing ineffectives over new systems need to be given serious thinking as it is necessary to identify the system-capacities in multi-dimensions with strong base, potential spread and have been accepted as historical representation.

- How the ethnic occupationability be defined, associated or modified towards ethical and non-ethical situations keeping in view the new aspirations, size, traditionalism, communication, development, compatibility, lifestyles etc.
- How the new systems can be made adoptable? Do mapping help the value delivery trends, preferable lifestyle adaptations, innovative thinking opportunities etc., are aspired to improve the way to shape and contours to a non-existing occupational situations need to focus on variables currently available *viz.*, lack of profile, focus and developmental means promote ridicule situations and manipulated performances.
- Do all new systems contribute towards new developments? Does it help ridiculing over the focus and drive new points of communication should be

developed by means of performances (by system manipulation/s). The strategies of development cannot be adopted here as the ethical views are different.

Creating an ethical brand, new habits, attitudes and initiations, the ability to develop a distinctive vision to accommodate innovation without the tedium of constant referrals of the success has a division (with a divided vision) and being promoted as splintered vision. It is always better to look at the condition with critical eye while initiating a new "learning by experience". Should we call the resource dependency as an ideal occupation? Do the occupational preference is strategically different from the mainstream of the country? Yet, it is worthy to mention that the backup of resource possession, the relaxations of accountability and responsibility, the protective measures (financial and non-financial nature) the economic and non-economic supportives are liberally promoted with least expectations result in the misused autonomy with a feeling of advantageous out of the system.

Developmental approaches viewed at personalized forms and implementations based on the inexperienced patterns lead to biased analysis and evaluation. The justification of occupational status is still in the warming up status. The new and innovative schemes promoted sound existing but the new idea is being understood in its conventional sense does not remain perpetually new. A leap only one step enables the state to grow in incremental form. An occupational sink being the condition prevalent where new threats to the prevailing systems adopted as is felt desirable with changing times. Such priorities enable "synergistic" benefits based on the true liberalism and dispassionate evaluation of the benefits in the fragmented structure/s.

Engineering Long-term and Short-term Growth

The progressive dimensions believe order amid change and preserve change amid order. The current occupational status seemed to have brought saturation and offering fewer opportunities for survival and growth to younger generation. The state has to examine its operations in the light of its occupational position and compensation trends where the per cent of large categories of small and medium nature occupy larger spaces. The rapidity of the growth is unlikely and the environments prepared for it only can survive and a mindset that encounter growth within the state.

Virtual Immobilities : Assumed Condition of Self-sustainabilities—What forms the basis for new opportunities?

The determinable abilities of new opportunities can be considered only by tapping their potentialities and associated threats. An in-depth understanding of SWOT must be carried out before introducing and entering new categories. It needs to look at the current players operating categories in the segments and the strength to develop enable :

- To do the consultancy over new occupational adaptations accommodating current portfolio of importance.
- To review current players' operational performance in terms of competencies prevailing and anticipate to be growth contributions in the system.
- To distinguish the low and high value addedness and to be innovative within its currently dominant areas ensuring a dualistic growth trend.
- To extend survival opportunities and expansions by offering conglomerated focus.
- Occupations which can grow independent with larger visions create models and independent but setting up an operation dependent on the occupational mindset.

The perceptions of their current strengths, core competences, governance, vision and definiteness of objectives need to be promoted by taking into concern each nuance need to be attended. The occupational stretch needs the capacity to produce solutions towards new knowledge, synchronizations, and adaptations of innovative styles in alignment with local possibilities. Is it that the context still permits the supremacy of conventional methods over new systems? Necessitating the concept at entry level the orbit of desirability evolves the need of introducing new practices and eases the current practices. The near term merits modelled in the lines of images define the occupational radius at low and high level based on the dependencies, outcome, and consequence. The extent of external help anticipated cannot influence the occupational market comparatives as the spirit of self-dynamism and external dependencies have been angled and perceived in alternative dimensions even if the spirit remains same. Having a joint strategy to influence the structural roles and procedures which the stakeholders exercise the decision-making power and to design occupational leverages. The approach with cutting edge over multiple issues including the succinct structures, process solutions and scalability, access to low costing market and to attend to key characters of value creating, building growth, vision, leadership, resource commitment, interaction and focus, leading to the stake developer (women) and occupational process. Mapping an ideal mix of big ideas with visionary leadership and sound occupational design with womens' determined participation enables to promise development of synthesizing effect.

Research Questions

1. *It is observed that the female occupational domain in Meghalaya can be ascertained to be in developing status. There is a necessity to identify the root causes which hinder their growth and development and do the similar constraints continue to hamper the future growth prospects?*

- The Meghalayan economy remains uncomparable with any other known economy as its distinguishable features prevalent are not possible characters of other economies. Its prevailing status is being the result of the contextual progression advocated and adapted by the system itself and its non-opposition reveal the adaptation of casualisation, informality and diversification in every developmental event include occupational. The root causes being preferred—isolation, loss of identity and least anticipation of the endangered situations of this wholly resource-based economy which have not been caring for its alter is deeply reliable on single formula of resource-dependency. Its other economic or socio-cultural values have been the bubbles of the large resource dependent economy currently been facing new loads. Added by the ethnic enforcements of clan promotion, accultured/extended and large families, meagre contribution and inattention towards learning, skills development, constrained social capital etc., are also potential contributors. The system need super leadership, idealized local transformations, synchronized growth and prototypical developmental strategies framed to suit its short and long-term requirements.

2. *The conventional occupational techniques (ideologies), which were previewed through multiple perceptional and characteristic forms, proved to be not-so-significant and it is more a pressing requirement to probe into the insights of feminine occupational/service possibilities, adoption and adaptation probabilities of new innovative occupational technologies.*

- If change is considered inevitable the Meghalayan economy too has been witnessing change. However, the package of ethical systems, if branded, to be the non-contributors there is an instant need to change the source (of contribution) as well as its domain. If it needs to be realized that new change can be possible with the conventional situations, such change remain a myth. Most of the prevailing systems when proved to be unworthy need to be replaced with immediate effect as the realizations and reactivities have not yet arrived saturation to dislodge the inefficient sources and to reengineer new ideological and growth orientations as extensions of the prevailing systems definitely cannot transform themselves into new embodiments of contributories ignoring their past. The domain which has been currently adopting micro approaches is only fit for narrow radius of development but a manifold growth context to be suitable for wider occupational aspirations cannot be justified with the prevailing set of tools used for system renovations.

3. *The transformation and dilution of feminine socio-occupational thought (in physical and psychographic terms) is inevitable due to its constant interaction with market externalities and internalities. What application patterns are temperamentally suitable to the tradition-bound and ethnic-oriented tribal segments?*

- It is rather a non-prerogative to assume a transformatory condition from the incoming external factors as these forms "multiple-arriving" with shallowed visions and part-provisions entering into the state with pre-determined motives. Having seen a wider framework the externalities aiming commercial and opportunistic stances represent domineering market turbulences, contractual/fragmented or even speculative forces intrude towards all undesirable opportunistic conditions erode the ethnic sanctities and cultural values. Meghalaya is understood as being a state which prefers its tribal identity for any understandable reasons has been rigid in its adaptation towards transformations. Temperamentally, it can accept the tailor made possibilities articulated by taking into concern the nuances which can rightly serve and abridge the gaps at inter- and intra-structural forms. The concept of occupation cannot flourish in isolation as it needs interconnects and inter-dependencies. Mutually and reciprocally acceptable developmental strategies applicable to the local context can be articulated by the stakeholders rather than prescribing ready-to-implement visionary plans from external system leading to non-contributions due to the defaults in practical and prototypical applications.

4. *The negative outlook formulated and established among both influencing and influenced may be consisting alternative situations and possibilities. The research explores the possibilities, which help facilitating conversion of negative (service threats) conditions to constructive situations (service opportunities) and there exist a need to observe what innovative strategies can promulgate new tailor-made "pro-ethnic" stratagems?*

- The state's physiological conditionalities pose serious problems associated with topography, climate, living habits, practices, food and clothing as well as language etc., create differences in preferences, accessibilities, exposure, inter-connects and aggressiveness towards living styles. The occupation is a wrapped up condition which need to be defined in the ethnic context as it is viewed in a totally different perspective as the composite and comprehensive context with a shared approach, limited contribution and expectation. Mere resource access too didn't contribute to the developmental way. The undesirable channel public in the guise of service-providers enables to hold the gamut of value-benefits arrived. The ethnic groups by nature are pleasure-loving, easy-going and dislike responsibility. The complexities borne by the people-groups in the other parts of the country are not being comparable with these tribal groups. The pro-ethnic strategies and the constructive situations remain leveraged between the acceptance and rejection of re-engineered strategies. The Meghalayan economy basically been cushioned with external and internal reflexes as internalities are manifold times wider and turbulent rather than the externalities. Meghalaya, if referred as a service economy has not yet well understood the real definition and scope of service spectrum. Its opportunities erupt from its own perceptions, knowledge, experience and determination/commitment and aggressive mindset but the aspirations for the promotive condition need taming to be tuned as per the segmental demands and especially of vulnerable groups inclusive of women.

5. *Occupational service technology, if forms an integral part of wide technology scope in which, if "female occupational status" is a given state of affairs—its services form a spectrum of issues. The portfolio issues under prevailing situations remain cautious i.e., mere occupation or mere resources apparently doesn't prove lucrative unless their congruency produces "synergistic effect?*

- The occupational definition need to be redefined over regional specializations of knowledge, technology and approaches in prescribed time frames nurtured by local ethno-cultural forms. Informal and implicit learning define the tacit knowledge indigenously grown has gained instant acceptance rather than the sophistications recommended by external systems. In most of the cases it is understood that there is ignorance and lack of understanding at every level and the relative implications could not be codified into localized terms resulted in making effective measures which ultimately turned non-contributive. The applicability and operability to the context remained significantly *nil* as there is no complete grasp over the gamut of events. Absence of organizational and administrative skills is evidently accompanied by lack of initiations, accountability and in-depth involvement created chaos especially those who have never been exposed to realistic situations. In short, the developmental strategies need to satisfy the "local" effect by co-existence modes and the primitiveness in the economy resulted due to non-exposure, ethnic rigidities, and lack of communication, interactivities and knowledge systems which bring in self-potentialities to drive the economy into contested form.

Hypotheses : Macro View-point

1. *Ethnicity forms domain of tribal ideologies however, in reality it is not necessarily an in-depth condition. The superficial veil of ethnic outlook once lifted, the underlying typical psychology towards feminine preferences remains similar and uniform irrespective of origin.*

- The hypotheses stand partially true as the Meghalayan tribes have adopted few distinctive practices *viz.*, matriliny, clan title sought after women's title, women's responsibility after marriage (man after marriage leaves his parental house to live with his wife in her or her parental house), property to the youngest daughter and adopting mother's title (rather than father's) etc. It is true that the ethnic women prefer to be more than a typical woman as their compulsions is cultural, situational as well as self-creative. If clan promotion is considered as prerogative it was found that the promotion and survival of the tribal cult remain in the hands of women and it is a desirable and revered concept accepted by all women. But this assigned responsibility is not shouldered by the companion is a serious consequence witnessed in majority of the households resulting in chaotic conditions *viz.*, single parents, living together, temporary relations etc., have their contributions down-sizing women's dignity and esteem. This seemed to be the distinctive motivational factors enabling the women hold the responsibility of self and nurturing familial and dependent responsibilities. Majority of women are observed with the character of meagre education, knowledge and economic support get crucified with this ethnic role of overloaded responsibility find occupation as an individual and social necessity for survival. It is not the concept of occupationality or the entrepreneurial skills which have been glorified but it is the living condition and preference taken to task in the due context to undertake the occupationalities at-convenience in order to meet the life needs. Therefore, the uniqueness displayed is occupation as a survival source, as a surrogate supportive towards clan-promotion, as a source of resource-exploitation, as a micro-force which satisfy the micro-participatory trends of informal segments and as a means to evidence conjugal relations, as a means to maintain external inter-connectivities with non-tribals and also as a definition to prescribe the women's authority and status supremacy over men. The occupation also pamper positivities as the women are self-motivated barring all conditionalities prefer to work or to be engaged in work. There are hardly few women who prefer (in Garos) to be dependent over men for their livelihood but at large all women displayed self-dignity and preference to work irrespective of the nature and status of work.

2. *Efforts to develop the female occupational possibilities pose a potential alternative or generate new occupational situations/delights are necessarily the privilege of innovative technologies. However, such situations, which grow beyond the "typical parameters", may face minimal opposition.*

- The hypothesis stands partially true as in majority of the situations women's status remain unquestionable. The matriliny stands true to its word and the feminine dominance is being highlighted in several spheres at multiple layers. The gender discrimination is high in several segments and women being domineering in several domains naturally acquire the authoritative stance in the field of occupation too. There is neither dearth for opportunities nor for externalities (both developmental and commercial of short and long perspectives) but the "preparedness" remains questionable. The ethnic groups within their self-imposed reservations distance themselves from any external activities aiming them to provide with a gamut of schemes, assignments, opportunities which have not been honoured nor relished. The fear of insecurity and losing current *status quo,* rigidities arising barriers in co-existence, inter-connectivities and inter-dependencies, lack of understanding and tolerance towards alien cultures and instead prefer to remain complacent in meagreness, simple living styles, proneness towards western culture, adaptations (preferences towards non-Indianisation) enabled them to be unique and distinctive segment. Adaptations of current day advancements are prone for occupational opportunities need due base with comprehensive understanding of the occupations suitable to the temperament of women/people segments, occupational environment with competencies to cope up with new technologies, awareness and training programmes of familiarization, handling the situations within the familiar and unfamiliar context, to reconciliate the situational and context-based differences to be prototyped within the ethnic purview.

3. *Transformations of occupational markets bring dilution and a passing phase is more permissive to overcome "negative consequences" otherwise difficult to be dealt with. Execution of radical changes in desirable direction tend to be easy in flexible condition rather than in stagnant (historical) service situations. The case remains similar in feminine context.*

- The hypothesis stands partially true as it remain as a mere wishful thinking if anticipated that the stagnant conditions prove to be merit-based. No system is free from change and the system adamancies of non-changeability need to be a more serious error as any impending change is instantly resisted ignoring its consequences. Refusal to change cannot be admitted as a prerogative as in long-term effect it results in stunted deviations and conventional systems lead to system collapse. The tribal women need to be identified as a vibrant force yet without much voice. The known conditionalities, familiarities and preferences deemed to be most favourite zones provided them with a carefree environment and identity. It cannot be mistaken that the entrepreneurship qualities have been the natural talents of women but prescriptions of behaviour remain sullen with the growing gaps in generation, technology, market forces, and business trends etc., found to be making their mark of indifference.

4. *For a "learned society" the offer of new technologies like female occupational involvement is prone for logical reactions but a society (social segment) never faced such situation, needs initiation. In former it is application emphasis but in latter it is an initiation process, which may or may not lead to application. The strategies tend to be different in both cases and ethnic districts of Meghalaya belong to the later category.*

- The hypothesis stands partially true. The governmental, institutional, and organizational involvement constantly and continuously been making efforts by introducing several developmental (new) schemes (prepared by state and centre) for various purposes have been offered so as to elevate the prevailing status. The intervening forces are too dominant and the inner ethnic motives form the core determinants pose reflections at different levels but a non-desirable reluctance and deliberate withdrawal is witnessed among several ethnic segments. The lack of enthusiasm towards change, growth, developmental/ promotional activities as well as inter-dependencies is most prone situational deliberations displayed. The concept of informality is rampant and the localization is the favourable context. The tribal segments have innate fear of being exploited with the possessions and value their carefree lifestyle and lack of responsibility etc. But the teeming numbers have been forcing them to adopt normal lifestyles making them to force their way towards dilutions. The boarder areas shared with neighbouring state and country promoted trade relations and exchange transactions are further strengthened with accultural acceptances transforming to conjugal/familial relations. The initialization processes are the most recommended situations for the informal value approaches yet there is dire need to perk into different systems which forms suitable to introduce a conscious and purposeful package of new occupational modes applicable at different layers and contexts applicable in tribal reference without antagonizing their sentiments.

Hypotheses : Micro View-point

1. *The priority vs. resource-orientations among occupational situations may present similar output tendencies irrespective of the occupational character.*

- The situation is partially accurate as there exists a need to understand the generic basis for resource-based economies i.e., the natural resource endure as a sole criteria for survival. Is it that the society's inclination towards resources as easy resort or the resource-proneness eventually lead to the dependencies is a matter to be investigated? But it is consequenced and witnessed as on the current day that majority are directly or indirectly dependent over natural resources endowed by the state. The primitiveness of the state can be witnessed by the choice options selected for its usage suggest absence of any potential alternatives viz., skills, technologies, market or business activities etc. The women segments irrespective of their stature are not versatile in the developmental issues especially the knowledge of total resource-base, access levels and the dependency status even at clan/community level. This is quite feasible—as much of the resource land has been in peoples' hands as private possession (individual or clan/community). These assets belong to the private owners granted with the liberty of using them in the exclusive manner they prefer. The government's role remain *nil* as to interfere nor make an estimation of the state's resources, take measures or enforce laws etc., to boost, monitor, supervise or regulate their decisions. This "private ownership" is detrimental to the state progression as the entire state resources irrespective of their nature be it forestry or mining activities. It is found that majority of the policy-makers themselves are resource owners and affluent personnel reject to pay any heed to cope up with any developmental activities. Boosting the occupational scenario in the state can be distanced due to its inept governmental position, the impossibilities of private owners to be sacrificing their rights and think for society, to expect a highly multi-layered competent occupational portfolio adopting the suitabilities of protective and producible modes.

2. *The occupational technologies tailor-made to the domestic requirements help ethnic-segments accept the innovative situations but may not evolve new "service" circumstances.*

- Deprival is being identified at every level which is the end-result of multiple consequences *viz.*, government, local bodies, traditional hierarchical systems, community and clanship, religious leaders, NGOs etc., play vital channels to approve any feasible systems to be reaching the people segments especially the vulnerable/grassroots levels. They form the decision-makers to judge or witness any new entry, acquisition, transaction and even permissiveness into the domain. This has been the hindering factor for free flow of information, commodities and services and people movement. Surprisingly the women's forces have not been a part of this machinery. Besides topographical difficulties there are innumerable practical difficulties as the background of non-exposure, language, cultural factors, time allocations, practicing methods, facilities, willingness, initiatives, and accommodations etc., which are made to create a "prone environment". The frugalities in the level of understanding, familiarity, resourcefulness, forgoing currently-in-hand occupational opportunities, lack of confidence over the lucrativeness of new opportunities, lack of assured availability of supplementaries and constant guidance till the new systems/technologies sink is being accepted as utility proven, recommended, been associated as an extension to occupational familiarity which is being in practice, should be easy to handle and memorize. Each of the new systems has been accepted in prototypical forms or for alternative uses. There is no appeal for any "breach of such agreement" as any external element is considered as intruder and any unpleasantness lead to grave consequences.

3. *The option of service syndication in occupations helps to influence the environmental situations in general and personification in particular. In other words it encourages the conversion of micro servicing into "service monopolies".*

- The portfolio of occupational opportunities has been limited and the micro approach is predominated option most suitable to the temperament, resource utilities and the local technologies. The personal and familial limits to a large extent restrict women to be active participant especially under constraints. The Doctrine of Private Property holds the law and the fundamental cause of the social imbalances resulting in its backwardness in several spheres. The proportion of resources-owners is limited and considerable number hold political power. It is the literal money and power game of significant few where majority of the rest have been compromising with minimum needs. The service monopolies can be interpreted as being a condition in micro participation where the private owners permit as the decision cannot be undertaken at grassroots level as it is a followers forum rather than decision-makers.

5. *The determinants of "variable" societal situations tend to remain rigid and static as compared to the flexible technologies. A successful end-result can be expected only when occupational technologies are competent to match the segmental-demand set.*

- The hypothesis hold true to a significant extent as the given economy is persistently learning to co-exist beyond its compromise. Several self-imposed systems have made their place of permanence and draw command over issues of varied importance. Few of them even become merged up with the native systems resulted in widely prone "pseudo systems" to some extent gained acceptance. Struggling to retain their identity in the "signified accultural environment" the micro segments adopting the route of rigidity in character. Flexibility arises when there is mutual acceptance of the systems especially when they tend to be dependent over each other. The strong external technological reasons vying to be merged in local systems cannot be accepted as long as such technology is not felt as a necessity for their survival. The adaptations pose difficulties and there is a need to make a sound ground work before such technologies are making entry into the system.

6. *Ethnic minority entrepreneurship has faced different issues from those that have been formally identified. Successful diversifications and development rely upon the effective networks and strategies rather than being promoting the conventional philosophies.*

- The conventionalism cannot be separated from its people's living behaviour and so its occupational patterns. It forms their life blood and possessing the very identity for which the women force has been directly or indirectly contributing in numerous forms. Survival of the tribe is the supreme aim and every member especially women are occupationally involved to nurture the tribal needs. The insecurities of being minority and the vulnerabilities resulting into aggressive options and behaviour which shaped into the perverted vision. Keeping in view the distinguished character of Meghalayan tribals the diversifications and developments have become the prescriptions over the diagnosis made by several external agencies where the local conditions could not assess the reasonability and effectiveness of those. The money concept was clear but not the associated responsibility and outcome which is missing. The conventional systems cannot altogether are not without their own methods such as unification, coordination and aiming for common objectives etc., if treated as informal systems the formal systems need to take the merit of these informalities to create a foolproof system.

7. *Innovative ethnicities and inter-generational relations often create culture-gaps between generations investigated. It is to be believed that the cultural-protection influence moreover the ethnic-identities than the occupational choices.*

- The statement prove partially true as ethnicities perceived by two generations definitely have differences in terms of involvement and value assessments as for the younger generation, the culture forms an insignificant influencer in their total life system. It is found that the youngsters' cultural dominance over decision-making and behavioural factors is much less than their seniors. The cultural norms and relative influence over occupational factors have minimal association as to work or not to work on specific day viz., extent of work continuity or discontinuity due to the family or clan celebration or calamity. But the women never really given up the work. The culture in its prescriptions never encouraged nor discouraged the work concept but the women voluntarily involve in work without any external pressure. It is easy to show a proper direction as the people are motivated and the personal preparedness or the zeal to be engaged in the specific tasks, does not remain as a norm. The women segments are definitely slow learners but keeping in view the long-term non-exposure and deprival factors the women seemed to be positioning themselves as vibrant lot to be worthy of occupationally extensive substance.

Recommendations

The role of women in the ethnic dominant social segment has definite role-dominance and there is a need to use this invaluable **measure** in its proper form so as to adopt the portfolio of priorities in aspirational dimensions. The growing concept of individualization which is the new system adaptation rather than the group think, to be over dependent on the medium which has minimal sustainable effect and to be selective in occupational implications towards skills, education or resources to create an outlook with positive mindset towards constructivism.

Navigating Multifarious Serformance-based Transformations

- Using the traditionally prevailing fragmented systems (clans) the domain need to be understood in terms of raising performances by overcoming the obstacles. There is a dire need to integrate both conventional and modernities as inputs to create an integrated effort.
- The short and long-term measures need to be demarcated to realize the value-addedness by means of alignments, criteria, reflexes and contributions to promote a paradigm shift in the mindset of the women groups layered in the system.
- To reduce the effect of prevailing "informality" in the system which is witnessing a stunted development, shallow penetration trends, minimal transaction and micro-visualizations reveal the rationale of insignificant producible competencies demand a total transformation.
- The brand image of socio-cultural isolates needs to be changed by progressive aesthetics into the corpus of rational endorsements. The synergistic impact need to be promoted by merging different systems to yield both pull and push strategies at prototypical levels.

Overcoming Possibilities of Non-familiarization

- Shaping the segmental behaviour : The behavioural trajectories currently groomed by cosmic changes need an in-depth understanding of survival and growth dimensions and differential treatments applicable and justifiable to the context.

- Conversion of marginal outlook into sustainable and wholistic approaches needed an aggregated effort unifying the determinants of prevalent and progressive introductions.
- Commodifying the heterogeneous structures and identifying the drivers of competency-based on resources, skills, experience, approaches, uncontrollables and perceptional references over the "preference + selectivity" dynamics to aim occupational alignment with new value determinants.
- Visualizing the occupation as a rationale to determine the centralities of constant/continuous evaluation so as to create an impact of managing aspirations, alignment of value and behavioural norms, work-life balancing which can reengineer the developmental trust in new systems of career growth to shape one future.
- Coping with context-based challenges in the process of building capacities and adopting the targeted developmental practices need stake of the local participant groups who explore alternative lifestyles and raise the opportunities from preliminary issues accommodating local policies and community norms.

Reinforcing New Occupational Ethos

- The variables over which the decision framework is constructed to define the life choices revealed by means of occupational choices to be collaborated with the value discrepancies and shared vision aiming both individual and community vision.
- Self-motivations and micro-entrepreneurships imbibed by the ethnic culture need to be glorified so as to hold the responsibility of sustainable framework for long term effects.
- Access to the occupational tools can be the incentive to improve the prevailing status of creative and value-oriented stringencies resulted in the neglect of regional responses.

- Promoting both internal (insider) and external (outsider) view enable to align the occupational conditions, need of organized patterns, collective support and experience in order to promote negotiation and appreciation to be advocated.
- Occupational mapping which can grasp different ideologies (alternatives) creating solutions to value added-professionalism, potential for producible opportunities, coordinated linkages of government, semi-government, facilitators, intermediaries of formal and informal forms to be formed as "occupational mechanism".

At macro level an appropriate conceptual and operational tool to promote facility of developing similar effects in the areas of agriculture, enterprise management, small/micro-industry development, resource management, community and infrastructural development to be merged into the prevailing systems and also to create an identity of their own. The core competencies have been forming the genesis of collective "inter-connect" support systems. A multi-dimensional contributory focus is an immediate necessity to establish linkages in the occupational spectrum. The new innovative system need to :

- promote a concrete shape to amend the current ineffective systems into more dynamic and embedded forms.
- initiate an ideal occupational domain to generate the *status quo* of the trends and drives determining avenues and opportunities for realistic transformations.
- for appropriate unified outcome the interconnections and linkages among internal and external forces with appropriate norms, enforcements and collateral measurables needed.
- collaborated occupational initiations ranging from low to high intensities with local appropriation, transactional access to ethnic proximities and localized applicabilities need to be reprimanded.

- resource base estimations and utility strategies help insuring the supportive contributions to be used over target systems by means of appropriate power balance and allocation (of the chain-partners).

Fostering Occupational Capacity Building Supportives

The ethnic women promise a dominant force but the question of calibre and contribution barring rural or urban status is in question. In-depth environmental familiarization in terms of value conditioning, with socio-situational enablement, boosting multifarious behavioural standards—prove to be effective and impressive but in terms of new situations of new inputs, information, new service spectrum quality maintenance, new counsel, developmental supportives and interactive diversifications. The concepts of sustainability, concepts of informality, individual and social networking need to be negotiated keeping in view the channel efficiencies attend to appropriate mechanisms for creative diverse, proper delivery and development service systems. Evolving local interest groups, exploring livelihood opportunities, promoting capacity building teams with power balances, developing in-house opportunities and assessments enable to explore short and long-standing options and embedded approaches. The prevailing "micro-professionalism and informality" development structures have become a sought-after trend well accepted and manipulated leading to new negotiable systems potentially viable and are operational through social networks and reciprocal relations using the "external-chain mechanisms" need an overall assessment of appropriate leveraging to evolve idealized systems.

Sum Up

To conclude, the ethical systems domesticated the women role-status to be under prescribed term by means of external enforcements or to be cornered to design the self-restrained condition due to lack of alternatives. The available opportunities in the state do not encourage a positive growth and the situations have been arrived as a consequence of policies which have been mutually accepted. The government is the most powerless system and the people deemed to be holding the real power of resource access and decision-making enabled the government as merely a disbursing agent. The women's force is totally autonomous and it is the individualized growth which can be systematized by encouraging the self-motivated systems to be put to operationalisation so as to arrive synergistic merits.

ANNEXURES

ANNEXURE-I

Details of the Districts, Blocks and Villages chosen for the Research Study

S.No.	*Districts*	*Blocks*	*Villages*
1.	**East Khasi Hills**		
1.1		Mylliem	Mawtawar, Mawkhar, Mawpat
1.2		Mawphlang	Marpna, Sohiong-Nongsen, Khrang-Nonglum
1.3		Mawkynrew	Rosang, Umshan, Mynriang
1.4		Mawryngkneng	Jarioit, Umphrup, Rynjah-Lapalang
1.5		Pynursla	Phernai, Mawkynjng, Lapalang
1.6		Khatarshong	Mawshaton, Mawbeh, Krhadem
1.7		Mawsynram	Mawkhan, Haptaka, Mawryngkneng
1.8		Shella Bholaganj	Disong, Umblei, Umdeng
2.0	**West Khasi Hills**		
2.1		Mawshynrut	Mawlan, Nongdom Synrang, Salpala
2.2		Nongstoin	Mawatrep, Mawkohar,Doledonga
2.3		Mairang	Teibeh, Kharthagurav, Nonpriang
2.4		Ranikor	Khasiadop, Punchiring,Thangrei
2.5		Mawkyrwat	Hiland, Mawjirsim, Awro
2.6		Mawthadriashan	Mahati, Mawlum, Pariong
3.0	**Jaintia**		
3.1		Thadlaskain	Mookynang, Madan Synrang, Saitsama
3.2		Laskain	Mushai, Mootyrshiah, Umsalang
3.3		Amralem	Amtra, Amsohrhong, Khonglah
3.4		Khleiriat	Mawthoi, Mukhasohshreh, Jalyiah
3.5		Saipung	Mynthiang, Tangnub, Kyrluh
4.0	**Ribhoi**		
4.1		Jirang	Nongrim Jirang, Umsohbar, Limrit
4.2		Umling	Umling, Umtyrnaga, Hatimaa
4.3		Umshning	Umlangling, Umiong, Mawka

(*contd.*)

S.No.	*Districts*	*Blocks*	*Villages*
5.0	**East Garo Hills**		
5.1		Rasublepara	Swalmari, Thapa Dajong, Rangagora
5.2		Dambo	Amralem, Lower Sambrak,Kama Gandim
5.3		Songsok	Dobu Bolsalgi, Doki, Damepal
5.4		Samanda	Nengmandal, Dewadepa, Suchilgre
5.5		Karkotta	Memilan, Jargilgittam, Sakware
6.0	**West Garo Hills**		
6.1		Selsella	Berupara, Pattarkata, Sidakandi
6.2		Deddangre	Dipogre, Chanupara,Holaidonga
6.3		Tikrikilla	Dobok Jokolggre, Didapara, Pedalboba
6.4		Rangram	Agalgre, Takitgre, Kamagre
6.5		Betasingh	Mangasangre, Asangre, Sonamitigre
6.6		Zikzak	Dhoramchas, Nachilpara, Kambakpara
6.7		Dalu	Dupakura,Chotobollang,Genepara
6.8		Gambegre	Kamilpera,Somongre,Durasongmagre
7.0	**South Garo Hills**		
7.1		Chokpot	Durabanda, Dayal,Rongrachi
7.2		Bhagmara	Badri, Rongdingaree,Sasatgire
7.3		Robgara	Mingmabel,Golasora,Chimitap
7.4		Gasuapara	Dasingre,Dalangre,Rongra kantalu

Urban Details of Meghalaya

S.No.	*District*	*Name*	*Status Population*
1.	East Khasi Hills	Shillong	Class I (1,00,000 and above)
		Cherrapunjee	Class IV (10,000-19,999)
2.	West Khasi Hills	Nongstoin	Class III (20,000-49,999)
		Mairang	Class IV (10,000-19,999)
3.	East Garo Hills	William Nagar	Class IV
		Rasubelpara	Class IV
4.	West Garo Hills	Tura	Class II (50,000-99,999)
5.	South Garo Hills	Bhagmara	Class V (5,000-9,999)
6.	Jaintia Hills	Jowai	Class III (20,000-49,999)
7.	Ribhoi	Nongpoh	Class IV

ANNEXURE-II

Mapping Rural and Urban Meghalaya

Map 1 : Rural Meghalaya

S.No.	Location (Districts)	Map-I	Map-II	Map-III	Map-IV	Map-V
I.	**West Garo Hills**					
1.	Selsella	D	D	A	B	A
2.	Dedangre	A	A	F	E	F
3.	Tikrikilla	B	D	F	A	F
4.	Rongram	D	F	B	B	A
5.	Betasingh	B	D	D	D	B
6.	Zikzak	B	F	D	F	E
7.	Dalu	C	E	B	C	G
8.	Gambegre	C	E	F	C	E
II.	**East Garo Hills**					
1.	Rasubelpara	B	D	D	B	A
2.	Dambo	D	F	D	A	B
3.	Songsok	D	D	F	C	G
4.	Samanda	B	E	C	A	B
5.	Karkotta	C	E	F	C	F
III.	**South Garo Hills**					
1.	Chokpot	E	C	F	B	A
2.	Bhagmara	C	F	C	A	E
3.	Rongara	D	E	B	C	D
4.	Gasuapara	C	C	E	A	C
IV.	**West Khasi Hills**					
1.	Mawshynrut	D	D	A	D	B
2.	Nongstoin	A	A	D	A	A
3.	Mairang	E	B	E	A	A
4.	Ranikhor	B	D	F	B	E
5.	Mawkyrwat	C	F	C	A	F
6.	Mawthadriashan	C	F	C	C	C
V.	**East Khasi Hills**					
1.	Mawphlang	B	A	E	C	A
2.	Mawkynrew	C	F	B	C	E
3.	Mawryngkneng	E	F	F	A	B
4.	Mawsynram	D	D	F	D	A
5.	Shella Bholaganj	A	D	C	D	B

(contd.)

S.No.	*Location (Districts)*	*Map-I*	*Map-II*	*Map-III*	*Map-IV*	*Map-V*
6.	Mylliem	A	C	D	B	A
7.	Pynursla	A	A	C	B	A
8.	Khatarshnong	B	B	A	F	E
VI.	**Ribhio District**					
1.	Jirang	B	E	F	D	A
2.	Umling	B	F	B	C	B
3.	Umshing	C	F	F	A	C
VII.	**Jaintia Hills**					
1.	Thadlaskain	D	F	C	A	C
2.	Laskain	E	A	B	B	D
3.	Amralem	E	F	C	A	A
4.	Khleiriat	E	A	C	B	D
5.	Saipung	A	A	D	C	E

Map-II : Urban Mapping of Meghalaya

S. No.	*District*	*Location*	*Map-I*	*Map-II*	*Map-III*	*Map-IV*	*Map-V*
1.	Jaintia Hills	Jowai	RP	Mut	C	A	E
2.	East Khasi Hills	Shillong	LP	RP	D	D	A
3.		Cherapunjee	RP	RP	F	E	B
4.	Ribhoi	Nongpoh	EP	EP	C	B	B
5.	West Khasi Hills	Nongstoin	MO	Int	B	B	C
6.	South Garo Hills	Bhagmara	MO	Mut	F	C	A
7.		Mairang	ET	Iso	E	A	D
8.	E. Garo Hills	Resubelpara	ET	Iso	B	C	G
9.		William Nagar	ET	Iso	D	F	F
10.	West Garo Hills	Tura	LP	Ext	A	C	G

Map-I : (i) EP; Ethnic Professionalism; (ii) MO : Micro-occupations; (iii) ET : Ethnicity; (iv) LP : Leveraging Performance; (v) RP : Resource Provisioning Map-II : (i) Int : Internal ; (ii) SS : Social Supportives ; (iii) Ext : External ; (iv) Mut : Mutuality; (v) Iso : Isolates ; (vi) Inf : Informality Map-III, IV and V : Parameters same as Rural

Key-I : Occupational Stretch and Direction

S.No.	*Attribute*	*Detail*
A.	**Status**	**Occupational Closeness and Ethnic Professionalism**
A1.	Reflection	Self-sufficiency
A2.	Effect	Self-promotion
A3.	Anticipation	Competency to cope up
A4.	Condition	Independent
B	**Status**	**Micro Occupational Perspectives (entrepreneurial)**
B1	Reflection	Scope of value added opportunities
B2	Effect	Preference for external support
B3	Anticipation	Dependency towards occupational branding
B4	Condition	Vulnerability
C	**Status**	**Ethnic Perspective**
C1	Reflection	Culture preference
C2	Effect	Religion dominance in life decisions
C3	Anticipation	Matriliny and femininity
C4	Condition	External dependency
D	**Status**	**Leveraging Performance Patterns**
D1	Reflection	Compromised view-point
D2	Effect	Context-based Accommodation
D3	Anticipation	Occupational Intent
D4	Condition	Reconciliation
E	**Status**	**Resource Possession**
E1	Reflection	Asset-based access and indigenization
E2	Effect	Decision flexibility and multi-tasking
E3	Anticipation	Robust but limited view
E4	Condition	Self-confidence

Key-II : Occupational Serve and Sub-serve Criteria

S.No.	Code	Description
1.	A	**Major influencer** : Internalities **Minor influencers** : Social Supportives; Externalities; Mutualities; Isolates; Informality
2.	B	**Major influencer** : Socio Supportives **Minor influencers** : Internalities; Externalities; Mutualities; Isolates; Informality
3.	C	**Major influencer** : Externalities **Minor influencers** : Internalities; Social Supportives; Mutualities; Isolates; Informality
4.	D	**Major influencer** : Mutualities **Minor influencers** : Internalities; Social Supportives; Externalities; Isolates; Informality
5.	E	**Major influencer** : Isolates **Minor influencers** : Internalities; Social Supportives; Externalities; Mutualities; Informality
6.	F	**Major influencer** : Informality **Minor influencers** : Internalities; Social Supportives; Externalities; Mutualities; Isolates

For Individual : Key-III : Feminine Occupational Decision-Consequence

S.No.	Code	Attributes
1.	A	Context appropriation in occupational segregation Intensity of localized complexities consequencing occupational stereo-typing
2.	B	Usage of local capacity in income diversification Micro participation and occupational stretch
3.	C	High magnitude of resource dependencies Occupational preference discrepancies and counter urbanization
4.	D	Focus over occupational radius Drives-based on external causes with internal effects
5.	E	Selt-centricism and feminine volatilities Anticipating decision consequences of occupational spectrum
6.	F	Anticipating decision consequences of occupational spectrum Lifecycle stages and activated occupational dynamism

For Clan : Key-IV : Coordinated Occupational Inclinations

S.No.	Code	Attributes
1.	A	Behavioural reactions based on conceptual and objective criteria At convenience socio-cultural norms Compromised inadequacies
2.	B	Leveraging transformational attributes Composite and comprehensive preferences Adaptabilities and advocations
3.	C	Extent of Limitedness in decision domain Lifestyle profiles Mobility and migration Allied (non-occupational) contributions
4.	D	Occupational selectivities Positivities in relation to opportunities and facilities Intrigue into occupational compatibilities and preference discrepancies
5.	E	Situational response : Occupational adequacies Ethnic professionalism Occupational insights and commitment
6.	F	Marginalized perseverances Access to the dependency-proven condition Impact of socio-cultural reconciliations

For Society : Key-V : Women's Occupational Self-direction

S.No.	Attributes
1.	Level of Interactivities and Connectivities
2.	Level of Permissiveness, Compromises and Cope up
3.	Level of Value Perception Discrimination
4.	Level of Behavioural Rigidities
5.	Level of Opportunistic Situations in Familiar and Non-familiar Conditions
6.	Level of Disproportionate Perseverance towards Need-gratification
7.	Level of Associative Tendencies Influenced by Subsequent Effect/s of Decision

Bibliography

Arce, A. "Knowledge relations : agricultural repositioning and new ruralities", XIV World Congress of Sociology, Montreal, Canada. Sociological Abstracts 98S33555/ISA (1998).

Archer, L., Francis, B., 2006. "Challenging classes? Exploring the role of social class within the identities and achievement of British Chinese pupils". *Sociology* 40, 29-49.

Arnon, Sara, "Influence of Socialization Agents on Leisure-time Activities of Youth Adolescents. (Report)" June 22, 2008.

Bevan, M., Cameron, S., Coombes, M., Merridew, T., Raybould, S., 2001."Social Housing in Rural Areas." Chartered Institute of Housing, Coventry.

Boeri,T., Del Bocae. D., Pissarides, C., (ed.). 2005. "Women at Work. An Economic Perspective". Oxford : Oxford University Press.

Bose, A., Nongbri and N. Kumar (Eds.) "Tribal Demography and Development in Northeast India", (1980), B.R. Publishing Corporation, Delhi.

Champion, T. and G. Hugo. 2004. "New Forms of Urbanization : Beyond the Urban-Rural Dichotomy", Bodmin. Cornwall : Ashgate Publishing Ltd.

Crompton, R. and F. Harris. 1998. "Explaining Women's Employment Patterns : Orientations to Work", Revisited. *British Journal of Sociology* 49(1) : 118-49.

Das. N.K., "Ethnic Identity, Ethnicity and Social Stratification in Northeast India", (1989). Inter India Publications, Delhi.

Davies, H. and H. Joshi. 2002. "Women's Incomes Over a Synthetic Lifetime". In : *The Gender Dimension of Social Change. The Contribution of Dynamic Research to the Study of Women's Life Courses,* eds. Elisabetta Ruspini and Angela Dale. Bristol : The Policy Press.

Halliday, J. and M. Coombes. 1995. "In Search of Counter urbanization : Some Evidence from Devon on the Relationship between Patterns of Migration and Motivation." *Journal of Rural Studies* 11 : 433-446.

Hakim, C. 2000. *Work-Lifestyle Choices in the 21st Century.* Oxford : Oxford University Press.

Heath, A., and Cheung. 1998. "Education and occupation in Britain." In : *From School to Work : a Comparative Study of Educational Qualifications and Occupational Destinations.* eds. Y. Shavit, and W. Müller. Oxford : Clarendon Press.

Jacobs, S. 1999. "Trends in women's career patterns and in gender occupational mobility in Britain", *Gender, Work and Organization,* 6 : 32-46.

Kenny, S. (2002). 'Tensions and dilemmas in community development : new discourses, new Trojans?' *Community Development Journal,* 37 (4).

Koston Roy, R. "Assortment from Tribal Research Institute, Meghalaya", (1978). Spectrum Publications Limited, Shillong.

Ngai, Steven Sek-yum, "The effects of service participation, friendship networks, and family support on developmental outcomes : a study of young people from low-income families in Hong Kong.(Report)", June 22, 2008.

NERC-ICSSR, Proceedings of the Seminar on the Status of Women in Tribal Cultures in Meghalaya, (1988), Shillong.

Pisati, M. and A. Schizzerotto. 2003. "The Italian Mobility Regime : 1985-1997". In : *National Patterns of Social Mobility", 1970-1999 : "Divergence or Convergence?",* (ed.)

Pugh, C. (ed.) (1996) *Sustainability, the Environment and Urbanisation.* London : Earthscan.

Schmidt, J.D. (1997). *The challenge from Southeast Asia : social forces between equity and growth.* pp. 2144.

Shukla, V. (1988). "Rural migration to an Indian metropolis : examining the micro foundations of the Harris-Todaro paradigm (a review and future research agenda)". *Indian Journal of Agricultural Economics,* 43(4) : 580-602.

Sullivan III, W.C. (1994). "Perceptions of the rural-urban fringe : citizen preferences for natural and developed settings. Landscape and Urban Planning", 1994, 29(2-3) : 85-101.

Tripp, A.M. (1992). *The impact of crisis and economic reform on women in urban Tanzania.* pp. 159-180.

Vance, I. (1987). *More than bricks and mortar : women's participation in self-help housing in Managua,* Nicaragua. pp.139-165.

Van Dijk, M.P. (1983). "Locational behaviour of small entrepreneurs in Ouagadougou", *Upper Volta. Tydschrift voor Econ, en Soc. Geografie,* 74(2) : 96-106.

Varley, A. (1996). "Women heading households : Some more equal than others"? *World Development,* 24(3) : 505-520.

Index